D1622569

Also available from Northwest Parent Publishing, Inc.:

OUT AND ABOUT

SEATTLE

WITH KIDS

The Ultimate Family Guide for Fun and Learning

BY ANN BERGMAN
AND STEPHANIE DUNNEWIND

SECOND EDITION

FROM THE PUBLISHERS OF

ACKNOWLEDGEMENTS

*Thanks to everyone who contributed to the book,
including Shelley Arenas, Rebecca Clarren,
Toddy Dyer, Susan Garrett, Mary-Leah Gordon,
Virginia Smyth, Tom Davis, Barbara Miller,
Nancy Reynolds, Tony Schenk, and Zachary.*

Edited and indexed by Miriam Bulmer

Production by John Rusnak

Printed in the United States of America.

Northwest Parent Publishing, Inc.
1530 Westlake Avenue North, Suite 600
Seattle, Washington 98109 U.S.A.
(206) 441-0191
www.nwparent.com

IBSN: 0-961462-69-8

TABLE OF CONTENTS

HOW TO USE THIS BOOK:

The listings were current at press time, but please confirm hours, prices, and location of selected destinations.

Tips boxes offer advice on how to make your outing more enjoyable and less stressful; Essentials boxes give information on basics such as parking, restrooms, and restaurants; Inside Scoop lets you in on things that only locals know about; and Neighborhood Notes boxes profile local neighborhoods from a family perspective.

Four icons appear regularly throughout:

Offers classes and/or workshops for children

Offers birthday-party packages

Offers field trips for schools or large groups

Features facilities that are accessible to persons in wheelchairs

INTRODUCTION

Since this book was first published by Northwest Parent Publishing in 1993, a lot has changed. Some things are obvious: prices have gone up, places have shut down, new ones have opened. Several children's attractions, such as the Children's Museum and the Pacific Science Center, have gone through major expansions. Seattle now hosts several new sports stadiums, with more on the way. Technology has made its mark as well, with numerous groups offering Web sites.

In addition to updating listings, the new edition adds several features, including "Neighborhood Notes," which profile neighborhoods such as Fremont, University District, Kirkland, Green Lake, and Madrona; and "Inside Scoop," which gives you insider tips on places to go on a summer night, for example, or where to fly a kite. Plus we've added dozens of new parks and attractions, expanding the coverage of the Eastside, and south and north King County.

The revised book follows the same principles as the earlier edition, providing parents with reliable information so they can get the most out of family time. As parents ourselves, we wanted to know what bike trails are suitable for wobbly rides, what to do indoors when kids start bouncing off the walls in the middle of winter, and where to eat without getting dirty looks from servers and other patrons. As editors for a company that publishes six monthly parenting newsmagazines in the Northwest, we knew how to best get that information and share it with other parents.

Outings can be more difficult with kids, but also more rewarding when familiar views and places are transformed by a child's wonderment and joy. We hope this book will help you share that experience with your children.

Chapter 1

ANIMALS, ANIMALS, ANIMALS

The great thing about animal outings is that adults and children are both enthralled. Granted, toddlers will likely be just as interested in the peacocks wandering around as they are in the endangered species. But parents can read the educational displays while kids enjoy the pure wonder of watching strange beasts.

And the Seattle area is wonderful for seeing animals: It offers an award-winning, top-rated zoo; a beautiful aquarium with a 400,000-gallon viewing tank; a zoo where elk and bison wander freely; and two city parks with barn animals.

Although the animals are in cages, Northwest zoos have tried to re-create their natural habitats, offering homes with trees, waterfalls, and playthings rather than sterile gray concrete.

Cougar Mountain Zoological Park

5410 194th Ave. S.E., Issaquah;
just south of I-90
(425) 391-5508
www.issaquah.org/zoo/zoo.htm
Open: March-Oct., Wed.-Sun.,
10 a.m.-5 p.m.; Nov. and Feb.,
Fri.-Sun., 10 a.m.-4 p.m.; Dec.
(Santa's Reindeer Farm only),
Wed.-Sun., 5-8 p.m.
Closed Jan., except prearranged
programs
Admission: $5.50/adults; $4/chil-
dren ages 4-15; $2.50/children
ages 2-3; free/children under 2
Directions: Take Exit 15 from I-90
and go south on Highway 900
(Renton-Issaquah Road). Turn right
onto Newport Way and travel west
to S.E. 54th. Follow 54th up the hill
to the zoo.

Established in 1972 by Cougar
Mountain Academy, a private
school, this 14-acre teaching zoo
specializes in threatened or endangered animals and birds, and is
home to such creatures as lemurs,
reindeer, and cougars. Bird fans will
be pleased with the large assortment
of exotic parrots and cockatoos, in
addition to emus and cranes.

Visitors can walk through the zoo
at their own pace or take a guided
tour; experienced volunteer docents
will answer questions. During school
field trips, docents will often take a
cougar out of its cage to give the
kids a rare close encounter.

This small zoo recently expanded,
adding several exhibits, including a
children's wildlife statue park with 24

TIPS

Santa's Reindeer Farm, where
kids can meet Santa, talk to elves,
and admire the reindeer team
(led by Rudolph, of course), is
open Wednesday-Sunday evenings
in December. Cost is included in
zoo admission. Videos and cameras
are welcome.

Don't bother paying $1 to buy
a small cup of fruit and vegetables
to feed the animals: All you can do
is throw it to the alpacas or nyalas
from above their pens or through
the chain-link fence.

bronze animal statues children can
climb on. Renovations were expected
to be completed by spring 1998.

ESSENTIALS

The zoo features a seasonal
snack bar and tables. Parking is
free. The paths are gravel, so
negotiating a stroller can be tricky;
bring a backpack for babies. The
zoo is small enough that even a
preschooler can walk through it in
half an hour. A rest room was built
as part of the renovation.

➤ **Nearby attractions:** All For Kids
Books & Music (Issaquah location), the
Herbfarm, Lake Sammamish State Park.

Farrel-McWhirter Park

19545 Redmond Road, Redmond
(425) 556-2300
Open: Daily, 8 a.m. to dusk
Admission: Free
Directions: Follow SR 520 east until it ends and turns into Avondale Road. Follow Avondale for one mile and turn right onto Novelty Hill Road. After a quarter mile, turn onto Redmond Road. Drive a half mile to the park, which is on the left.

Driving through second-growth forest in this 68-acre park, you'd never guess that hidden behind the trees is a farm with ponies, pigs, goats, and rabbits. Expect to make at least two rounds past the pens of friendly animals. Even the rest room, located in a converted silo, is worthy of exploration—it has a fun lookout on top.

If you can drag the kids away from the animals, this park on the eastern edge of Redmond also encompasses a large open field, an orchard, and two miles of trails.

Children can visit with barnyard animals, including baby pigs, at Farrel-McWhirter Park in Redmond.

Charlotte's Trail, an asphalt trail that is wheelchair accessible, runs the length of the park. There is also a 1.5 mile equestrian loop.

In the 1930s, the McWhirter family built the farm for a summer home. Elise Farrel-McWhirter, a horse trainer, willed the property to the city of Redmond. Upon her death in 1971, the land became a public park.

The Redmond Parks Department hosts a variety of excellent programs for children of all ages at Farrel-McWhirter, including farm activities, preschool classes, breakfasts with the animals, pony-riding classes, and summer day camps.

Forest Park Animal Farm

802 Mukilteo Blvd., Everett
(425) 257-8300
Open: April-Sept., daily,
9 a.m.-5 p.m.
Admission: Free
Directions: Take the 41st St. exit from Interstate 5 north. Go left on 41st and follow it as it winds around, passing Broadway and Rucker. The street turns into Mulkiteo Blvd.; the park is on the left.

The barnyard is home to rabbits, pigs, goats, ducks, ponies, calves, and two llamas. Free pony rides are offered from 2-3 p.m. daily June to August, weather permitting. Children can get a handful of feed for a quarter. Popular farm programs include "Breakfast With the Animals," "Barnyard Birthdays," and "Mommy and Me." Educational tours are also offered for groups by reservation.

Kelsey Creek Park is the beautiful setting for a farm, walking paths, and preschool playground.

The park also has a new playground and summer sprinkler pool.

Kelsey Creek Community Park/Farm

13204 S.E. Eighth Pl., Bellevue
(425) 455-7688
www.ci.bellevue.wa.us/bellevue/kelsey.htm

Open: Dawn to dusk year-round; public viewing of animals daily, 8 a.m.-4 p.m.

Admission: Free

Directions: Take Exit 12 (SE Eighth Street) from I-405 and go east on S.E. Eighth. Follow this road through the intersection at Lake Hills Connector to the stop sign at 128th Avenue S.E. and turn left; follow 128th to S.E. Fourth Place and turn right. The park is just ahead.

If someone in your family either loves or doesn't recognize rabbits, chickens, horses, cows, goats, donkeys, and pigs, this farm-in-the-big city is well worth a visit. Farm in

TIPS

Spring brings the arrival of many baby animals at Kelsey Creek. If you want to give your child a chance to watch a birthing scene or see some new babies, call in early spring to find out the EDTs (Expected Delivery Times) of the pregnant animals.

Craft and animal care classes are offered year-round; special events include sheep shearing in mid-March and the Farm Fair in early November.

Group tours for preschools, schools and parties are $1.50/person.

this case means a lovely, big red barn and adjacent small buildings that house the usual assortment of farm animals. Behind the barn are corrals for the horses. Children can wander through the barn at their own pace, enjoying up-close views of their favorite farm animals. Down along a pretty creek is a first-class playground for the toddlers and preschoolers. This 80-acre expanse also offers paved and gravel trails, plenty of open lawns, and a covered picnic area, so take lunch and enjoy the setting.

ESSENTIALS

Parking is free. Park in the first parking lot. The barn is accessible by stroller, though toddlers can easily handle the walk.

Rest room facilities are available near the playground but not at the barn. Food and drink are not sold at the park, so bring your own.

➤ *Nearby attractions: Bellefield Nature Park, Bellevue Botanical Gardens, Bellevue Art Museum, Rosalie Whyel Museum of Doll Art*

Northwest Trek Wildlife Park

11610 Trek Dr. E., Eatonville; 17 miles south of Puyallup
(800) 433-TREK
www.nwtrek.org
Open: Year-round. March-Oct., daily; Nov.-Feb., Fri.-Sun. and holidays. Opens at 9:30 a.m.; closing time depends on the season.
Admission: $8.25/adults; $7.75/seniors; $5.75/children ages 5-17; $3.75/children ages 3-4;

free/children 2 and under
Annual membership: $45/family
Directions: Take Exit 142B from I-5 and travel south on State Route 161. Northwest Trek is 17 miles south of Puyallup on SR 161. Total distance is about 55 miles from Seattle, 35 miles from Tacoma.

You know you're not in a typical zoo when the naturalist tour guide has to nudge American bison out of the road so she can drive a tram through, asking passengers how much clearance she has. Or when she warns that even if she sees a moose, she's not stopping the tram to look because it's rutting season and the male moose are very aggressive.

Hourly tram tours take visitors through 435 acres of free-roaming habitat to search for eight kinds of big hoofed animals, including

Wildlife, such as the American bison, gets up close and personal at Northwest Trek.

STEPHANIE DUNNEWIND

STEPHANIE DUNNEWIND

A beaver family enjoys lunch in the zoo area.

bighorn sheep, elk, caribou, mountain goats, and deer. This trip can be either wonderful, such as when the keeper feeds the animals along the road and they are so near you can take pictures of their nose hairs, or disappointing, such as when the animals are hanging out away from the road. But the drive itself is pretty, passing through forest, meadows, and wetlands, and kids will probably enjoy the whole "hide-and-seek" aspect of the tour. The guides also provide plenty of interesting information about the behavior of these magnificent animals, which will hold the attention of most school-age kids.

The park owes its existence to the generosity of Dr. and Mrs. David T. Hellyer, who in 1971 donated 600 acres of beautiful land to the Metropolitan Park District of Tacoma to create a protected place where Northwest wildlife could roam freely.

In addition to the tram tour, a more traditional zoo area offers close-up views of raccoons, beavers, badgers, river otters, skunks, wild cats, bears, and wolves. (The beavers and otters can also be viewed underwater.) The exhibits are spaced somewhat apart from one other, so

expect a healthy walk. Strollers and wheelchairs can easily navigate the wide, paved paths.

At the Cheney Discovery Center,

TIPS

Try to allow at least three hours to take in all the activities at Northwest Trek: the one-hour tram tour, hands-on activities at the Discovery Center, a visit to the walk-through area, browsing in the gift shop, and lunch in the cafe. Arrive early in the off-season, because the Discovery Center closes at 3 p.m. and the last tram leaves at 3 p.m. Naturalists say the early tours are better for seeing animals; the free-roaming animals are more likely to be resting in the shade or sleeping in the afternoon. Since animals can be anywhere, there is no obvious advantage to either side of the tram. Also, if you get a bum tour or enjoy it so much you want to do it again, additional tram rides are free, but you need new tokens from the front office.

Trek holds special activities year-round, including hayrides, photo tours, breakfasts, animal-care camps, elk bugling tours (Sept.–Oct.), and Hoot 'N' Howl (for Halloween). Spring is the best time to see baby animals; Trek holds a baby shower in May.

kids can touch frogs and garter snakes, pet animal fur coats, have their picture taken with a (stuffed) bear, and try out the many learning boxes, which offer activities such as listening to a tape of animal sounds and trying to identify them.

ESSENTIALS

Parking is free. Strollers can be rented for $3. Northwest Trek features over 5 miles of hiking trails through wooded areas, as well as a paved .75-mile loop easily accessible to strollers and wheelchairs. A changing table is located in the women's rest room. Guides to native plant life are available at the trail entrance and the office. There are plenty of tables for picnicking. The cafe offers dining inside or out; on chilly days you can warm yourself by the fireplace. The food is basic (burgers, chicken sandwiches, etc.), tasty, and not outrageously priced. Bottled juice and some salads are also available.

➤ **Nearby attractions:** *Pioneer Farm (in Eatonville). See Chapter 9.*

Olympic Game Farm
1423 Ward Road, Sequim
(360) 683-4295 or (800) 778-4295
www.northolympic.com/gamefarm
Open: Year-round. Walking tours available during summer only.
Admission: Driving tour, $6/adults, $5/children ages 5-12, free/children age 4 and under. Guided walking tour and driving tour, $8/adults, $6/children ages 5-12, free/children age 4 and under.
Directions: Take the Edmonds or Seattle ferries to the Olympic

Peninsula and take Hwy. 104 north to Hwy. 110. Follow this to Sequim.

The farm, started by animal trainers, is a haven for injured wild animals, endangered species and animals retired from the movies. Many of the animals have been in Walt Disney Studio productions, including "Never Cry Wolf" and "The Incredible Journey." You can drive your car through to see animals such as llamas, yaks and deer up close. Animals such as bears, tigers and wolves are kept behind safety barriers. During the summer, guided walking tours are offered. You can purchase a loaf of bread to feed to certain animals. There is also an aquarium, petting farm, prairie dog town and fishing pond.

ESSENTIALS

A snack bar is open during the summer. You can bring food for a picnic, but no sharing with the animals is allowed.

TIPS

There is a small per-inch fee for trout caught at the fishing pond. Fish can be taken home or given back to the game farm to be shared with a bear of your choice.

Elephants are one of the many animals at Point
Defiance Zoo, which has a Pacific Rim theme.

The Point Defiance Zoo and Aquarium have a Pacific Rim theme, focusing on animals from countries bordering the Pacific Ocean. This means you might see some animals not commonly seen in Northwest zoos, such as beluga whales, walrus, and tropical sharks. The zoo's 29 acres house more than 5,000 animals, including penguins, polar bears, and, of course, elephants. Several of the animals that like to swim can also be viewed underwater. A popular stop for children is the farm, where a

Point Defiance Zoo and Aquarium

5400 N. Pearl Street, Tacoma
(253) 591-5335
www.ckmc.com/pdza/
Open: Daily year-round, except Thanksgiving Day and Christmas Day. Labor Day-Memorial Day, 10 a.m.-4 p.m.; Memorial Day-Labor Day, 10 a.m.-7 p.m.
Admission: $7/adults; $6.55/seniors and disabled adults; $5.30/children ages 4-13; free/children 3 and under
Annual membership: $45/family
Directions: From I-5 take Exit 132, and follow signs to Highway 16. Turn left on at the Sixth Avenue exit from Highway 16, turn right onto Pearl Street, and follow the signs to Point Defiance Park, home of the zoo and the aquarium.

TIPS

Each December, Zoolights transforms Point Defiance Zoo and Aquarium into a fantasy land where more than 530,000 lights cover pathways, trees, and buildings, and outline illuminated animals, nursery rhyme characters, and local landmarks. Try to visit Zoolights early in December, as this attraction gets busy later in the month.

During the spring and summer months, the zoo and aquarium host ZooSnoozes for children of all ages. These overnight camp-outs include activities designed to teach children about animals who make the sea their home.

See Chapter 9 for more information about the rest of Point Defiance Park.

quarter buys a handful of food to feed the goats —a real thrill for little city slickers. Naked mole-rats—ugly, rodent-like creatures that burrow in tunnels—and other animals that have unique ways of fitting into their environments are part of the "World of Adaptations" exhibit, located near the park entrance.

The popular North Pacific Aquarium and side exhibits feature marine life from the cold-water regions of the Pacific Northwest, including playful sea otters, octopuses, wolf eels, jellyfish, and other species native to this area. The Discovery Reef Aquarium is devoted to life in warm waters and is home to sharks and dozens of colorful tropical fish. Watch out! Your 2-year-old may not like being face-to-face with a huge shark!

ESSENTIALS

Parking is free and located conveniently adjacent to the zoo; stroller rentals are available on a first-come, first-served basis for $3. The two gift shops—one at the main gate, the other in the aquarium—feature a good assortment of souvenirs and gift ideas. Bring a picnic, grab a snack at one of the snack bars located throughout the park grounds, or order lunch in the cafe at the zoo. The cafe prices are reasonable ($2.99 for a kid's meal), and the food is quite good.

Seattle Aquarium and Omnidome
Pier 59, Waterfront Park, Seattle
(206) 386-4320 (Aquarium),
(206) 622-1868 (Omnidome)
www.seattleaquarium.org/

Open: Year-round. Labor Day-Memorial Day, 10 a.m.-5 p.m.; Memorial Day-Labor Day, 10 a.m.-7 p.m.
Admission (Aquarium): $7.75/adults; $7/seniors and disabled adults; $5.15/children ages 6-18; $1.95/children ages 3-5; free/children 2 & and under
Admission (Omnidome and Aquarium): $13/adults; $11.25/seniors; $9.50/children ages 6-18; $5.50/children ages 3-5; free/children age 2 and under
Annual Aquarium membership: $45/family

The Seattle waterfront offers a wide variety of attractions for the entire family, but the Seattle Aquarium has to be one of the best. Set right over the water on Pier 59, the Aquarium's view of Elliott Bay shows a variety of boats and ferries. The Aquarium also offers visitors a beautiful view beneath the waters of Puget Sound and a chance to learn about sea creatures from around the world.

Entering the Aquarium, visitors can escape into a world of color and movement. The lights are dimmed, setting off the colors within the many lighted tanks.

The first stop is the Principles of Survival exhibit, which features elegant seahorses, spiny lionfish, and an electric eel. The cichlids don't look like anything special, but be sure to read the descriptive blurb out loud to kids: one type of cichlid sucks out and eats other fishes' eyeballs! Next comes the Local Inverte-

TIPS

The Seattle Aquarium is a good first outing for an infant in a backpack—the bright fish colors are captivating. Visitors' maps are free and offer an overview of the featured exhibits. Allow some time for browsing in the Sandpiper Gift and Book Store, which you enter as you exit the exhibit area. Keep your Aquarium receipt in order to leave and re-enter the Aquarium.

A lot of tanks are just above eye level for small children, so expect to do a lot of picking up.

brates exhibit, where a Pacific octopus, crabs, and shrimp should keep kids' interest. And don't expect kids to let you past the Discovery Lab, where you can touch tide pool favorites such as starfish, anemones, and sea urchins. Nearby is a felt board where kids can make their own sea visions. "Jaws" —well, a model of a great white shark— hangs above the entry to the Pacific Coral Reef exhibit. (Puget Sound is home to seven kinds of shark.)

In Building 2, visitors start out at the common entry to the sea—a beach setting, complete with waves—and take a journey that leads into the middle of the ocean in the Underwater Dome. Next is an extensive exhibit devoted to salmon;

it boasts the only aquarium-based salmon run in the world, featuring a fish ladder and interesting information about the migration of these fascinating creatures. (Late summer and early fall are the best viewing times.)

The stunning Underwater Dome is a 400,000-gallon, glassed-in area where families can sit on benches and observe life under the sea. Even an infant will be mesmerized by the action in this "inside-out" aquarium. If you schedule your visit for about 1:30 p.m., you'll witness the Aquarium's divers feeding the dome residents. You'll probably also see the divers cleaning: They wipe 85 to 100 windows a day!

After checking out the graceful underwater ballet of the fur seals, head to the open-air "Otters and Seals" exhibit, where playful sea otters twirl and romp. Catch feedings at 11:30 a.m. and 2 and 5 p.m.

Although the Aquarium is a wonderful attraction now, the city plans to make it even better. In 1997, the Seattle City Council gave the Aquarium the go-ahead to look for funding and start designing a new facility, to be located two piers to the north, that would be double the size of the existing one. Construction is slated to begin in four to six years.

Adjacent to the Aquarium is the Omnidome Theatre, featuring films that put you so close to the action, you feel you are a part of it. Whether it's a ride in a helicopter viewing the destruction of Mount St. Helens or a dive with giant whales, these movies offer breathtaking footage accompanied by entertaining and informative

ESSENTIALS

Parking is available across the street from the Aquarium using either meters or the Public Market parking garage. Stock up on quarters if you use the meters; a dollar's worth buys only an hour. Parking in the outside lot is $8 to $10 for two to four hours (depending on the season); parking inside the garage costs $6.75 for two to three hours. Metro buses don't run along the waterfront, but the Waterfront Trolley travels between the International District and Pier 70, with several stops along Alaskan Way ($1/adults non-rush hour; $1.25/adults rush hour; 75 cents/children).

Stroller rentals are usually available at the Aquarium, but call ahead to be sure they are in service. Aisles and ramps are easily accessible to strollers and wheelchairs. If you want to walk outside on the pier to read informative displays or watch the otters and seals from outside viewpoints, dress for the weather.

King County residents with proof of residency receive admission discounts (be sure to tell the cashiers, because they won't necessarily ask). Joint annual family memberships for the Seattle Aquarium and Woodland Park Zoo are available for $85.

Steamers, a spot with tasty fish and chips, is located right outside the Aquarium. (Kids' meals run $2.99.) Several places to snack are located just south at the Bay Pavilion on Pier 57. On the Hillclimb —the stairs leading to the Pike Place Market—you'll find El Puerco Lloron, a very good, inexpensive Mexican restaurant.

narrative. Warning: While these movies are typically a great hit with children age 5 and up, younger kids may be frightened and overwhelmed by the huge screen. And anyone susceptible to motion sickness might get a queasy stomach. Each film is about 45 minutes long.

Omnidome admission can be purchased separately ($6.95/adults; $5.95/children ages 6-18; $4.95/children ages 3-12; free/children under 3), or in combination with admission to the Aquarium (see above).

► *Nearby attractions: See Chapter 8/ Waterfront for other waterfront attractions. Across the street from the north entrance to the Aquarium, you'll find steep stairs (aptly called the Hillclimb) leading to the Pike Place Market. For more information on these areas, see Chapter 8's section on Pike Place Market.*

Wolf Haven International

3111 Offut Lake Road, Tenino (about 10 miles south of Olympia) (360) 264-4695

www.teleport.com/~wnorton/wolf.shtml

Open: May-Sept., 10 a.m.-5 p.m.; Oct.-April, 10 a.m.-4 p.m. Closed Tuesdays.

Admission: $5/adults; $2.50/children ages 5-12; free/children under 5

Directions: Just south of Olympia, take Exit 99 from I-5 and go east onto 93rd Avenue. Follow 93rd to Old Highway 99 and turn right. Drive south for about 4 miles and turn left onto Offut Lake Road. Wolf Haven is 0.3 mile ahead.

Wolf Haven International, a non-profit organization, was established in 1982 to provide a sanctuary for captive wolves and to help educate

COURTESY OF WOLF HAVEN

Wolf Haven provides sanctuary for captive wolves.

the public about the activities—hunting, poisoning, trapping, and habitat destruction—that have led to the near disappearance of the wolf. Wolf Haven is currently home to about 40 wolves of various subspecies of the gray wolf, *Canis lupus.* In addition to hourly guided tours of the 80-acre sanctuary, Wolf Haven offers outreach programs to schools, civic organizations, and

TIPS

If you'd like to directly affect a wolf's life, you can "adopt" a wolf through Wolf Haven. Howl-ins are special events held Friday and Saturday nights from May through September, featuring a tour, storytelling and sing-alongs around the campfire, and howling with the wolves. Cost is $6/adults and $4/children ages 5–12. Reservations are required; call (800) 488-9653.

others within the community. The organization is dedicated to educating the public about the importance of wildlife and habitat.

Woodland Park Zoo

5500 Phinney Ave. N., Seattle
(206) 684-4800
www.zoo.org
Open: Daily year-round, from 9:30 a.m.; closing time varies with the season
Admission: $8/adults; $6.25/seniors; $5.50/children ages 6-17 and disabled adults; $3.25/children ages 3-5; free/children age 2 and under
Annual membership: $50/family
Directions: Take Exit 169 (for N. 50th Street) from I-5. Go west on N. 50th about 1.3 miles to the south gate of the zoo, located at the intersection of N. 50th and Fremont Avenue.

Rated one of the 10 best zoos in

STEPHANIE DUNNEWIND

Orangutans enjoy a naturalistic home with trees and a waterfall.

Giraffes roam in the African Savannah at Woodland Park Zoo.

STEPHANIE DUNNEWIND

the United States, the Woodland Park Zoo is an outstanding example of what a zoo can be when time and money are spent to re-create natural habitats. Located just 10 minutes from downtown Seattle, the 92-acre zoo features an extensive array of animals, many in wide-open areas, not cramped cages. Giraffes, zebras, and hippos roam within the African Savannah exhibit; elephants plod, play, and demonstrate their strength and intelligence in an exhibit that looks like a Thai logging camp in the midst of a jungle; gorillas go native in their jungle home. The Tropical Rain Forest exhibit makes a vivid impression as visitors ascend from the floor of the forest to high up in the canopy. In the Northern Trail area, wolves, sea otters, and grizzlies live as if they were on the Alaskan tundra. Kids can crawl into a cave and find a bear sleeping in the back (separat-

ed by a shield, but up close nonetheless). On the Trail of Vines, orangutans hang out among trees and waterfalls, while siamangs make themselves known with extremely loud shrieks.

The Nocturnal House is a favorite with children; there bats, raccoons, lizards, and other denizens of the dark carry on their routines in a nighttime environment. The Nocturnal House is linked to the Reptile House, which is equally popular with kids, and likely to get a few oohs, ahhs, and eeks. Strollers must be left outside.

In the Temperate Forest exhibit, the Family Farm features the usual farm animals, including sheep, rabbits, chickens, and pigs. The Contact Area, where kids can pet the animals, is open daily during the summer and on weekends in spring and

ESSENTIALS

Parking is available in lots next to the north and south entrances to the zoo; cost is $3.50. Wheelchairs and strollers can be rented for $3 at the ZooStore next to the south gate. Bring a picnic lunch or stop by the Outback Cafe or the Rain Forest Food Pavilion, which offers a variety of restaurants, including Pizza Hut, Chili Peppers, Burger King, Rain Forest Deli, and Dreyer's ice cream. Summer concession stands offer hot dogs, soft drinks, popcorn, and other goodies. King County residents with proof of residency receive admission discounts. Joint annual family memberships for the Seattle Aquarium and Woodland Park Zoo are available for $85.

fall. Sure to be a hit is the new Bug World, with plenty of creepy-crawlies of all sorts. If kids get sick of sitting in a stroller, head to the Habitat Discovery Trail, where they can climb up a giant rope spider web, slide down otter slides, or pretend to be a mole squirming through a simulated mole burrow.

➤ **Nearby attractions:** *Green Lake, Hiram M. Chittenden Government Locks, Woodland Park. See Chapter 3.*

TIPS

If you live in the area, consider investing in a family pass so you'll feel free to make unlimited visits. A leisurely zoo outing on a cloudy winter day is an altogether different experience than a trip to the zoo on a hot, crowded weekend in the summer.

The Education Center, located by the south gate, is open daily, 8:30 a.m.–5 p.m. Visitors can stop by to pick up informational brochures, participate in educational programs, or explore the Discovery Room (weekends only), which offers young visitors a variety of hands-on experiences.

Pony rides are offered in the northwest corner of the zoo daily during the summer months. The hours are limited, usually 11 a.m.–3 p.m., and the cost is $2. Children must be at least 2 years old; the maximum weight is 120 pounds. There is often a line, and the rider is led just once around the corral, but this is a big thrill and very popular, especially with very young children.

The zoo presents Zoo Tunes Jr., a summer concert series that takes place outdoors on the North Meadow, on Monday nights during July and August. Cost is $5/children. Children age 12 and under receive discounted admission to the adult concerts performed on Thursday evenings. For more information, call the zoo at (206) 684–4800.

If you're running out of time or if the kids are bored, skip most of the Temperate Forest exhibit and take the alternate access directly to the Family Farm and the Discovery Trail. The double sets of doors that keep birds contained in the Temperate Forest exhibit make it difficult to navigate with a stroller.

INSIDE SCOOP Seeing Salmon

Kids can't help but be fascinated by salmon as the fish visibly struggle up rivers and creeks to spawn. If you come at the right time, you might see hundreds or even thousands of fish at these two local hatcheries. Both offer free self-guided tours. The best time to see salmon is early September to the second week in November. Chinook arrive in September, while coho show up in mid-October.

Green River Hatchery, 13030 Auburn-Black Diamond Road, Auburn. (253) 931-3950. Open 8 a.m.-4:30 p.m. daily. The hatchery, located off Highway 18, features a small ladder and a holding pond with 100 to 10,000 fish.

Issaquah Salmon Hatchery, 125 E. Sunset Way, Issaquah. (425) 392-1118. Open daylight hours. About 1 million juvenile salmon are put in Issaquah Creek each spring. Issaquah celebrates the salmon's return each fall with a Salmon Days Festival in October.

Chapter 2

HARVESTS

In the urban and suburban world of 24-hour grocery stores and we-have-everything warehouses, it is easy for a child to forget about the real source of food and plants: land. And though the convenience of being able to buy your food, pumpkins, and even Christmas trees at the local supermarket is undeniable, there is much to be said for the experience of going out to the farms where these goods are grown.

Luckily, you don't have to drive too far to get back to nature, and the minute you are out of city traffic you'll be glad you made the effort. The sweet fragrance of a strawberry field, the cool frost on a pumpkin patch, the braying and neighing of farm animals—these rural sights and smells and sounds are quite alluring, and the entire family will be better off for a bit of country air.

SPECIAL FARMS

Biringer Farm

Hwy. 529 north of Everett and
south of Marysville
(425) 259-0255

Families can pick berries in the
summer, select pumpkins in October, and ride the "Jolly Trolley" tractor shuttle to chop down a Christmas tree in December. Other attractions include a farm market, tours,
and picnic area. Call for information
about special events.

Carnation Farm

28901 N.E. Carnation Farm Road,
Carnation
(425) 788-1511
School tours by reservation in the
spring; call well in advance.
Public hours vary (usually summer
Saturdays); call to check
Free admission

This 900-acre working dairy farm
is open for group tours in the spring
and includes a nice, self-guided
walk along spotless paved pathways. The maternity barn and calf
nursery are great stops for kids,
who love to pet the young calves. A
visit to the milking barn will prove
once and for all where the creamy
white liquid originates. The tour can
be easily completed in about an
hour, making it a good field trip for
preschool and kindergarten classes.

Fall City Farms

3636 Neal Road, Fall City
(425) 222-7930
Open July-November

The farm opens in July with U-
pick garlic, organically grown rice,
and herbs. It offers garlic-braiding
lessons as well as tours for school
groups and the general public. Later
in the season it features specialty
garlic, corn, pumpkins, apples,
cider, and gourds. Special events
include Garlic Weekend in August,
Apple Day in September, and Winter Weekend in December.

The Fat Hen Farm

28040 152nd Ave. S.E., Kent
(253) 631-9553
Open March-December

Kids can visit with the farm animals while adults wander through
display gardens with more than 300
varieties of herbs, perennials, and
everlastings. Herb, craft, and cooking classes are also offered.

Remlinger Farms

32610 N.E. 32nd, Carnation
(425) 451-8740; www.rfarm.com
Open April to mid-Dec.
Free admission; costs vary for
classes, activities and festivals

Remlinger Farms, boasting a
270-acre "working farm that really
works," offers a wide variety of special events and activities. Harvest

STEPHANIE DUNNEWIND

Old farm equipment is one of many attractions at Remlinger Farms in Carnation.

strawberries in June, raspberries in July, pumpkins in October, and Christmas trees in December, or pick up fresh vegetables and fruits, plus homemade jams and soups, from the General Store. From May to October, a variety of classes are offered for children, including spring planting, fall harvesting, how the farm works, and wildlife on the farm. Other attractions include farm tours, a steam train, birthday parties, and a petting farm, as well as special events and festivals on weekends throughout the year.

Children's Garden
4649 Sunnyside Ave. N., Seattle
(206) 633-0451
Summer classes; tours in spring and fall
Prices for classes vary

The Seattle Tilth Association's

Children's Garden offers a series of Peawee Patch Workshops for children ages 7-12 at its garden in Meridian Park in the Wallingford neighborhood. Children plant and tend their own plot in the garden, draw, keep journals, sing, play games, and more. Workshops are offered June through August, with EarthSteward tours in the spring and fall; call to register.

The Herbfarm
32804 Issaquah-Fall City Road, Fall City
(206) 784-2222;
www.theherbfarm.com
Open daily year-round,
10 a.m.-5 p.m.; extended hours April-Sept.
Free admission

This is a pleasant outing if your group feels like a drive into the

country and a walk among 17 lovely herb gardens. Your family will
learn more about herbs than you
ever thought possible (more than
most kids want to know)—from
cultivation to cooking. Guided tours
are given on summer weekends at
1 p.m. Special theme weekends
include lavender in July, basil in
August, and scented geraniums in
late summer. The outdoor gardens
feature rows and rows of an amazing variety of potted herbs to purchase for your home garden.

Although it's unlikely that the
majesty of these gardens will hold
children's attention for long, kids
will enjoy visiting with llamas. The
Herbfarm also offers picnic areas
on the grounds, so bring a lunch
and enjoy the rural surroundings.
The restaurant, which burned
down early in 1997, will reopen in
1998. Initially only dinners will be
served, with lunches slated for
1999. Though exquisite, the meals
are not for kids—too refined, too
slow, and too expensive.

Classes for children ages 8-12
are taught year-round; call for a free
activity schedule and visitor's guide.

Seattle P-Patch Community Gardening Program

City of Seattle, Department of
Neighborhoods
(206) 684-0264

If the preceding information
makes you wish you and your kids
had a garden of your own to plant
and harvest, but you just don't have
the space, consider participating in
a community P-Patch Program.

The Department of Neighborhoods, in conjunction with the non-
profit Friends of P-Patch, allows
Seattle residents to organically grow
vegetables, small fruits, and/or flowers in one of 36 neighborhood garden sites. The P-Patch Program also
serves refugees, low-income, disabled (some gardens are wheelchair
accessible), and youth gardeners.
Any surplus is given to local food
banks; the program donates seven to
10 tons of fresh produce each year.
The P-Patch plots range in size from
100 to 400 square feet, for an annual
fee of $21 to $53. Gardeners must
be Seattle residents, contribute eight
hours per year of volunteer time,
attend a group work party, and provide their own seeds. Call early so
you'll be ready for spring planting.

BERRY PICKING

Just about the time summer
vacation begins, ripe strawberries,
raspberries, and blueberries are
ready for picking. Boxes are usually
supplied at U-pick farms; a staff
member will assign you and your
kids to a row where you can pick
to your hearts' content. When
you're finished, someone weighs
your berries and you pay by the
pound. Reservations are not necessary, but call ahead to make sure
berries are available. Try to go early
in the day, when the selection is
best. Many fields are pretty bare by
the end of the day. It's hard work,
but the rewards are immediate!

Each year *The Farm Fresh Guide*

is published in April, listing names, addresses, crops, and hours of operation for many of the U-pick farms throughout King, Pierce, Skagit, and Snohomish counties. The guide is available free at public libraries and Chamber of Commerce offices beginning in April or May. You can also send a stamp along with a self-addressed mailing label to: Sue Kinser, Puget Sound Farm Markets Association, 1733 NE 20th Street, Renton, WA 98056.

Local berry farms include:

Biringer Farm, Hwy. 529 north of Everett and south of Marysville; (425) 259-0255. Strawberries.

Blueberry Farm, 12109 Woods Creek Road, Monroe; (360) 794-6995. Blueberries; has a playground and picnic area.

The Blueberry Patch, 10410 54th Pl. N.E., Everett; (425) 334-5524. Blueberries.

Blue Heron Blueberries, 8628 Fobes Road, Snohomish; (360) 568-0192. Blueberries.

Bybee-Nims Farms, 42930 S.E. 92nd St., North Bend; (425) 888-0821. Blueberries.

Cruz-Johnson Farms, 22243 Frager Road, Kent; (253) 872-8017. Raspberries.

Due's Berry Farm, 14003 Smokey Point Blvd., Marysville; (360) 659-3875. Strawberries.

Grandpa's Farm, 26825 S.E. 208th St., Maple Valley; (425) 432-4269. Strawberries.

Harvold Berry Farm, 32325 N.E. 55th, Carnation; (425) 333-4185. Strawberries and raspberries.

John Hamakami Strawberry Farm, 14733 S.E. Green Valley Road, Auburn; (253) 833-2081. Strawberries.

Kennydale Blueberry Farm, 1733 N.E. 20th St., Renton; (425) 228-9623. Blueberries.

Lydon's Blueberry Farm, 14510 Kelly Road N.E., Duvall; (425) 788-1395. Blueberries.

Overlake Blueberry Farm, 2380 Bellevue Way S.E., Bellevue; (425) 453-8613. Blueberries and raspberries.

Remlinger Farms, 32610 N.E. 32nd, Carnation; (425) 451-8740. Strawberries and raspberries.

Serres Farm, 20306 N.E. 50th St., Redmond; (425) 868-3017. Strawberries.

Snow's Berry Farm, 18401 Tualco Road, Monroe; (360) 794-6312. Raspberries.

Sunny Acres Berry Farm, 17516 SR 203, Monroe; (360) 794-8855. Strawberries and raspberries. ■

TIPS

When berry picking, use sunscreen and hats, and bring food and plenty of drinks. Also, show the kids how to maneuver between the rows of plants carefully. Make sure they understand which berries are ripe for picking (there are little secrets the farmer might share), and don't pick more than your family can eat or process in a few days, because berries spoil quickly.

PUMPKIN PATCHES

J ust when the fallen leaves have been drained of their last vestiges of color and the dreary drizzle of autumn has settled in, Halloween comes along and rejuvenates our spirits (quite literally, according to some). Children adore this holiday: creating fun costumes, trick-or-treating, and, of course, carving their jack-o'-lanterns for display on the window or porch.

Many pumpkin farms offer an array of special activities throughout October, including hay rides, haunted houses, scarecrows, and costumed characters. Call ahead to confirm hours of operation and to verify special events, since they're apt to change from year to year.

Pumpkin-themed scenes entertain October visitors to Craven Farm in Snohomish.

Alden Farms
19604 Tualco Road, Monroe
(360) 805-0911

U-pick pumpkins and hay rides are offered. The original Victorian farmhouse, built in 1900, has been restored. Open weekends, 10 a.m.-5 p.m.

Biringer Farm
Highway 529, north of Everett and south of Marysville
(425) 259-0255

The month-long schedule of activities and attractions during October includes a cornfield maze, story barn, pony rides, a fishing hole, and wagon rides to the pumpkin patch. There is an admission fee (about $3), with additional cost of $1 to $4 for some attractions. Call ahead to confirm hours and events.

Craven Farm
13817 Shorts School Road, Snohomish
(360) 568-2601

The farm features a collection of about a dozen pumpkin-themed scenes, such as "Snow White and the Seven Pumpkins." Other attractions include a "live" pumpkin who greets the children and tells them a story about the farm, a friendly witch who introduces the kids to the farm animals, and pumpkin harvesting right from the vine. Weekday reservations for preschool and elementary school group tours are

TIPS

At most farms, pumpkins have already been cut from the vine and are lying free in the fields. The cost of the pumpkins varies from farm to farm but is usually determined individually by weight. Remember to dress warmly, wear your boots, and bring the camera!

required, but the public can drop in on weekends. A small fee (about $4 per child) includes the tour, a cookie, and a pumpkin; adults are free.

Fall City Farm
3636 Neal Road, Fall City
(425) 222-7930

Weekday organized tours for a minimum of 10 include a talk about what farmers do, a wagon ride, a visit to the animal barn, and a turn at helping to make cider. Price varies by age and size of group. Call for an appointment. The public can stop by for free on weekends to enjoy a corn maze, U-pick and picked pumpkins, and a store with produce and prepared foods.

Hands-On Pumpkin Farm
15308 52nd Ave. W., Edmonds
(425) 743-3694

This farm offers educational field trips for all ages. Children are led on a 40-minute tour of the farm, which includes time to pet and feed some of the animals before picking pumpkins. Reservations are required. The fee of $3.50 per child includes a pumpkin; adults are free with school groups. The barn and the pumpkin patch are free for visitors who purchase a pumpkin; $2 per person to visit only.

The Herbfarm
32804 Issaquah-Fall City Road, Fall City
(206) 784-2222

Storytelling, scarecrows, barn animals, a thousand-bale hay maze, and the Great Pumpkin are annual Herbfarm favorites. Weekend activities range from crafts and games to pony and hay wagon rides. Weekday visits are by appointment ($5/person); call ahead for reservations. The public is welcome to drop in on Saturdays and Sundays ($7/person). Fees include most activities and a pumpkin.

Remlinger Farms
32610 N.E. 32nd St., Carnation
(425) 451-8740

The granddaddy of pumpkin patches, Remlinger hosts the annual regional Giant Pumpkin Contest in early October. That event kicks off a month of activities, including weekday tours with a steam train ride,

STEPHANIE DUNNEWIND

Remlinger's barn is decorated to celebrate Halloween.

hay maze, petting farm, and puppet shows. Weekends include all the daily attractions plus pony and wagon rides. The Land of Orange pumpkin patch has thousands of pumpkins. Weekday visits are by reservation ($5/person); call (425) 333-4135. Weekends are open to the public ($6.50/adults; $7.50/kids).

Smaller pumpkin patches include:

Cruz-Johnson Farms, 22243 Frager Road, Kent; (253) 872-8017.

Peter's Pumpkin Patch, 23724 Dockton Road S.W., Vashon Island; (206) 463-3256.

Serres Farm, 20306 N.E. 50th St., Redmond; (425) 868-3017.

Top of the Hill Pumpkin Patch, 16533 36th Ave. W., Lynnwood; (425) 743-4250.

Tasty Pumpkin Seeds

Once you have scooped the insides out of the pumpkins, rinse the seeds thoroughly (or boil them), spread them on a baking sheet, and coat them with butter and any of the following: paprika, garlic, salt, or seasoning salt. Bake at 425 degrees for 15-20 minutes (stirring a few times), until they are golden brown and crisp.

Optional: Sprinkle pumpkin seeds with Parmesan cheese. ■

CHRISTMAS TREE FARMS

Bundle up the family and visit one of the area's Christmas tree farms for a special outing during the winter holidays. Many farms offer hot cider, coffee, and holiday goodies, as well as special attractions such as tractor rides and visits with Santa. Each year,

TIPS

As romantic as they sound, family outings to find a Christmas tree have the potential to turn into a tortured experience in failed group decision-making. Whether you search for your tree at a Christmas tree lot in the city or venture out to a tree farm, remember that this is not a ride into the snowy woods in a one-horse open sleigh. Discuss in advance how the group will choose a tree (a lesson in compromise) and caution the kids (and adults) that the perfect tree WILL NOT BE FOUND. You don't want to be one of those families that come home with a tree for each family member out of sheer desperation (and fear of frostbite). Dress warmly and bring plenty of snacks.

the Puget Sound Christmas Tree Association publishes a guide with its member Christmas tree farms, including addresses, phone numbers, and hours of operation for each farm, as well as any special amenities. This free guide is available during November and December at Chamber of Commerce offices and public libraries throughout the Puget Sound area. The Northwest Christmas Tree Association also publishes a guide covering Washington and Oregon, which is available locally during the holidays. Call (503) 364-2942 to receive a free copy or for more information.

The **U.S. Forest Service** issues permits for $10 to cut your own tree in selected areas. Call the local ranger station for areas and permit information: Darrington, (360) 436-1155; Skykomish, (360) 677-2414; Verlot (Granite Falls), (360) 691-7791; Mountlake Terrace office, (425) 775-9702.

Biringer Farm and Remlinger Farms (see Special Farms at beginning of chapter).

Pilchuck Secret Valley Christmas Tree Farm
Hwy. 9 north of Arlington
(360) 435-9799

Offers 100 acres of U-cut trees, as well as a children's patch of small trees, a Grandma's tree patch, and a special touring area of trees from around the world. Visitors can also purchase refreshments and crafts.

Shults Christmas Tree Farm
4528 E. Heggenes Road, Clinton
(360) 341-5868

The tree farm on Whidbey Island offers fresh Christmas trees, wreaths, and swags, as well as complimentary hot cider, coffee, and candy canes. Kids can also enjoy pony rides on the weekends (weather permitting). Located 10 minutes from Mukilteo/Clinton ferry.

Trinity Tree Farm
14237 228th Ave. S.E., Issaquah
(425) 391-TREE

After selecting and cutting a tree, you can enjoy complimentary hot drinks by a bonfire, visit Santa on weekends and buy decorations and ornaments from the gift shop.

Aunt Stina's Pepparkakor

This Scandinavian recipe is especially popular with kids because the final product can either be eaten or hung on the tree (or both), and the cookies are very tasty. It will yield enough cookies to trim a small tree and can be doubled successfully. The dough keeps well in the freezer, if you want to plan ahead.

Combine:
2 sticks butter or margarine
1 cup granulated sugar
1 cup dark corn syrup
1/2 pint sour cream

Blend well, and add:
1 tsp. allspice
2 T. cinnamon
1 T. ginger
1 T. cloves

1 tsp. baking soda
4-5 cups flour

Chill dough until firm. Roll out portions on a well-floured board. Transfer to an ungreased cookie sheet and roll dough with a floured rolling pin to one-eighth-inch thickness on the cookie sheet. Cut out dough with cookie cutters or cut around your own cardboard patterns with the point of a sharp knife.

Bake at 325 degrees for 10-15 minutes, or until browned. Cool cookies on the pans before removing.

Decorate cookies with white decorative icing from a tube. Use regular sewing thread and a fine needle to pierce and hang the cookies.

—Sonia Cole

FARMERS MARKETS

E ven if you don't have the time or inclination to grow your own vegetables, you can still get them fresh from one of the area's many farmers markets. Rich in colors, sights, smells, and sounds, these markets present a plentiful array of fresh-from-the-garden vegetables, fruits, and flowers, as well as clothes and jewelry made by local craftspeople, and street artists. A guide to local markets is available May 1 by calling (425) 710-2064.

Bainbridge Island Farmers Market
Municipal Parking lot, 410 Madison Ave. N., Winslow
Easter-Oct., Saturdays, 9 a.m.-1 p.m.
(206) 842-7431

Country Village Farmers Market
Country Village, 23730 Bothell-Everett Hwy., Bothell
June-Sept., Fridays, 10 a.m.-2 p.m.
(425) 483-2250.

Edmonds Summer Market
Downtown Edmonds
July-end of Sept., Saturdays,
9 a.m.-3 p.m.
(425) 347-2790.

Everett Farmers Market
Everett Marina on W. Marine View Drive, north of the Navy Homeport and Marina Village
June-end of Sept., Sundays,
11 a.m.-4 p.m.
(425) 347-2790.

Fremont Farmers Market
N. 34th St. and Evanston Ave.
May-Oct., Sundays, 10 a.m.-4 p.m.

The popular University District Saturday Market often offers special activities, such as classes and a petting zoo.

Issaquah Farmers Market
Community Center, 301 Rainier
Blvd. S., Issaquah
Open April-Oct., Saturdays,
9 a.m.-3 p.m.
(425) 392-2229

Kent Market
Corner of Second and Smith
streets, downtown Kent
April-Oct., Saturdays, 9 a.m.-
4 p.m.; Sundays, 10 a.m.-3 p.m.
(253) 813-6976

Pike Place Market
First Ave. and Pike St.,
downtown Seattle
Open year-round
Monday-Saturday, 9 a.m.-6 p.m.;
Sunday, 11 a.m.-5 p.m. (Sunday is
an optional day for vendors; not all
stores or booths may be open.)
See Chapter 8 for details.

Redmond Saturday Market
7730 Leary Way,
downtown Redmond
May-Oct., Saturdays,
8 a.m.-2 p.m.
(425) 882-5151

Snohomish Farmers Market
First Ave., two blocks west of
bridge, Snohomish.
May-end of Sept., Thursdays,
5-9 p.m.
(425) 347-2790

Tacoma Farmers Market
Broadway between S. Seventh
and S. Ninth, Tacoma
June-early Sept., Thursdays,
10 a.m.-3 p.m.
(253) 272-7077

Tacoma - Proctor Farmer's Market
3916 N. 26th St.
June-Aug., Saturdays,
9 a.m.-2 p.m.
(253) 756-8901

**University District Saturday
Market**
University Heights Community
Center, University Way and N.E.
50th St., Seattle
June-Oct., Saturdays,
9 a.m.-2 p.m.
(206) 633-1024

Vashon Saturday Market
Downtown Vashon,
on the Vashon Highway
April-Oct., Saturdays,
10 a.m.-3 p.m.
(206) 463-6557

Woodinville Farmers Market
Downtown Woodinville,
next to City Hall
May-Oct., Saturdays,
9 a.m.-4 p.m.
(425) 788-3697

Chapter 3

PARKS

If you think your local park is the best in the area, you are not alone. Families all over Puget Sound feel the same way about their parks, which can mean only one thing: We have an abundance of top-notch parks. King County alone manages 18,000 acres of park land and some 200 miles of trails.

Seattle-area parks offer such diverse attractions as a salmon-shaped slide, dragon-shaped spray gun, human-powered trolley, sandy beaches, and giant wind chimes. So next time your children want to go to the park, make it a new adventure instead of a routine skip down the block.

M ost parks departments publish excellent guides that feature listings of parks and other recreation areas, maps, and details about various facilities. For more information, call King County, (206) 296-4232 or www.metrokc.gov/parks; Seattle, (206) 684-4075 or www.pan.ci.seattle.wa.us/seattle/park s/home.htm; Bellevue, (425) 452-6881; Issaquah, (425) 391-1008; Kirk-land, (425) 828-1217; Mercer Island, (206) 236-3545; Redmond, (425) 556-2300; and State Parks Information Center, (800) 233-0321.

All of the parks in the region offer good picnic spots, but if you are planning a get-together with a large group and want to be sure you'll have enough tables, sheltered sites may be reserved year-round. In Seattle, picnic sites may be reserved at 20 parks, including Alki, Carkeek, Gas Works, Golden Gar-dens, Lincoln, Seward, and Lower Woodland. Picnic shelters are $25 for all day; picnic tables, $7.50. Reservation applications are sent out in February. Phone and walk-in reservations are accepted beginning in April. Reserve early for the best sites (206-684-4081).

Alki Beach
Alki Ave. S.W., Seattle

When the first Seattle settlers landed on Alki, they were optimistic that eventually the area would become a bustling town. The name they gave their settlement was New York Alki (Alki meaning "by and by" in Chinook jargon). No matter what those pioneers envisioned, one can be sure it *wasn't* the Cali-fornia beach scene that occurs on hot summer days. The sandy 2.5-mile strip skirting Puget Sound and an adjacent walkway are hugely

STEPHANIE DUNNEWIND

The popular strip of beach along Alki is best visited off-season or on a weekday if you don't want crowds.

NEIGHBORHOOD NOTES

WEST SEATTLE

A good **bike trail** runs from Alki to Lincoln Park (see Chapter 4). Other parks in West Seattle include **Camp Long** and **Lincoln Park** (described elsewhere in this chapter) and **Schmitz Park** (see Chapter 4).

Alki Point Lighthouse, (3201 Alki Ave. S.W.) is open for tours from 12-4 p.m. on weekends from Memorial Day to Labor Day. For more information, call the U.S. Coast Guard at (206) 217-6120.

The **Log House Museum** (3003 61st Ave. S.W.; 206-938-5293) features historical information about "The Birthplace of Seattle," including displays on the Duwamish Indians, West Seattle's pioneer families, and Luna Park, the area's early-1900s amusement park. Videos show a reenactment of the city's founding; heritage kits and a historical library are available for teachers and students. Each year the museum, housed in a 1903 log house, celebrates the anniversary of the landing of the Denny party at Alki Beach on Nov. 13. Admission is by donation. Hours are Tues., noon to 7 p.m.; Fri.-Sat., 10 a.m.-4 p.m.; Sun., noon- 3 p.m.

If you're interested in more history, pick up a copy of *West Seattle Wanderings* at the Chamber of Commerce (4750 California Ave. S.W.; 206-932-5685). The illustrated guide, which costs $1.25, shows 17 places of West Seattle historical note.

Eleven murals on various buildings within a few blocks of the Chamber of Commerce office offer additional glimpses of West Seattle history. The Chamber sells a $1 pamphlet with a map and descriptions of each mural.

Check out the local Web site— www.westseattleherald.com—for an events calendar, tips on discovering West Seattle, and a dining guide.

Hungry? Across the street from the beach are numerous boardwalk eateries. **Spud Fish and Chips** (2666 Alki Ave. S.W.; 206-938-0606), which offers some of the best fish and chips in the area, is known for their good-sized chucks of fresh ling cod coated in cornmeal and fried in canola oil. If the kids don't like fish or clams or oysters, they can still carbo-load on the delicious fries, which are peeled, cut, and fried fresh every day.

continued on next page

Pegasus Pizza (2758 Alki Ave. SW; 206-932-4849) serves up fabulous pizza (try the Greek pizza) in an attractive setting with plenty of windows facing the fine views. Dine inside or use the take-out window and picnic on the beach. Pegasus is open daily, for dinner only. **Alki Cafe** (2726 Alki Ave. S.W.; 206-935-0616) offers baked goods, seafood, and pasta, and is open for breakfast, lunch, and dinner. **Pepper-dock's Restaurant** (2618 Alki Ave. S.W.; 206-935-1000) serves up grilled hamburgers, seafood, and ice cream.

Elsewhere in West Seattle, **Zatz A Better Bagel** (2348 California Ave. S.W.; 206-933-8244) bakes 20 varieties of bagels fresh each day. **Luna Park Cafe** (2918 S.W. Avalon Way; 206-935-7250), serves breakfast, lunch, and dinner amid funky '50s decor (see Chapter 11).

popular with cyclists and sunbathers, Rollerbladers and beach walkers. Expansive views of downtown Seattle (with the Space Needle just peeking out) and the Olympic Mountains are an added attraction.

However, the crush of humanity that flocks to the shore when the sun shines is not around most of the year. Year-round the beach offers families fine beachcombing and fresh salt air. Take along hot dogs and marshmallows if the weather is decent (small beach fires are allowed) and bring a kite to fly upon the sea breezes. Rest rooms are located at 57th Ave. and 60th Ave.

If your kids get tired of sand, or if the beach gets too windy, head over to **Alki Park** at 59th Ave. S.W., which features a playground at either end. The northern one is older, with a wooden boat and swings; the southern play area features newer climbing toys, slides, and decorative tiles painted by children.

(For information on trails, see Chapter 4.)

Camp Long

5200 35th Ave. S.W., Seattle
(206) 684-7434
Lodge hours: Tues.-Sun, 8:30 a.m.-5 p.m.; closed holidays
Directions: Take the West Seattle Freeway exit from Interstate 5. Follow the freeway to the first light and turn left onto 35th Ave. S.W. Take 35th to S.W. Dawson and turn left into the parking lot.

With 68 acres of forest, nature trails, overnight cabins, a 25-foot artificial climbing rock, and plenty of open areas, Camp Long is the ideal park to visit when the family wants to get away from it all without driving far.

For many years, Seattle Parks

and Recreation operated Camp Long exclusively for organized groups. Today the cabins are open to the public as well, making it the only city park with overnight camping.

At the beautiful old lodge next to the parking lot, you'll find an

Kids will enjoy scrambling up "Glacier" at Camp Long.

TIPS

Camp Long naturalists lead free nature walks on most Saturdays for families with children age 5 and up. Advance registration is required the week of the walk; call (206) 684–7434. Free introductory rock-climbing classes are offered occasionally for age 7 and up; more advanced classes are also available for a fee. Reasonably priced educational programs for school groups of preschoolers to fifth-graders focus on topics such as pond ecology, forest discovery, and basic rock climbing.

For a back-to-nature overnight, not too far from latté land, rent one of the 10 rustic cabins in the park, complete with double bunk beds and electricity, for $30/night Tuesday through Saturday. Bring your friends: The cabins sleep up to 12 people. Six cabins are wheelchair accessible. The wheelchair-friendly Rolling Hills Trail starts at the parking lot and provides access to these cabins.

Whispering of the Woods, available for $4 at the lodge, is an outstanding teacher's guide full of interesting facts and suggested activities to make a trip to Camp Long more meaningful.

interesting historical and wildlife exhibit and an informative ranger who will give you the run-down on how to enjoy the park.

The Nature Trail, a half-mile loop through the woods, is perfect for young hikers who are long on enthusiasm but short on endurance. To get to the trail, follow the path down the hill from the lodge to the open field below. Take a left on the service road, passing Polliwog Pond on the right. At the north end of the pond, leave the road as it curves right and instead follow the path past the large, flat stone compass set in the ground to the sign marking the start of the trail. Start on the left fork. Longer trails loop around the eastern portion of the park.

Schurman Rock, an artificial climbing structure, is at the northern end of the park. Nearby Glacier, a series of rock slopes built down a wooded hill, is used to train climbers in rappelling, but kids love the challenge of scrambling to the top (closely supervised by an adult).

The enormous open field in the middle of Camp Long is ideal for games that require plenty of space. A large campfire pit surrounded by benches lies at the south end of the field.

Carkeek Park

950 N.W. Carkeek Park Road
Seattle
(206) 684-0877

You can see real salmon here in the fall or you can slide down a salmon's mouth and come out its tail all year round! Carkeek Park is tucked away down a narrow road, but it's well worth finding. An imaginative playground features the aforementioned slide, in the shape of a giant salmon, a trail with a bridge and dry creek, riding toys in shapes of sea animals, and two rock cave shelters.

TIPS

Carkeek is a great place to see salmon up close since Piper Creek is small and shallow. You can look down from a bridge or stand nearby to watch the struggle. Park stewards offer impromptu talks on weekends from late November to early December; call to confirm the salmon's arrival. In the spring, impromptu walks of the wetlands and beach are offered, including a look for intertidal critters at low tide. Call to see when volunteer naturalists are scheduled.

Other programs include free "walk-and-talks" for families on selected weekends, a junior naturalist club and family programs for a small fee. Group tours and classes are available.

Kids can't resist the salmon slide at Carkeek Park.

STEPHANIE DUNNEWIND

A pedestrian bridge to the beach crosses over railroad tracks, offering the closest view you'll ever get of a train without riding one. The long set of stairs is steep for little ones, so be prepared to carry them.

Several miles of trails wind through the park, including a paved trail along Piper Creek and a raised wooden walkway over wetlands.

Children's Park
Island Crest Way, Mercer Island

This pleasant little park was designed by the Mercer Island Preschool Association especially for small children. The play equipment is imaginative and fun, two tennis courts are nearby, and several short trails meander through the shady grounds.

Gene Coulon Memorial Park
1201 Lake Washington Blvd. N., Renton

Located at the southeasternmost tip of Lake Washington, next to Boeing's Renton plant, Coulon Park is the city's pride and a youngster's delight. The major attraction is the large sandy swimming beach. The kids will quickly target the play area, which sits near the beach and is equipped with slides, swings, climbing toys, and a big sandbox. A

> ## ESSENTIALS
> Slightly north of the beach at Gene Coulon Memorial Park you'll find Ivar's Fish Bar and Kidd Valley Restaurant, where you can sit outside and enjoy fish and chips or burgers, respectively, while watching the action on the water. If you'd rather take your own picnic, the large, covered pavilion nearby has outstanding picnic facilities, including several barbecue grills. If the park has one drawback, it's the abundance of geese: Be prepared with washable blankets or towels to sit on!
>
> There is usually plenty of parking, even on the sunniest days.

foot bridge crosses to a small island that is kept as a nature preserve. Other attractions include a 1.5-mile paved trail with raised walkways over the water, and volleyball and tennis courts.

Dash Point State Park
5700 S.W. Dash Point Road
Federal Way
(253) 661-4955

Dash Point's day-use area features a playground, picnic tables, and a sandy beach fronting Puget Sound. About 14 miles of trails traverse the woodsy, 475-acre park. Mountain bikes are permitted.

The campground, which is open year-round, offers 138 campsites, including 30 hookup sites for RVs. Cost is $10/standard tent site, $15/hookup site, $5/hiker-biker site. Reservations can be made for dates from April 15 through Sept. 15 by calling Reservations Northwest at (800) 452-5687. For general information, call (800) 233-0321. Rangers lead interpretive programs and nature walks on summer weekends.

Discovery Park
3801 W. Government Way, Seattle
(206) 386-4236
Visitor Center: Open daily, 8:30 a.m.-5 p.m.; closed holidays
Daybreak Star Center: Open Mon.-Sat, 10 a.m.-5 p.m.; Sun., 12-5 p.m. Phone: (206) 285-4425.

Discovery Park is the largest and most diverse park in Seattle, boasting 534 acres of forest, meadows, cliffs, beaches, self-guided interpretive loops, short trails, jogging trails, man-made ponds, and a thriving population of birds and animals. It's a spectacular nature sanctuary that invites exploration and learning, as well as sport and play.

When the Secretary of the Army announced in 1964 that 85 percent of the land at Fort Lawton in Magnolia would become surplus, local and federal politicians went to work on obtaining the land for public enjoyment. In 1972, the federal government gave the site to the city of Seattle, which was aptly named the park Discovery (after Puget Sound explorer Captain George Vancouver's flagship, the H.M.S. *Discovery*). A handful of buildings and trucks are the only reminders of this park's military past.

The South Meadow, once maintained as an athletic field for military personnel, is an inviting open space with a majestic view of Puget Sound and the Olympics. It is a fine spot to spread a blanket and delve into a good book, while the kids romp or fly a kite (there is always a stiff breeze off the Sound). The South Bluff, east of the meadow, also offers a spectacular vista of the islands and mountains beyond, but the cliffs are steep and treacherous, so be careful to hold on tightly to your curious preschooler. One of the most popular attractions at this bluff is a big pile of sand (fondly referred to by locals as "the dunes," despite its singularity), upon which such games as King of the Mountain and Bury the Feet can be played. At the higher point of the South Bluff are signs that point the way down to the South Beach and the West Point area, renowned for some of the best marine bird-watching and tidepooling in Seattle. The beach, like the park, is mixed terrain: There are sandy areas, rocky beds, and mud flats (when the tide is low). The West Point Lighthouse, built in 1881, is maintained by the Coast Guard.

TIPS

If you have children age 5 and under, ask for a parking permit so you can drive to South Beach and thereby skip the 3-mile round-trip hike.

Discovery Park rangers offer an exceptional variety of nature programs for adults and kids (some for as young as age 2). The popular Night Walks, on which rangers lead families on a search for nocturnal life in the park, are just one example of the many activities offered. Naturalists arrange education programs for preschool and kindergarten classes, as well as nature day camps during the summer. The classes and workshops are low cost (or free) and invariably top-notch. Call (206) 386-4236 for information.

Several bald eagles live at the park, so ask the rangers at the Visitor Center where you can spot their nests. Bring binoculars!

The North Bluff was once the site of military barracks and the noncommissioned officers' club. It offers another spectacular view and several picnic tables. On the area of land below the bluff, the Shilhoh people lived until early in this century. To the left of the picnic area is a trail leading down to the North Beach, another ideal spot for exploring tidepools. Look for crabs, sea stars, sea anemones, and sea urchins. Remember to tell the kids to look but leave the sea life undis-

turbed. Luckily for the animals, the days of hauling sea creatures home in buckets have passed.

(For information on hiking trails, see Chapter 4.)

One highlight of Discovery Park that is not nature-made is Daybreak Star Center, a Native American cultural/educational center in the northwest corner of the park. Twelve Native American artists were commissioned to create artworks for this beautiful building, and most of the pieces are large murals and carvings depicting legends and traditions that children will find interesting. Daybreak Star's gallery features a variety of contemporary and traditional Native American art. A gift shop sells books, calendars, and stationery.

On three weekends in December, Daybreak Star hosts an Indian Art Mart from 11 a.m.-4 p.m. It usually includes an authentic Native American lunch of salmon, corn, and Indian fry bread; cost is $8.50/person.

There is no charge to visit Daybreak Star Center. If you park in the north parking lot, it is a short walk to the center. Check the map in the southwestern corner of the north lot for directions.

ESSENTIALS

The park can be entered at the main gate at W. Government Way and 36th Ave. W., the south gate at W. Emerson near Magnolia Blvd. W., and the north gate near W. Commodore Way and 40th Ave. W. Unless you know where you are going, it is easiest to enter at the main gate on the east side, where you'll find a good map and a short history of the park and the Visitor Center just ahead on the left. The Visitor Center features environmental interpretive exhibits.

Just south of the Visitor Center are tennis courts, a basketball court, and an exceptionally good playground geared to younger children (none of which is visible from the parking lot). Picnic tables can be found at a number of locations: along the North Bluff, near the playground (south of the Visitor Center), at West Point, and at the Daybreak Arts Center.

Rest rooms are a good thing to scope out when taking little kids to this big park. You'll find them at the Visitor Center, South Meadow, North Bluff, and West Point.

Five Mile Lake
36429 44th Ave. S., Federal Way

Swim in the lake, fish off the pier, enjoy a children's play area, or play tennis or basketball at this 26-acre park. Bring a picnic; the park boasts 135 tables and 19 barbecues.

Flaming Geyser State Park

23700 S.E. Flaming Geyser Road,
Auburn
(Located 2.5 miles south of Black
Diamond)
(253) 931-3930

Don't go to this lovely park expecting an Old Faithful sort of display from its namesake. The geyser lets out natural gas that is lit on summer weekends to create a small flame. The lame flicker hardly seems worth naming a park after, but there are plenty of other attractions to make a visit worthwhile, including a nice playground. Trails follow a creek through lush lowland forest; another goes along the river. The large picnic area is usually filled with people carrying rafts and inner tubes to float down the river. The water moves pretty quickly, so it's more for wading than swimming. A separate area serves as a remote-controlled airplane site.

Gas Works Park

2101 N. Northlake Way, Seattle

When park designers first presented the idea of incorporating the old gas works plant perched at the north end of Lake Union into a new park, critics complained noisily. But today, the grotesque remnants have become a familiar part of the cityscape, and the 20-acre park is a premier spot to enjoy a picnic and panoramic views of the downtown skyline.

This was a working gas refinery until 1955, and about one-third of the old machinery still stands. The old boiler house, with its overhead maze of pipes, has become a bright-ly painted play barn. There is also a small playground.

A grassy man-made knoll has become a favorite gathering spot for kite-flying enthusiasts. Look for a giant sundial, built in the ground near the top of the hill. The 28-foot diameter dial is made of inlaid and

TIPS

The Burke Gilman Trail runs through Gas Works Park and is a good place for walkers, runners, bikers, and skaters to take a rest room stop and stretch their legs. It's also a very popular picnic spot on a summer nights. A spectacular fireworks display is held here each Fourth of July.

Because residual contaminants in the soil and ground water remain from the park's former use as a coal and oil gasification plant, be especially careful to insist on good hygiene here. Ask your children to wash their hands after playing and before eating. Don't let them dig in dirt other than at the play area, and make sure little ones don't eat dirt. Also, don't allow them to swim or wade in the lake.

In case children ask, the six tall towers (kept behind cyclone fencing for safety) were oxygen gas generator towers used to convert crude oil to heating oil.

cast bronze, shells, ceramic, and found objects that have been embedded in multicolored concrete. To tell time, the viewer stands on a central oval and becomes the gnomon for the sundial, casting a shadow toward the mosaic hour markers at the perimeter. Children will delight in closely examining the dial to discover small figures, sea life, and other objects set in this beautiful piece of public art.

Golden Gardens
North end of Seaview NW, Seattle

If you hanker for a beach fire and salt air, head to Golden Gardens on Shilshole Bay, at the west end of Ballard. The water is frigid, but there is a warmer stream running into the Sound that is just right for water play. Ice cream and fish and chips are within easy walking distance. No lifeguards on duty.

A small play area features a climbing toy and swings. If your

NEIGHBORHOOD NOTES

FREMONT
Fremont cultivates its funky image by calling itself the "Republic of Fremont" and insisting that its motto is "Freedom to be Peculiar."

OK, whatever.

Drive north over the Fremont drawbridge on Fremont Ave. N., find somewhere to park on the street, pick up a free Walking Guide to Fremont brochure at various kiosks, and search for Fremont's fun public art. The basic area you want to explore includes N. 34th St., N. 35th St., and N. 36th St. from about Evanston Ave. N. to Aurora, plus Fremont Place.

At the north end of the Fremont Bridge is "**Waiting for the Interurban**," a group of five aluminum commuters who are usually decorated in some sort of fashion.

"**The Fremont Troll**," a huge statue devouring a real Volkswagen Bug, is tucked under the Aurora Bridge at Aurora and N. 36th St. The **rocket**, a colorful projectile, is attached to a storefront at Evanston Ave. N. and N. 35th St. Several spots around the neighborhood have markers with information on Fremont's history, art, and landmarks. The **History House** museum (790 N. 34th St.; 206-675-8875) focuses on the history of Seattle's neighborhoods, with photo displays, interactive computers, and video programs. It's open 11 a.m.–6 p.m. Wed.–Sun.; admission is free. School groups are welcome.

If your kids can handle a walk of several blocks or if you have a stroller, head for the path along the **Ship Canal**

continued on next page

and watch all manner of boats pass by. **Canal Park** offers grassy areas and an overlook at its western edge.

The quintessential Fremont place to eat is **Still Life in Fremont Coffeehouse** (709 N. 35th St.; 206–547–9850). The sturdy wooden tables and chairs are kid-friendly, and the menu offers hearty soups, salads and sandwiches ($1.95–$5.95). The enormous Vegetable Pie ($5.25) is like a quiche on steroids (in a positive way); the hefty portion of Tortilla Pie could easily fill an adult and child. Leave room for one or more of the baked desserts. Breakfast is served on the weekend.

Fremont is home to a number of shops worth peeking into. **Edge of Glass Gallery** (513 N. 36th St.; 206–547–6551) is a gallery and studio that features glass-blowing demonstrations on weekends, 11 a.m.–3 p.m. **Painted Fire** (3601 Fremont N.; 206–545–2816) a paint-your-own-ceramics studio, is at Fremont Village Square. **Redhook Ale Brewery** (3400 Phinney Ave. N.; 206–548–1305) offers daily tours. At **B.Y.O.B.** (102 N.W. 36th St.; 206–634–BREW) kids can make their own soda pop with custom-designed labels. One batch of 40 bottles is $50. (If you're exploring on foot, this is several blocks west on 36th.) If you continue west on 36th, it turns into Leary Way. Here you'll find the **Collectible Doll Company** (4216 Sixth Ave. N.W.; 206–781–1963), with

porcelain dolls, doll furniture, and doll supplies. It also offers classes, tours, and a toy museum. East of Aurora, on the opposite side of the neighborhood, is a bizarre toy store called **Archie McPhee & Co.** (3510 Stone Way N.; 206–545–8344). Older children will undoubtedly love the odd mix of toys, coin-operated machines, and self-described "wacky kitsch."

From spring to fall, check out the **Fremont Farmers Market**, N. 34th St. and Evanston Ave., on Sundays, 10 a.m.–4 p.m. The **Fremont Outdoor Cinema** is held at the same spot on Saturdays from June to Labor Day. Classic movies are projected on the side of a building, while people watch from lawn chairs they bring and set up in a parking lot. Seating starts at 7 p.m.; movies begin at dusk. Cost is $5/person. Call (206) 634–2150 for more information. Other seasonal events include the **Solstice Parade** and the **Fremont Street Fair** in June and **Trolloween** on October 31. An **ArtWalk** is held the first Saturday of every month; maps and listings are available at galleries or at various markers.

If you'd like a guided tour, try **Troll Tours** (206–632–3170) on nice weekends. **Web sites** with info on events, food, shopping, arts, and even an electronic walking tour are www.fremont.com; www.scn.org/fremont; and www.seattleweb.com/cities/fremont/fremont.html.

TIPS

For a fabulous beach walk, head out to Golden Gardens at a minus tide and walk north along a wide expanse of sand and rocks. If you walk far enough, you might run across geoduck diggers uncovering those grotesque mollusks. From out on the sand, you're likely to see a few trains pass by on the tracks above the beach, always a good diversion for young kids.

Two wetlands were recently restored at North Beach and a short, paved loop offers three view-points of the Sound.

a playground (at the east entrance), lifeguarded beaches from mid-June through Labor Day, a big wading pool (northeast corner), a community center, boat rentals, an indoor swimming pool, and many nearby places to grab a tasty snack or meal. The recently repaved jogging/bicycle trail, which runs along the water's edge (about 2.8 miles), is very popular on sunny weekends and gets dangerously crowded for wobbly young walkers, skaters, and bikers. A new playground features a sandbox, jungle gym, and swings.

Hamlin Park
16006 15th Ave. N.E., Shoreline

The 73-acre forested park offers play fields, a playground, and a series of interlocking hiking trails through a natural area. It is also

kids don't like dogs, avoid the upper part of the park, where there is an off-leash area.

Green Lake
E. Green Lake Dr. N. and W. Green Lake Dr. N., Seattle

Many Seattleites exercise religiously, and Green Lake has long been their Mecca. Joggers, roller skaters, cyclists, and boaters (non-motorized crafts only) of all shapes, sizes, and abilities make their pilgrimage to the lake whenever weather permits (and often when it doesn't). Families, too, flock to Green Lake, because it offers plentiful picnic areas, as well as activities and amenities for all ages, including

TIPS

The popularity of Green Lake threatens to ruin the pleasure, especially when families extra-burdened by hauling kids and their assorted paraphernalia have difficulty finding a place to park on a hot day. It is best enjoyed with little kids when the weather is less than spectacular and the crowds have dwindled. See Chapter 4 for more information on outdoor activities and Chapter 5 for information on the swimming pool (Evans).

NEIGHBORHOOD NOTES

GREEN LAKE

If you get hungry after playing at Green Lake Park, here are some recommendations for restaurants to visit.

Starbucks Coffee (7100 E. Green Lake Dr. N.; 206-523-9594), at the southeast corner of the lake, features all the regular Starbucks drinks and treats, plus a line of sandwiches from Briazz. The peanut butter and jelly sandwich (no crusts, of course) is a definite kid pleaser. But the best reason to come to this Starbucks is a rooftop deck that overlooks the lake. Kids will love the view and the birds that hang out up there.

Honeybear Bakery (2106 N. 55th St.; 206-545-7296) is about six blocks east of the lake, and well worth the detour. The Green Lake institution makes divine cinnamon rolls and cookies, as well as soups and homemade breads. Kids will enjoy the live music that starts in the early evening (before bedtime) on weekends.

Zi Pani Breads Cafe (7200 E. Greenlake Dr. N.; 206-524-3369) is a family-friendly cafe with healthy choices sure to please. Fresh-baked muffins, breads, bagel sandwiches, salads and satisfying soup breadbowls.

Urban Bakery (7850 E. Green Lake Dr. N.; 206-524-7951) is another great spot on the north side of the lake that serves up delicious homemade

continued on next page

sandwiches and to-die-for pies and cookies. Ask for your food to go and enjoy a picnic on one of the fishing piers that jut out into the lake just across the street from the restaurant.

Marbletop Creamery (7900 E. Green Lake Dr. N.; 206-526-9810), inside the new Lakeside Plaza, is a fun place to visit for customized ice cream. You pick one of six ice cream or frozen yogurt flavors, then choose a candy, topping, or fruit you want mixed in. They put the ingredients on a marble board and mix them together in front of you. The creations are served in a waffle cone or a dish, topped with whipped cream and a cherry. A personal favorite: chocolate ice cream mixed with caramel, cookie dough, and Butterfinger candy pieces. Less adventurous ice cream fans can go to **Baskin-Robbins** (7110 E. Green Lake Way N., at the southeast corner of the lake, next to Starbucks) or **Haagen-Dazs** (6810 E. Green Lake Way N., at the south side of the lake, near Albertson's). Other restaurants in the Lakeside Plaza are **Guido's Pizza**, **World Wrapps**, and **Ed's Juice and Java**. Stop in at any of them for a great quick bite.

popular with mountain bikers.

Hiram M. Chittenden Government Locks

3015 N.W. 54th, Seattle
(206) 783-7059;
www.nws.usace.army.mil/opdiv/lwsc
/lakewsc.htm
Open: Daily, 7 a.m.-9 p.m.
Visitor's Center: Oct.-May, Thurs.-Mon., 11 a.m.-5 p.m.; June-Sept., daily, 10 a.m.-7 p.m.
Public tours: Sat.-Sun., Oct-May, 2 p.m.; June-Sept. 1 and 3 p.m.

Most people, regardless of age, are fascinated by the remarkable sight of boats and water rising and dropping right before their eyes. The difference between the water level of Puget Sound and Lake Washing-ton varies by anywhere from 6 to 26 feet. The locks protect the ecosystem of the lake by preventing salt water from entering Lake Washington when boats go from Puget Sound into Lake Washington or vice versa.

On a warm afternoon, bring a picnic to enjoy on the grassy knoll above the locks and watch the boat traffic parade past. Sundays are great for boat watching because many people are returning from a weekend in the San Juans; during the summer, free band concerts play every Sunday at 2 p.m.

Fish ladders next to the locks offer underwater viewing of salmon as they struggle to return to their spawning grounds. Salmon arrive from mid-June to late October; the best viewing is in July.

The Visitor's Center shows a 12-

minute video with the history of the locks. A marble maze game allows children to pretend to be a salmon facing many obstacles to get home; they can also play lock master and move a boat through a model of the locks. A bookstore, open on weekends, sells videos, souvenirs, and posters.

Weekend public tours begin in the Visitor's Center, then proceed to the gardens, the locks, and the fish ladders.

Keep an eye out for seals and sea lions, especially from December to May.

Lakewood Park
11050 10th Ave. S.W.,
White Center

Besides the usual ballfields, tennis courts, and trails, Lakewood has a nine-hole disc golf course. It also offers two play areas, a swimming beach, fishing, and three picnic shelters. A public boat launch is next to the park.

Lincoln Park
Fauntleroy S.W. and S.W. Webster,
Seattle

Spread out on 130 acres at one of the most scenic vantage points in the region, Lincoln Park offers breathtaking views of the Olympic Mountains and Puget Sound, as well as shady woods, wide-open playing fields, a fine stretch of beach (less crowded than nearby Alki), and Colman Pool, an outdoor saltwater swimming pool. A short hike down a forest bluff takes you to the beach, which features plenty

TIPS

Though Colman Pool started as a tide-fed swimming pool, it is now an outdoor, heated saltwater pool. Situated right at the edge of the beach in Lincoln Park, Colman is maintained by the Seattle Department of Parks and Recreation and is open summers only. Kids will love the "monster water slide." Special events include Kids Carnival, Monster Splash Day, and Wild 'n' Wacky Olympics. Call (206) 684-7494 for more information.

The short, easy trek from Lincoln Park's parking lot, through deep woods, down to the saltwater beach is likely to seem much longer and much steeper to the little ones when it's time to go home after a frolic on the beach. Be prepared to bribe and coax your short-legged hiking companions up the hill, or bring a carrier to tote them on your back.

(An on-street bike route connects Lincoln Park with Alki Beach. See Chapter 5 for more details.)

of sand and a long, paved path along the water. Trails wind through the park; a nice one meanders along the bluff over the beach. There are two play areas: The one on the north side, near the wading pool, has a toddler climbing structure plus a larger one with slides and riding toys. The playground in the southern part of the park is being renovated in 1998.

The park is located right next to the Vashon–Southworth ferry dock;

kids will enjoy watching the ferries come and go.

Luther Burbank Park
2040 84th Ave. S.E., Mercer Island
(206) 296-4438

NEIGHBORHOOD NOTES

MADRONA

If you want to visit by bus, take Metro No. 2 east on Union St. to come to the heart of the small business district. Jump back on for a ride down to the lakefront.

Besides Madrona Beach, there are a couple play areas to visit. **Madrona Playfield**, located between Spring and Marion on 34th Ave., has a playground geared to younger kids, though a basketball court, tennis courts and large grassy area appeal to older ones.

Al Larkins Park, corner of 34th Ave. and Pike St., has a small but enjoyable selection of meandering, gently rolling sidewalks, making it a perfect spot for small children to ride toys or tricycles. Flowering fruit trees make it an appealing place to visit in the spring; in the fall, the apples and pears can be easily picked.

The **Madrona Sally Goldmark Library** (1134 33rd Ave.; 206-684-4705) is best for young children during school hours before the very popular after-school program begins in the evenings. Storytimes are held Wednesday

mornings. It boasts a Madrona authors' section.

The small Madrona business district has several family-friendly restaurants and indeed, families can often be seen wheeling their way to breakfast, lunch or dinner on bikes, trikes, or riding in wagons. Here are local favorites.

Cool Hand Luke's Cafe (1131 34th Ave.; 206-324-2553) is a casual restaurant decorated with bright blue walls which serves breakfasts on weekends (Mickey Mouse pancakes not on the menu but willingly prepared on request) and lunch and dinner Tues.–Fri. Kid favorites include Chicken Sticks (teriyaki chicken grilled on bamboo sticks that come with two sauces for dipping); Pot Stickers and Imperial Mix (scallions and Portuguese sausage scrambled with eggs), and, of course, PBJ and grilled cheese sandwiches. Pies are made on Fridays; chocolate chip cookies are baked daily.

Plenty (1404 34th Ave.; 206-324-1214) is a mostly vegetarian grocery store and restaurant that offers eat-in or take-out entrees, salads, and sweets.

This county park, which covers 77 acres on the eastern shore of Mercer Island, is a favorite among local families. The clean, sandy beach, with its shallow swimming areas and ideal sand castle spots, is a paradise for young children. And if that's not enough to keep the kiddos occupied, a wooded trail along the water's edge will take them to a playground full of slides, tunnels, swings, balance beams, and crawling nets.

ESSENTIALS

Luther Burbank's north parking lot provides access to the playground; go to the south parking lot if you are headed for the beach. Try not to pack too much, as it's still a good walk from the parking lot to the beach. If you plan to bring food, keep in mind that the picnic area by the beach (which has barbecue grills) gets crowded on summer weekends. Call ahead for reservations if you are bringing a big group.

Madrona Beach
South of the intersection of Lake Washington Blvd. and Madrona Dr., Seattle

Huge logs, arranged as if tossed onto the beach by a winter storm, and large rocks encourage climbing at this sandy beach along Lake Washington. Children will spend hours playing with a child-sized spigot, which supplies water for a stream that kids can make dams to control or footbridges to cross. There is a bathhouse and lifeguards on duty during the summer. Older children will enjoy swimming out to a floating dock and diving board. A large, grassy area with picnic tables and covered cooking spot is adjacent to the beach. In late summer, you can pick blackberries that grow nearby.

Spectrum Dance Studio, located in the bathhouse, offers classes. South of the beach is a fishing dock, but forget any notion of fishing on a sunny day when, regardless of signs prohibiting the activity, the dock becomes a favorite for swimming and sunbathing. On other days, the dock is great for young anglers.

Magnuson Park
Sand Point Way N.E. and NE 65th St., Seattle

This 193-acre park lies on the western shore of Lake Washington, next to what remains of the Sand Point Naval Air Base. Due to its relatively recent conversion from a military air base to a park, it is a rather desolate strip of land, barren of the lush woods that characterize other large city parks. Nonetheless, the paths along the shore are ideal for walkers as well as novice cyclists and skaters. Other features include a good swimming beach (with lifeguards), abundant picnic tables, softball and soccer fields, and six tennis courts. With its long shore and open layout, the park rarely feels crowded.

Matthews Beach
N.E. 93rd and Sand Point Way N.E., Seattle

Matthews Beach is popular with families during the summer. The

TIPS

At the north end of Magnuson Park lies one of the most charming outdoor art sites in the city. Passage through a gate at the end of the park walkway marks the end of the city park and the start of NOAA (National Oceanographic and Atmospheric Administration) property. NOAA developed its 114-acre site by integrating the shoreline walk with artworks that emphasize the relationship between man and nature. The result is a wonderful place to experience art and the outdoors with your kids.

A short distance past the gate separating the NOAA site from the park, walkers cross a footbridge lined with passages from Melville's "Moby Dick." Just to the left of the bridge, a short path leads to Sound Garden, a sculpture of steel towers holding aluminum pipes that wail eerily when the wind blows. Listeners have to be very still and quiet to hear the soft and haunting sounds emanating from the sculpture, so convince the kids to sit down on one of the benches and take advantage of a few calm moments. The NOAA site is open daily, 6:30 a.m.–7 p.m.

If you go in the summer, bring a bucket and some gloves because the park is a great place to pick blackberries.

lifeguarded beach is an exceptionally good swimming area, and easily accessible from the parking lot—a real plus for parents who are packing the usual assortment of beach and kid equipment. Located close to the Burke Gilman Trail, Matthews is also a good place to get off the bikes and enjoy a quick swim and a picnic. A snazzy playground adds to the fun.

Myrtle Edwards Park
3130 Alaskan Way W., Seattle

Located just north of Pier 70 on the Seattle waterfront, Myrtle Edwards is a scenic strip along Elliott Bay with two paved 1.25-mile paths: one for walking and one for cycling (see "Biking" in Chapter 4). The grassy areas are limited, the

> ### ESSENTIALS
>
> Myrtle Edwards is a good place to take a stroll at sunset, after a big meal at the Old Spaghetti Factory (see "Restaurants" in Chapter 11).
>
> If you want to get from Myrtle Edwards to Pioneer Square or the International District, you can take the Waterfront Trolley, which leaves from the park's southern entrance. See Chapter 8 for more details.

benches abundant, but don't think that's all the park has to offer. In its short stretch you will discover a grain terminal (that huge white monstrosity); a fishing pier (Pier 86), replete with a bait and tackle shop (see "Fishing" in Chapter 4); a sand pit between the two trails, about midway down the strip; and a gigantic rock sculpture, "Adjacent, Against, Upon," to climb and explore (near the south entrance). Cool sea breezes and a panoramic view are the finishing touches.

Richmond Beach Saltwater Park

2021 N.W. 190th St., Shoreline
(206) 546-5041
Directions: Take the N. 175th St. exit from Interstate 5 and head west on N. 175th until you reach Hwy. 99. Turn right, go to N. 185th St., and turn left. Follow N. 185th, which turns into Richmond Beach Road, for 2.5 miles. At 20th Ave. N.W., turn left. Follow 20th Ave. for three blocks to the park entrance. Park in the lower lot to go to the beach.

This 40-acre park offers a sandy beach on Puget Sound, hiking trails, a playground, and picnic shelters and tables. It also offers a panoramic view of the Sound and mountains. Special beach events are offered throughout the year at low tide, when naturalists are on hand to identify sea creatures. Watch (and listen) for sea lions.

Saltwater State Park

25205 Eighth Pl. S., Des Moines
(253) 661-4956
Directions: From Interstate 5, take exit 149 (Hwy. 516, Kent-Des Moines) west. Drive west to SR 509 (Marine View Dr.) until it veers left. Follow signs to the park.

Put 88 acres of forest park on the edge of Puget Sound and designate it as one of the few overnight camping sites in the Seattle–Tacoma region. Add boating, hiking, scuba

TIPS

The park offers 53 tent sites for $11/night from April through September. Some sites accommodate RVs, but there are no hookups. The campground is filled seven days a week in July and August, so come early to find a spot. No reservations are taken. A concessions stand sells snacks. Because the park can be so crowded, it is not a good place to let kids wander alone, especially on trails.

diving, and water play, and you get the most-used state park in the area. Many of the overnight camp sites lie next to McSourley Creek, which winds down the park's ravine; the steep, wooded hillside absorbs the noise of the nearby bridge traffic to give campers and hikers some unexpected quiet. You don't have to be a camper to enjoy this park, but you'll likely wait in line at the gate on sunny summer weekends (no fee for day use). Try going after Labor Day to avoid the crowds, and be sure to seek out the sandy beach—it's one of the best on the Sound.

Seahurst Park

13059 16th S.W., Burien
(206) 244-5662
This 185-acre park features a 2-mile-long beach, hiking trails, fishing, a picnic shelter, and a play-

ground with a view of the Olympic Mountains.

Seward Park
Lake Washington Blvd. S. and S. Juneau St., Seattle

Situated at the end of a long scenic drive along Lake Washington Blvd., this 277-acre park covers an entire peninsula. A paved 2.5-mile loop around the perimeter is very popular with walkers, joggers, and cyclists (see "Biking" in Chapter 4). The status of the fish hatchery on the east side of park was unclear at publication, but kids will still have fun playing in the small creek and waterfall off the path. The park also holds six picnic shelters. There are places to play in the sand along the northern edge of the park, or a life-guarded swimming beach in the summer near the Art Studio.

Though the part of the park next to the lake jumps with action on hot summer days, the old-

STEPHANIE DUNNEWIND

The small waterfall is a good stop on a walk around Seward Park.

growth forest above remains cool and tranquil. Several broad trails penetrate the woods in the park; the closed road that leads to the top of the park, past the preschool playground and amphitheater, is perhaps most inviting for strolling.

TIPS

The Seward Park Art Studio (206-722-6342) offers pottery classes for both children and adults.

An Audubon guide and naturalists lead bird walks for families with children age 7 and up on the second Saturday of each month. Pre-registration is required; call (206) 684-7434.

Volunteer Park
15th Ave. E. and E. Prospect, Seattle
Conservatory: Open daily, May 1-mid-Sept., 9 a.m.-7 p.m.; mid-Sept.-April 30, 9 a.m.-5 p.m. Free.

This elegant old park on Capitol Hill is home to the Seattle Asian Art Museum, a 75-foot-tall brick water tower with stairs to climb (daily, 8:30 a.m.-5:30 p.m.), a conservatory, and "Black Sun," a sculpture by Isamu Noguchi, which overlooks the reservoir and frames a spectacular view of the city and the Olympic Mountains beyond. The circular, black granite

The conservatory at Volunteer Park is a great place to visit in winter.

sculpture is irresistible to children, who like to crawl through the slippery, big opening in its center.

Volunteer Park's conservatory, located at the north end of the park, envelops its visitors in lush greenery, sweet heavy fragrance, and humid air. This splendid glass structure houses monstrous cacti, breathtaking orchids, and other flora that will capture most children's attention. The tropical warmth of the conservatory is especially welcome on a cold wintry day.

Just east of the conservatory is a wading pool and a great playground with slides, climbing toys, and an interesting sculpture kids can climb on.

Woodland Park and Lower Woodland Park

N. 50th St., Aurora Ave. N., and Green Lake Way N., Seattle

Just east of the Woodland Park Zoo, Woodland Park offers one of the most popular spots in town for big picnics. With plenty of covered shelters, lots of open space, and close proximity to the zoo and Green Lake, it is a good place to settle for a lazy summer afternoon of barbecuing and Frisbee tossing. Soccer, baseball, and softball fields and a running track are located at the bottom of the east slope of the park; tennis courts can be found at the south side and down near the soccer fields. A 2.5-acre rose garden by the south entrance to the zoo has delighted noses and eyes since 1922. To get to Green Lake, take a footbridge over Aurora Ave. and walk across Lower Woodland Park. (Also see entries for Woodland Park Zoo in Chapter 1 and for Green Lake earlier in this chapter.)

Eastside

Beaver Lake Park
24400 S.E. 24th, Issaquah

Older folks might remember Beaver Lake Park as Camp Cabrini, a wilderness summer camp run by the Catholic Youth Organization for 28 years. Now it is a 86-acre county park with ball fields, picnic tables, a shelter with barbecue pits and fireplace, a fishing spot, trails, and a playground. Totems stand near the shelter, on the lakeshore, and near the park entrance.

Interpretive nature programs are offered periodically at the renovated Issaquah Lodge.

Downtown Park
N.E. Fourth and 100th Ave. N.E., (south of Bellevue Square) Bellevue

This island of green space is a pleasant place to unwind after a shopping spree at nearby Bellevue Square. You can walk along a 1,200-foot-long canal through wide grassy areas. Other features include a cascading 240-foot-wide waterfall

and a preschool play area with a bright castle toy. The park is a great place to fly a kite and a popular spot for public concerts and special activities during the spring and summer months.

Bothell Landing Park
4919 N.E. 180th St., Bothell
(425) 486-3256

Bothell Landing Park, which sits across the river from the Sammamish River Trail, features a small playground, an interpretive trail through wetlands, lots of waterfowl, and an amphitheater and plaza (under construction through the end of summer 1998). The Bothell Historical Museum (open Sunday afternoons) is housed in one of the area's original homes and is decorated with authentic furnishings.

Blyth Park
16950 W. Riverside Dr., Bothell

Sand diggers, a long slide, and a tower of tires make this play area special. There is equipment for toddlers as well as older children. A covered picnic area and a grassy space are great spots to eat lunch before walking on trails that cut through woods around the park or lead down to the Sammamish River Slough.

Farrel-McWhirter Park
19545 Redmond Road, Redmond
See Chapter 1.

ESSENTIALS

There are plenty of fast-food restaurants close to Downtown Park (including several in Bellevue Square), so if you are hankering for a picnic on a nice day but you don't feel like packing a lunch, you have several convenient options.

Grass Lawn Park
N.E. 70th St. and 148th Ave. N.E., Bellevue

Located where Redmond, Bellevue, and Kirkland intersect, Grass Lawn Park offers plenty of space and activities for all ages. A play area, featuring climbing apparatus and swings, is set in a woodsy, nicely shaded spot. Children, both preschool-age and older, will enjoy riding their bikes and trikes along the paved pathways. Baseball and soccer fields and tennis courts are also available.

Juanita Beach Park
9703 Juanita Dr. N.E., Kirkland

During the summer, this 35-acre county park, with its large, sandy beach and enclosed swimming area, is very popular with families with small children. A long dock circles the swimming area; other amenities include ball fields, a picnic shelter, a small playground, and a large grassy area.

Kelsey Creek Community Park/Farm
13204 S.E. Eighth Pl., Bellevue
See Chapter 1.

Lake Sammamish State Park
20606 S.E. 56th St., Issaquah
(425) 455-7010

A large, sandy swimming beach is the main draw of this huge park at the south end of Lake Sammamish. Don't expect a quiet, peaceful outing, though, because you can't get away from the buzzing drone of Jet Skis out on the lake. A great wheelchair-accessible playground has a triple slide, miniclimbing wall, and tire swing. The park offers food concessions and dozens of picnic and barbecue areas. Bring your own net for volleyball or horseshoes to throw in the sand pit. Reserve your picnic tables if you are bringing a big group. Fishing is allowed in the lake but not in Issaquah Creek, which runs through the park. There are also hiking trails. If you tire of the beach, Gilman Village on the south side of I-90 offers good browsing and numerous snack places.

Marina Park
25 Lake Shore Plaza, Kirkland
(425) 828-1217

With a beach surrounded by a cement bench, a long dock, and close proximity to downtown Kirkland's ice cream shops and restaurants, Marina Park is a great place

TIPS

One-and-a-half-hour cruises of Lake Washington leave from Kirkland City Dock year-round: November through March at 1:15 p.m.; April through May, 1:15 and 3:30 p.m.; June through September, 11 a.m. and 1:15 and 3:30 p.m.; and October, 1:15 and 3:30 p.m. Cost is $18.15/adults, $8.95/children ages 5–12, free/children age 4 and under.

The beach at Lake Sammamish State Park is its main draw.

to watch boats, dip your feet, and throw pebbles in the water.

South of downtown Kirkland, scattered along Lake Washington Boulevard, are several more easy-to-spot waterfront parks, with sandy beaches, docks, and brightly colored playground equipment. **Houghton Beach** (5811 Lake Washington Blvd.) is especially nice. North of downtown is secluded **Waverly Beach** (633 Waverly Park Way).

Lake Wilderness Park
23601 S.E. 248th, Maple Valley

This forested, 108-acre park has a swimming beach, boat launch, playground, walking trails, arbore-tum, barbecues and picnic area, play fields, and tennis courts. King County naturalists often lead educational programs, including a natural-history lecture series, at the Lake Wilderness Center.

Marymoor Park
6064 W. Lake Sammamish Pkwy. N.E., Redmond

Covering 638 acres, Marymoor is the second-largest park in the King County park system. In addition to the numerous athletic fields that make the park a popular center for soccer and softball games, Mary-moor features two playgrounds, a

NEIGHBORHOOD NOTES

KIRKLAND

You can't walk very far in downtown Kirkland without coming across one of a dozen bronze sculptures, many of them whimsical creations children will appreciate.

The main areas to explore are Marina Park, Lake Street, Central Way, and Park Lane. You can pick up a map at local stores or from a display near Marina Park. Free two-hour parking is available in a lot near the park at Lakeshore Plaza or on the street; a free all-day lot is located off Market Street, north of the park.

At Marina Park, you'll find two sculptures:

"Puddle Jumpers," a group of children, and the **Centennial Fountain**. Coming up from the park, walk along Lake Street. To the right (south) are a **Baskin-Robbins** outlet and **Little Prince**, a restaurant with gourmet Italian ice cream. You can sit next to **"Mary**

Dawn" as she rests after a run. **World Wrapps** (124 Lake St. S.; 425-827-9727) and **Pasta Ya Gotcha** (123 Lake St.; 425-889-1511) offer more substantial food. **Stamping Room Only** (117 Lake St.; 425-803-0700) has a huge selection of stamps and art supplies. Down the street to the left, at the corner of Lake Street and Central Way, is the **Triple J Cafe** (101 Central Way; 425-

"The Puddle Jumpers" play at Marina Park.

822-7319) which has good sandwiches, pasta dinners, and breakfasts for $4–$6.50. The cozy atmosphere, complete with couches surrounding a central fireplace, was marred by unfriendly and unhelpful staff on one visit. Outside the

continued on next page

cafe, on opposite sides of the street, are "**Close Quarters,**" two cuddling bunnies, and "**The Cow and the Coyote,**" a howling coyote perched on the back of a large cow. West toward the lake on Central Way are local outposts of **Taco del Mar** (104 Central Way; 425-828-3002), and **Cucina Presto!** (90 Central Way; 425-739-9344). (See Chapter 11 for reviews.) Up a block in the other direction is **Eastside Trains** (217 Central Way; 425-828-4098), a store not to be missed if you have any train fans along. The large store has every type of model train, plus several working layouts. Nearby on Main Street is the video arcade **Quarters** (206 Main St.; 425-889-2555). Around the corner on Kirkland Avenue is the **Dakota Art Store** (209 Kirkland Ave.; 425-827-7678), which has art supplies for children. Up a block is the **Kirkland Library** (308 Kirkland Ave.; 425-822-1459), which features an outdoor sculpture garden with a rotating collection. Artwork is also displayed inside the library. Outside the main entrance is "**Carousel.**" North of the library is Peter Kirk Park (described elsewhere in this chapter), where "**The Valentine**" couple sits on a bench and "**Gossips**" make themselves at home on the grass.

Special events in Kirkland include an **Art Walk** sponsored by 13 galleries the second Thursday of each month, from 6-9 p.m. Free **concerts in the park** are performed at Marina Park from July through August. Marina Park is also the site for **Summerfest,** a festival with arts and crafts booths, entertainment, and hands-on activities in July, and **TASTE! Kirkland** in September.

velodrome for bicyclists, a climbing rock, miles of walking and bicycle trails, and lots of wide-open spaces perfect for kite flying or Frisbee. There's even a picturesque windmill near the park entrance.

If you're at the park on a clear evening, drive past all the sports fields to a dedicated remote-controlled airplane area, where most kids will be thrilled to watch the model aircraft buzzing around. For guaranteed action, show up on a Tuesday night between May and September, when the airplane club holds training sessions. Older kids can join the club and fly without buying a model.

The spiky 45-foot-tall climbing rock on the edge of the park has some low rock holds to challenge older children, who might also enjoy watching climbers in harnesses and ropes crawling up and then belaying down the high pinnacles. It is open daily from 8 a.m. to dusk. Call (206)

296-2964 for more information.

The Sammamish River Trail begins at the park, and a walk or bike ride will take you from Marymoor to Woodinville and its wineries (see "Biking" in Chapter 5). Also, folks who want to spend some lazy hours drifting upon the Sammamish Slough in inner tubes

TIPS

James Clise, a Seattle banker, purchased this land in 1904 for use as a bird-hunting reserve. The 28-room lodge that he built is called the Clise Mansion and houses the Marymoor Museum (425-885-3684). Museum exhibits highlight the history of the Eastside and the park. Admission is by donation; hours are Tues.-Thurs., 11 a.m.-4 p.m.; Sun., 1-4 p.m. King County naturalists lead interpretive nature programs regularly at the park; these usually start from the mansion.

Parents with kids who don't like dogs should avoid the park's southern portion, which serves as a 40-acre off-leash site.

See Chapter 6 for details about bike races at the Velodrome.

The Heritage Festival, held over Fourth of July, is a fun event for families. Go early and expect heavy traffic getting into the park.

or rafts often start at Marymoor. For obvious reasons, the park is usually jammed on hot summer days.

(For hiking suggestions, see Chapter 4.)

Meydenbauer Park
419 98th Ave. N.E., Bellevue

Located on the shores of Meydenbauer Bay in Bellevue, this park is nestled—almost hidden—among tall trees and residential areas. A small playground with swings and climbing equipment is above the beach; there is also a dock. There are plenty of shady picnic areas, but try to pack light, as the walk from the car is a long one if you're loaded down with gear.

Newcastle Beach
4400 Lake Washington Blvd. S., Bellevue

The 28-acre park, located on Lake Washington between Bellevue and Renton just south of Newport Shores Marina, is wonderful for kids. It's flat and wide open with a nice, shallow swimming area and a sandy beach. Near the beach is a first-rate playground with swings, slides, and climbing equipment. The park, which has its own wildlife reserve, also features nature trails and a fishing dock.

Peter Kirk Park
202 Third St., Kirkland

This 12-acre park in downtown Kirkland is the city's recreational centerpiece, with ball fields, a small playground with wooden toys, tennis courts, a skateboard park, paved pathways, and outdoor swimming and wading pools. Be sure to check out several pieces of public art scattered around the park, including a horse, a bronzed couple sitting on a bench, and a group of "gossips" in a circle on the lawn. (See "Neighborhood Notes" for Kirkland earlier in this chapter.)

Pine Lake Park
228th Ave. S.E. and S.E. 24th St., Issaquah

You can fish from a pier, launch a boat, or swim at the beach at this 16-acre county park, which also features a playground, tennis courts, baseball field, and three picnic shelters.

St. Edward State Park
1445 Juanita Dr. N.E., Bothell
(425) 823-2992
Directions: Take I-90 or SR 520 east to I-405. Drive north on I-405 to exit 20A (N.E. 116th St.). Go west on N.E. 116th to 98th Ave. N.E. in Kirkland. Cross the intersection and continue on Juanita Drive. In about 4.75 miles, turn left on N.E. 145th St. In 0.2 mile, turn right and drive straight ahead to reach the parking lot.

When the Catholic diocese closed the seminary that had occupied this 316-acre forested property since 1931, the state snapped it up. It was a wise purchase, considering that the area has 3,000 feet of waterfront, the largest remaining undeveloped shoreline on Lake Washington.

Also included in the deal were a gymnasium, tennis courts, outdoor handball courts, baseball fields, indoor swimming pool, soccer fields, picnic areas, and about seven miles of trails. Many of the trails lead to the beach, but swimming is not advised, as there are no lifeguards and the shoreline drops away abruptly about 30 feet out. Expect at least a .6-mile walk to get to the sandy shore.

The park is popular with mountain bikers, who are allowed only on designated trails.

TIPS

The 25-yard-long swimming pool is part of the King County parks system and is open for public swims most mornings and evenings year-round. Cost is $1.25/person. Call (206) 296-2970 for more details.

The newly renovated gym offers fitness and sports programs. There is no playground at the park.

Tolt-MacDonald Memorial Park
Carnation-Fall City Road and N.E. 40th St., Carnation
(206) 296-2966

This 264-acre rural park is the only county park with a campground. It has space for recreational vehicles (but no hookups), car camping, and walk-in sites. Several ball fields and a playground are also on-site. If you explore the park's hiking trails, keep an eye out for such wildlife as bears, deer, coyotes,

Wilburton Hill Park has a charming play-ground.

bald eagles, and red-tailed hawks.

If you don't mind heights, you can walk over a 500-foot-long suspension bridge swaying 28 feet above the Snoqualmie River.

The historic Dutch Colonial barn was renovated in 1995 to serve as a picnic shelter. The rest of the park was built in 1976 by more than 20,000 Boy Scouts who cleared debris, leveled areas, and built campsites and picnic shelters.

Wilburton Hill Park

Main St. and N.E. Second St., Bellevue

This 103-acre community park has a charming children's play area with play houses, a boat, climbing structures, and a spiderweb. More than three miles of trails wind through the park, which also offers ball fields, tennis and basketball courts, and group picnic facilities.

The park is home to the **Belle-**

vue Botanical Garden (12001 Main St.; 425-688-8551), which features 10 different gardens, including a rock garden with a zigzagging path. Kids will immediately be drawn to the fountain located near the visitor center, which gurgles out and runs down a path to a small pond. Trees and an arbor are lit up during December in the Garden D'Lights display.

North

Ballinger Park

23000 Lakeview Dr., Mountlake Terrace

This city park offers athletic fields, boating and fishing, a tennis court, a picnic area, and a playground.

Edmonds City Park

Third St. S. and Howell Way Edmonds

The 14.5-acre park is stuffed with playing fields, a playground, horseshoe pits, picnic tables, trails, natural area, special garden, amphitheater and wading pool.

Edmonds Waterfront Parks

The beaches on Puget Sound in Edmonds are very popular with families. **Underwater Park** at Brackett's Landing is popular with divers (they do an underwater pumpkin-carving contest there each October), as well as beach walkers. It has creature-filled tidepools at low tide.

3333322333222221211

INSIDE SCOOP

Urban Camping

Want a bit of the outdoors without traveling far? Try these parks.

Camp Long, 5200 35th Ave. S.W., Seattle; (206) 684-7434. Rustic cabins.

Dash Point State Park, 5700 S.W. Dash Point Road, Federal Way; (800) 452-5687 (reservations) or (800) 233-0321 (general information).

Saltwater State Park, 25205 Eighth Pl. S., Kent; (253) 661-4956. Fifty-three tent sites.

Tolt-MacDonald Park, Carnation-Fall City Road and N.E. 40th, Carnation; (206) 296-2966. Car camping with tents, walk-in sites, and group site.

Olympic Beach, Dayton Street and Admiral Way, is a small park with a picnic area, trails and fun public art that kids will have fun climbing on or posing next to for photos. **Marina Beach Park**, Admiralty Way S., offers a basketball court, playground, picnic area, and a little hill for flying kites.

Forest Park

802 Mulkiteo Blvd., Everett

Forest Park hosts an animal farm (see Chapter 1), the city's swim center, and a new playground with separate areas for toddlers and older children. During the summer, a giant sprinkler in an old wading pool douses kids. The city's Music in the Park family series is held here on Sundays in the summer.

Heron Park

2701 155th St. S.E., Mill Creek

Swings, climbers, and sculptures will entertain kids before you can entice them for a walk along a winding nature trail with small ponds. A large covered picnic area provides a pleasant place to eat lunch.

Legion Park

146th and Alverson Blvd., Everett

In May 1998 Legion Park should have a new playground with towers and a bridge. It also hosts the city's summer music program for children on Tuesdays at noon in July and August.

Lynndale Park

18927 72nd Ave.W., Lynnwood

This 38-acre park in a residential neighborhood has a play area, hik-

DID YOU KNOW?

The largest species of salamander in the world lives in King County. The Pacific giant salamander can grow up to 13 inches long and is one of the most poisonous amphibians in the world. But don't worry: Picking it up won't hurt you. Just make sure you wash your hands afterwards to be safe.

—King County Parks

INSIDE SCOOP   Favorite Playgrounds

Logan Park in Bothell has a climbing structure and triple slide, plus a human powered trolley.

Carkeek Park, 950 Carkeek Park Road (off Third Ave. N.W. and N.W. 110th St.), Seattle. Giant salmon slide, adventure trail, caves, and animal prints.

Forest Park, 802 Mukilteo Road, Everett. Interactive playground equipment.

Lake Sammamish State Park, 20606 S.E. 56th St., Issaquah. Triple slide, mini-climbing wall, and a tire swing.

Licton Springs, N. 97th and Ashworth Ave. N., Seattle. Artwork by children and professional artists, games painted on ground, and a large play structure.

Logan Park, 1411 Logan Road, Bothell. Fun equipment, including a long tube slide and a triple slide, is offered for kids from toddlers on up, but a human-powered trolley ride is the highlight for all ages.

Madrona Park, 853 Lake Washington Blvd., Seattle. Concrete and pebbles look like a natural beach; children can control a water fountain in the summer.

Matthews Beach Park, N.E. 93th St. and Sand Point Way, Seattle. Spider rope climber.

Pratt Park, Lavizzo Water Play Area, 20th Ave. S. and Yesler, Seattle. Summertime water-spray area features giant water cannons shaped like animals; in a water maze, sensors in the ground cause water to squirt up when kids step on them.

Phinney Playground, northeast corner of Woodland Park, N. 59th St. and Phinney Ave. N., Seattle. Log playhouse, rock cave, and a spiral pathway up mound of rocks.

Roxhill Playground, 29th Ave. S.W. and S.W. Roxbury St., Seattle. Huge, castle-like wooden play structure.

ing trails, softball fields, an amphitheater, and an orienteering course. The picnic area can be reserved for large groups.

Lynnwood Neighborhood Park
4612 189th Pl. S.W., Lynnwood

Teens will enjoy the two covered basketball courts here, while younger kids will love the spray dragon and the wading pool in the summer. There is also a walking path and a picnic shelter.

Thorton A. Sullivan Park at Silver Lake
1140 W. Silver Lake Dr., Everett

This city park offers a sandy beach with a roped-off swimming area that is watched by lifeguards in the summer, as well as canoe and paddle boat rentals, boating classes for age 7 and up, and a new playground (to be finished in fall 1998).

DID YOU KNOW?

If you stretched out Puget Sound's 2,000 miles of shoreline, it would reach from Seattle to Disneyland. The area also has 16,000 miles of rivers and streams. More than 10,000 species inhabit Puget Sound, including people.
—King County Parks

Yost Memorial Park
96th Ave. W. and Bowdoin Way Edmonds

The serene, forested park is delightful on hot summer days, when the trees keep it deliciously cool. The 48 acres hold a tennis court, playground, picnic area, and trails. It's also the site of an outdoor swimming pool, open during the summer.

Chapter 4
OUTDOOR FUN

Northwest families are eternally optimistic about the great outdoors despite the area's rainy climate. Every season brings a new array of outdoor opportunities for kids, from skiing and sledding to fishing and hiking. The greater Seattle area boasts many places to bike, skate, and ride horses year-round. And no matter where you are in the area, you're not far from water. Puget Sound and local lakes offer lifeguarded summer beaches and limitless options for boating. Don't let a lack of experience or equipment stop you from taking a trip to the mountains or a bike ride to a scenic picnic spot—many places in the area offer instruction and rentals.

WALKING/ HIKING

To hike with kids, forget the old adage about how getting somewhere is half the fun. On a hike, getting there has to be *all* the fun. Picking up slugs, climbing stumps, crossing bridges, dipping toes into freezing cold streams—those are the reasons kids like to hike.

For more detailed information about many of these trails, check out "Nature Walks In & Around Seattle: All Season Exploring in Parks, Forests and Wetlands," by Cathy McDonald and Stephen Whitney, published by The Mountaineers.

Urban Trails

Cougar Mountain Regional Wildland Park

Issaquah

(206) 296-4171

Directions: From Interstate 90, take exit 13 and drive west on Newport Way. Turn south at 164th Ave. S.E. and go up the hill 1.7 miles to Lakemont Blvd.; turn right and follow it 1.4 miles to the Red Town trailhead.

Hiking at Cougar Mountain, you'll find it hard to believe you're only a few minutes from the bustling Eastside. The 3,010-acre county park, part of the foothills known as the Issaquah Alps, features more than 30 miles of trails through forests of Sitka spruce, cedar, hemlock, and Douglas fir. Prospectors and coal miners worked

TIPS

King County naturalists lead guided walks at Cougar Mountain during the summer. Call (206) 296-4171 for more information.

Issaquah Alps Trails Club members lead free hikes for all ages and skill levels year-round on the mountains and plateaus in the greater Issaquah area, including Cougar, Tiger, and Squak mountains. Some are designated as family hikes, but all hikes are rated by length and climbing difficulty, so hikers can tell if a particular outing will be appropriate for their children. Parents should also check with the hike leader. Children under 13 must be accompanied by an adult. Hikers meet at the Stationmaster's House on the corner of First and Bush (across the street from the community center) in Issaquah at an appointed time, and then carpool to the trailhead. A $15/year family membership includes a newsletter and calendar. Call the Issaquah Alps Hotline at (425) 328-0480 for a complete hike schedule and more information.

The club offers a booklet, "Eastside Family Hikes," for $3 by mail. The booklet describes family hikes and notes whether strollers are appropriate.

Pretend trolls live under the steep bridges at Kubota Gardens in Seattle.

Cougar Mountain for a century, finally leaving it alone in 1963. Most of the old-growth forests were logged, but some fragments can still be found near Wilderness Peak. Some easier trails to try include Coal Creek Trail, a 2-mile round trip on level ground, and the Wildside/Mill Pond Loop, a level 1.5 miles. Both begin at the Red Town trailhead.

Discovery Park
3801 W. Government Way, Seattle
(206) 386-4236

The trails that penetrate the park each offer a different view of Discovery. Exercise buffs can work up a sweat on the fitness trail (with workout stations); nature lovers will enjoy the Loop Trail, a 2.8-mile loop full of curves and twists through wood and meadow. A great walk for families is the Wolf Tree Nature Trail, a lovely half-mile path through one of the least disturbed areas (last logged in the 1860s). Half a dozen bridges, raised wooden walkways, and numbered posts will keep kids interested in trudging along. The posts designate points that correspond to an excellent nature booklet, available for purchase (35 cents) or free (if you return it) at the Visitor Center (located inside the east gate, to the left). To get to the trail from the main east gate entrance, follow the park road to the north parking lot. At the southwest corner of the lot is an information sign with a map of the park. The Wolf Tree Trail begins at the northwest corner of the lot.

There are also free drop-in nature walks led by knowledgeable and enthusiastic park rangers most Saturdays at 2 p.m. Meet at the Visitor Center.

Juanita Bay Park
2201 Market St., Kirkland
(425) 828-1217

The 113-acre park features trails, boardwalks, observation areas, and interpretive signs that help identify plants and animals in the wetlands. Kids will enjoy crossing bridges and raised wooden walkways. Volunteer rangers offer a free interpretive tour of Juanita Bay Park on the first Sunday of each month at 1 p.m., beginning in the parking lot. Registration is not required. Bring binoculars.

Kubota Gardens
55th Ave. S. and Renton Ave. S., Seattle
Admission: Free

Trails run through this 20-acre display garden, leading to waterfalls, prayer stones, and lush lawns. Kids will like the steep, brightly colored bridges (you can make your walk even more fun by suggesting trolls live underneath). The high point of the property offers a view of the gardens, the Cascade mountain range, and the Eastside.

Lakeridge Park
10145 Rainier Ave. S., Seattle

A .75-mile trail follows a stream through this forested, 36-acre park tucked away in a natural area known as Deadhorse Canyon.

Marymoor Park
6064 W. Lake Sammamish Pkwy. N.E., Redmond

With all the action at Marymoor, it is easy to overlook the Marymoor Interpretive Trail, a short (just under a mile) path to the Lake Sammamish overlook, featuring informative signs about the plants, animals, and birds that thrive in this wildlife preserve (no dogs allowed). The walk can be lengthened by taking the boardwalk north along the Sammamish River and walking over open fields to the parking lots for a loop almost two miles long.

As you walk along the trail, impress your kids by telling them that between 1964 and 1970 archaeologists from the University of Washington identified four pre-Columbian sites, two in Marymoor Park and two more just outside the park along the river. The oldest tools found were made 6,000 years ago, the rest around 3,000 years ago.

Mercer Slough Nature Park
2102 Bellevue Way S.E., Bellevue
(425) 462-2752
Directions: From I-90, take the Bellevue Way exit and head north past the South Bellevue Park and Ride. Look for the blue "Winters House" sign on the right.

With 320 acres, this nature park encompasses the largest remaining wetland on Lake Washington and offers more than five miles of year-round trails through marshes, meadows, and forests. Wildlife watchers can try to spot more than 100 species of birds, plus coyotes, beavers, and muskrats. A 12-nest heron rookery tree is located at the northern tip of the park. Rangers lead free guided nature walks every

Sunday at 11 a.m., beginning at the Winters House. All ages are welcome; children must be accompanied by an adult.

Other Bellevue nature trails include the 2-mile-long **Lake Hills Greenbelt Trail,** which connects Larsen and Phantom lakes as it threads through 150 acres of woods and wetlands. Rangers lead walks every Saturday at 11 a.m. from the ranger station (15416 S.E. 16th St.). The ranger station is home to demonstration plots for hummingbird and butterfly gardens, grassland sanctuaries, and forest edge gardens.

An easy 1-mile loop trail through 10 acres of woods can be found at **Robinswood Community Park** (148th Ave. S.E. and S.E. 22nd St.) which also features a pond, a horse arena, and a picnic area.

A 2.5-mile asphalt trail loops around **Phantom Lake**, where great blue herons, red-winged blackbirds, and other feathered friends hunt along the shores. You can leave your car at the parking lot at 1200 164th Ave. S.E., or at Phantom Lake Park (156th Ave. S.E.

TIPS

at S.E. 20th St.). The trail intersects the **Spiritridge Trail**, a 2.5-mile wooded loop around the Boeing Service Center. Park at Spiritridge Park (16100 S.E. 33rd Pl.).

Ravenna Park
N.E. Ravenna Blvd. and Cowen Pl., Seattle

This forested ravine just north of the University of Washington is hidden from the cars zipping along nearby on 15th Avenue N.E. Easy walking paths follow both sides of a little stream and steeper trails lead up to a picnic area and play fields off N.E. 55th Street on the west end of the park. For safety's sake, plan to be out of the park by dark.

Schmitz Preserve
S.W. Stevens and S.W. Admiral Way, Seattle

Home to one of the last stands of old-growth forest in Seattle, 50-acre Schmitz Park in West Seattle is a good place to visit if nearby Alki gets too windy or the kids have gotten too much sun. Rustic paths follow a stream through lush forest and over several bridges. You can drive here and park in the lot or access a paved trail from the south

INSIDE SCOOP

Good Places to Fly a Kite

Discovery Park
Gas Works Park
Magnuson Park
Marymoor Park

side of Alki Community Center (5817 S.W. Stevens).

Washington Park Arboretum
Lake Washington Blvd. E., between E. Madison and Hwy. 520, Seattle (206) 325-4510

The 200-acre Arboretum features miles of walking paths, mossy ponds, and the finest display of native Northwest plants found anywhere in the region. A definite kid-pleaser is the Waterfront Trail, a half-mile trail that crosses bridges and extensive wooden walkways to get from Marsh Island to Foster Island. You can pick up the trail near the Museum of History and Industry (2700 24th Ave. E.). Kids will also like watching the boat traffic on Lake Washington.

Gardens within the Arboretum, which contains more than 5,500 kinds of plants, include Azalea Way, a .75-mile promenade with flowering cherries, azaleas, and dogwoods; Loderi Valley, with rhododendrons, Loderi hybrids, magnolias, and conifers; Rhododendron Glen, with dozens of rhododendron species and hybrids; and the Joseph A. Witt Winter Garden, which is best visited from November through March.

The Japanese Garden offers a peaceful reprieve from city activity. One of the Arboretum's highlights, this authentic Japanese stroll garden, designed by Japanese landscape designer Juki Iida and maintained by the Seattle Department of Parks and Recreation, is open from March through November; visitors are welcome to pick up a brochure at the garden's entrance and walk through the fenced area on their own or take a guided tour from a trained docent (by reservation only). Each season offers something new in the garden, from blooming cherry trees in the early spring to rhododendrons and azaleas throughout the summer to colored foliage during the fall. Turtles and 50 carp can be spotted in the landscaped ponds. If you want to see a public tea ceremony, stop by on the third Saturday of each month from April through October. The half-hour narrated demonstration starts at 1:30 p.m.

TIPS

Volunteer guides offer free tours of the Arboretum most Saturdays and Sundays at 1 p.m. Guided hikes are also available by appointment for families and organized groups of children in kindergarten through 12th grade; $5/group. For a small fee, families and groups can check out Explorer Packs, backpacks full of equipment, field guides, and tools; reservations are necessary. For more information or to make an appointment, call (206) 543-8800.

A fun way to enjoy the Arboretum is by rowboat or canoe, available for rent from the Waterfront Activity Center (see "Boating" elsewhere in this chapter).

The Japanese Garden is located on Lake Washington Boulevard between E. Madison and 23rd Ave. S. Admission is $2.50/adults, $1.50/children age 6 and up. Groups are always welcome; special discount rates apply. Hours are 10 a.m.-6 p.m. or 8 p.m.; closing time varies according to the season. Call (206) 684-4725 for more information.

Snoqualmie Pass

If you want to get out of the city, here are some suggestions for short hikes around Snoqualmie

Twin Falls is a 2.6-mile hike for older kids.

INSIDE SCOOP

Blooming Gardens

For Mother's Day or just to enjoy the spring flowers, take a walk in any of these gardens. Admission is free except as noted.

Bellevue Botanical Garden, Main St., Bellevue.

Japanese Garden, 1502 Lake Washington Blvd., Seattle. Admission fee.

Kubota Garden, 9817 55th Ave. S., Seattle.

Parsons Garden, Seventh Ave. W. and W. Highland Dr., Seattle.

Washington Park Arboretum, 2300 Arboretum Dr. E., Seattle.

Woodland Park Rose Garden, 5000 Fremont Ave. N., Seattle.

Pass, courtesy of the North Bend Ranger District.

Twin Falls (2.6 miles round trip; elevation gain, 500 feet). The trail follows the South Fork of the Snoqualmie River, then climbs to an overlook at .8 mile. It then heads up for an up-close view of both the lower and upper falls; a wooden bridge crosses between them. Some portions of the trail drop off steeply, so watch small children. To get there, take exit 34 off Interstate 90 and turn right onto Edgewick Road. After half a mile, right before a bridge, turn left onto S.E. 159th Street. The road dead-ends at the trailhead in .75 mile.

Asahel Curtis Nature Trail (1.25-mile loop; elevation gain, 60 feet). The nature trail is an easy walk through one of the last stands of old-growth forest in the Snoqualmie Valley. Kids will enjoy the bridges as the trail crosses Humpback Creek several

INSIDE SCOOP

Best Birding/ Wildlife Spots

Camp Long, Seattle

Carkeek Park, Seattle

Cougar Mountain Regional Wildland Park, Issaquah

Discovery Park, Seattle

Juanita Bay Park, Kirkland

Lincoln Park, Seattle

Mercer Slough, Bellevue

Richmond Beach, Shoreline

Seward Park, Seattle

Tolt-MacDonald Park, Carnation

Washington Park Arboretum, Seattle

times. During the summer, the path is punctuated with interpretive signs and plant labels. To get there, take exit 47 from I-90 and turn right at the stop sign. Turn left at Road 55 and drive .5 mile to a large parking lot; the trail begins at the east end.

Franklin Falls (2 miles round trip; elevation gain, 250 feet). An easy walk along the South Fork of the Snoqualmie River leads to Franklin Falls, a nice place for a picnic or sunbathing. To get there, take exit 47 from I-90. Turn left at the stop sign, then right at the T. In .25 mile, turn left onto Denny Creek Road No. 58 and follow it 2.5 miles.

Turn left on a paved road just past the campground. In 200 feet, you'll find parking on the left; the trailhead is on the right.

Resources

The Mountaineers

300 Third Ave. W., Seattle
(206) 284-6310
www.mountaineers.org

The Mountaineers is the largest outdoor organization in the region, currently comprising 15,300 members. The club is dedicated to offering a wide array of outdoor activities for all ages, including hiking, cross-country skiing, backpack trips, kayaking, and more. A family activity committee organizes hikes and backpack trips geared for families. Each individual has his or her own membership, but spouses and juniors are at a discounted rate. Children under 13 are free.

Evergreen State Volkssport Association

(800) 828-WALK

Children are welcome at volkssporting events, usually 5- or 10-kilometer organized walks, though some clubs also sponsor bike rides and swims. Walks are rated by difficulty and information is available on whether the trails are suitable for strollers or wheelchairs. The free events are open to anyone. Call the state organization for information about the club nearest you.

TIPS

Mountaineers Books publishes two excellent guides: "Best Hikes With Children in Western Washington & the Cascades," volumes 1 and 2. These guides are available at local bookstores or by contacting The Mountaineers.

The club also maintains four mountain lodges near ski areas where members can stay with children age 5 and up.

For privately guided family hiking, backpacking, or rock climbing trips, contact Cascade Alpine Guides in Bellevue at (425) 688-8054, or Mountain Madness in Seattle at (206) 937-8389.

Wilderness Awareness School
26311 N.E. Valley St., Duvall
(425) 788-1301;
www.speakeasy.org/~was-net/

Tracking and nature awareness classes and camps for children and families can enhance your outdoor time.

STEPHANIE DUNNEWIND

The Waterfront Trail in Washington Park Arboreteum goes from Marsh Island to Foster Island.

BIKING

B*icycling* magazine ranks Seattle as one of the top cities in the country for bicycling, and it's easy to see why. The city and King County have worked with many avid bicyclists (Seattle is home to the largest cycling club in the United States) to develop an impressive network of bicycle trails, along with comprehensive maps, highlighting both on- and off-road routes. You can receive a free Seattle Bicycling GuideMap by calling (206) 684-5087, or by going to the Seattle Transportation Department (Municipal Building, seventh floor, Seattle). The King County Bicycling GuideMap is available at REI stores for about $4. The city of Bellevue offers a free bicycling map; call (425) 688-2894.

Biking/In-line Skating Trails

The following multi-use trails are utilized by bicyclists, inline skaters, runners, and walkers. Some separate wheeled and non-wheeled users; use caution on those that don't.

Alki

S.W. Florida St. to Duwamish Head
Seattle
Length: 1.7 miles one way

One way to enjoy beautiful Alki Beach is to hop on bikes and take a short but delightful ride along the water from Alki Beach Park to Duwamish Head at the tip of West Seattle. The safe, 12-foot-wide trail features a separate path for pedestrians that varies from 6 to 12 feet wide. The faster riders and racers

ESSENTIALS

Nearby bike and skate rentals on Burke-Gilman in Seattle: Al Young Bike & Ski (bikes and in-line skates), (206) 524-2642; The Bicycle Center (bikes), (206) 523-8300; Urban Surf (in-line skates), (206) 545-9463.

Nearby bike rentals on the Eastside: Bothell Ski & Bike, (425) 486-3747; Redmond Cycle, (425) 885-6363; Sammamish Valley Cycle, (425) 881-8442; Spoke & Ski in Woodinville, (425) 483-6626.

tend to stay on the roadway, making the bicycle path pretty safe for kids.

Families with older children can stretch their trip to 14 miles one way by taking a street route west along Alki Avenue S.W. and south along Beach Drive S.W. to Lincoln Park. There isn't a designated bike path, but signs mark the route.

Burke Gilman Trail and Sammamish River Trail

Eighth Ave. N.W. in Seattle to Marymoor Park in Redmond
Length: 27 miles one way

This amazing trail makes local bicyclists the envy of casual riders in every other Northwest city. The route takes you more than 50 miles round-trip on a level, scenic path from Eighth Ave. N.W. (Gas Works Park is the easiest place to start, however), past the University of Washington, around the north end of Lake Washington, through Kenmore and Woodinville, to Marymoor Park in Redmond. Although too far for most young children (and many adults), the route gives riders many shorter options and allows you to start wherever is most convenient. One nice family ride is the 10-mile round-trip

TIPS

Special family bicycling events are scheduled by various organizations throughout the Puget Sound area, especially during the summer months. The 5,000-member Cascade Bicycle Club (206-522-BIKE) offers loads of information for novice and experienced bicyclists, as well as classes and group events. Its Web page, (www.cascade.org) includes tips for riding with children.

From May through September, the Seattle Parks Department designates one Bicycle Saturday and Bicycle Sunday per month. With the help of the Seattle Engineering Department, Lake Washington Boulevard from Seward Park to Mount Baker Beach is closed to vehicle traffic between 10 a.m. and 6 p.m. Bicycle safety checks and first-aid stations are set up along the route.

Whatever bike route you choose, try not to rush it. Pack a lunch and, instead of setting a distance goal, just ride for the fun of it, stopping along the way to relax and unwind.

Don't forget helmets for the whole family.

stretch from Marymoor Park to the wineries in Woodinville. The segment from Gas Works Park to Matthews Beach is about 15 miles round-trip.

The Burke Gilman Trail (Seattle to Kenmore) and the Sammamish River Trail (from Kenmore to Marymoor) are paved and often heavily traveled, especially on weekends. Plan to make a park your starting and end point, so you have access to bathrooms and a place for kids to play after the ride.

Cedar River Trail
Mouth of the Cedar River in Renton to Landsburg
Length: 17 miles one way (6 miles paved)

One segment of the trail follows the Cedar River through downtown Renton to where it eventually spills out into Lake Washington. Fans of airplanes will enjoy walking past one of Boeing's fields (be warned, it can be noisy); pick up this portion of the trail from Renton Memorial Stadium. The trail can also be accessed from the Renton Community Center (1717 Maple Valley Hwy., Renton). Bicycling is discouraged (but not prohibited) on the section through the downtown area. Heading the other direction, the trail mostly parallels SR 169, with a cleared parking area off SR 169 north of its junction with SR 18. The trail becomes crushed rock and continues to Issaquah-Hobart Road and 276th Avenue S.E.

Discovery Park

3801 W. Government Way, Seattle
(206) 386-4236

More than five miles of paved roads now closed to cars are great for biking. Bicycles are not allowed on dirt trails, however.

Elliott Bay Bicycle Path

Pier 70, north through Myrtle Edwards Park
Length: 1.25 miles one way

This trail is rarely crowded, although it attracts a large number of downtowners who are trying to get some exercise and fresh air at lunch time. Take the kids on a nice spring or summer evening, stop at the fishing pier, and watch the sun set over the water.

Green Lake

Between N. 59th and N. 77th, just northeast of Woodland Park
Length: 2.8-mile loop

The trail around the lake is flat and paved; a playground and grassy areas are scattered along the way. On almost every sunny day, however, it gets very crowded with cyclists, joggers, couples, roller skaters, baby strollers, and dogs. A line divides wheeled and non-wheeled traffic. It is more enjoyable and less risky to ride on cloudy days or weekday mornings.

ESSENTIALS

Nearby Greenlake rentals: Gregg's Greenlake Cycle (bikes and in-line skates), (206) 523-1822; The Good Sport (in-line skates), (206) 526-8087.

Green River Trail

I-405 to S. 192nd St., Kent
Length: 2 miles one way (additional portions are about 1 mile each)

The Green River Trail follows the scenic Green River as it winds through the Kent Valley. A good place to park your car and pick up the trail is Briscoe Park (S. 190th St., Kent), situated at one of the bends of the river. From there you can travel north or south along the flat, paved, uncrowded trail. Briscoe Park has picnic areas, a boat launch, and play fields as well, so the day can be broken up with several activities if you wish. Other portions of the trail include: S. 143rd Street to Fort Dent Park (along the Duwamish River), 1 mile; Pacific Avenue S. to 42nd Ave. S., 1 mile; Russell Road Park to West Valley Hwy., 1.5 miles. The southern segments can be connected by riding on the street. The eventual goal for the Green River Trail is to have it stretch 30 miles from Alki Point to Auburn.

Interurban Trail

Strander Blvd. in Tukwila to Third Ave. in Pacific
Length: 14 miles one way

The Interurban Trail runs underneath Puget Power's power lines and is flat and paved. Parking is available at many sites along the trail, but one of the more convenient places is located at S. 182nd St., just south of S. 180th, off the West Valley Highway on the west side of the river. You can pick up the Green River Trail or the Interurban Trail here, or take some time to relax in the park, which has a play area with swings. Another trailhead is at 259th Street just east of Highway 167.

Lake Washington Boulevard Trail
Seward Park to Mount Baker Park
Length: 3 miles one way

The scenic paved path along the lake is popular with walkers and joggers.

Preston-Snoqualmie
Interstate 90 at Preston to Snoqualmie Falls
Length: 6 miles one way

The paved trail ends two miles east of Lake Alice Road with a view of Snoqualmie Falls. There is no way to make a loop, so it's an out-and-back ride. Access is off 308th Avenue in Preston.

Seward Park Loop
East end of Seward Park parking lot, Seattle
Length: 2.5-mile loop

This short loop around the perimeter of Seward Park along Lake Washington is an ideal place for even the wobbliest rider to enjoy fabulous scenery and a flat, easy ride. The trail is a road that has been closed, so it is plenty wide. The views here are exceptional, with Mount Rainier to the south and the city skyline to the northeast. Plan to swim at the lifeguarded beach at the end of your ride if it is a hot day.

Soos Creek Trail
S.E. 208th St. at the 13700th block in Kent, south to S.E. 264th St. and 150th Ave. S.E. (a few blocks east of Lake Meridian)
Length: 4.5 miles one way

This scenic, paved trail stretches along Soos Creek, east of Kent. Parking is available at the trail's north end at Gary Grant Park (13700 block of S.E. 208th, Kent), where families can take advantage of a picnic area. You can also access it at the central trailhead (148th Ave. S.E., between S.E. 240th and S.E. 256th streets, Kent) or the Meridian South trailhead (152nd Way S.E., .25 mile north of Kent-Kangley Rd., Kent). The route is mostly flat, especially at the north end, and is divided for horse and bike traffic. It is not heavily traveled.

MOUNTAIN BIKING

Though mountain bikes are the most popular type of bicycles, many people never ride them off-road. If your family is looking to hit the dirt, try the trails at St. Edward State Park in Bothell, Dash Point State Park in Federal Way, or Hamlin Park in Shoreline (see Chapter 3 for more details on these parks). For more information, check out the book "Kissing the Trail" by John Zilly. He notes which trails are easy and suitable for children.

Snoqualmie Trail
Duvall to Tokul Road (north of Snoqualmie Falls)
(206) 296-4232
Length: 18 miles one way (20 miles by fall 1998)
Extension: 10 miles
Surface: Crushed rock

This path along a former railroad right-of-way winds by farms and open space. By the end of summer 1998, the trail should extend an additional two miles north to Duvall Park. For a shorter ride, you can access the trail at Nick Loutsis Park (Entwhistle St., Carnation), from a dirt parking area off the trail at N.E. 11th Street, south of Carnation, or from a parking area east of Fall City on 356th Ave. (head north from SR 203). For a longer ride, you can reach the extension from the trail by riding on the street (Tokul Road to Mill Pond Road). The trail picks up again in the Three Forks Natural Area and goes through North Bend to Rattlesnake Lake. It can also be accessed at the intersection of Fourth Street and Ballarat Avenue in North Bend. At Rattlesnake Lake, a connection with the Iron Horse Trail, a former railroad grade that runs all the way to the Columbia River, should be finished in spring 1998.

Tolt Pipeline Trail
Woodinville to Snoqualmie Valley
Length: 6 miles one way
Surface: Dirt access road

The trail, also popular with equestrians, runs alongside a giant pipe. You can leave your car in a small parking area at the 15000 block of 155th Ave. N.E. in Woodinville, or where the trail crosses Avondale Road at approximately the 14500th block. The trail ends at West Valley Road, but parking is not available there.

Crystal Mountain
(360) 663-2265
Hours: Open daily, June-Sept., 10 a.m.-5 p.m.
Tickets: $10/adults, $7/children ages 7-17, free/children age 6 and under, $30/family day pass for par-

---

TIPS

Even if you don't mountain bike, riding to the top of the mountain on a sunny day offers stunning views. Kids will be thrilled (if they're not afraid of heights). The mountain can be chilly even in summer, so bring a light coat.

ents, grandparents, and children

Hikers and mountain bikers can ride the chairlift to 6,872 feet, allowing access to walking trails and intermediate to advanced bike trails. The resort also offers picnic areas, horseshoes, tennis courts, and camping.

Summit at Snoqualmie Mountain Bike Center

(206) 236-7277, ext. 3372
Summer Activity Line:
(206) 236-1600
Season: May-Sept., Fri.-Sun. and holidays

During the summer, a chair lift transports riders and their bikes up the mountain for easy access to trails. Most trails are rated intermediate to advanced. The facility also offers guided rides, lessons, bike camps, and rental bikes.

Resources

Backcountry Bicycle Trails Club

(206) 283-2995
www.dirtnw.com/bbtc

The club organizes free rides every weekend year-round, as well as a three-hour mountain bike boot camp that covers off-road riding basics. A discount is offered for kids learning with their parents. The club also publishes a monthly newsletter and event schedule. Membership is $10/students, $30/families.

BOATING

Seattle is surrounded by Puget Sound, Lake Washington, Lake Sammamish, and dozens of smaller lakes, so it's no wonder boating is so popular here. The state has one of the highest ratios of boats per capita in the country. Boating is a wonderful family activity, providing your child isn't stir-crazy. Most kids are thrilled to sit in a small boat dragging a stick or a toy boat on a string, trying their hand at paddling, and just watching other boats go by.

ESSENTIALS

Boating, like any water sport, can be dangerous, so take proper precautions before you push off. Check the weather conditions, and make sure everyone, even the best swimmer, is wearing a PFD (personal flotation device, or life jacket).

When you are out on the water in the summertime, protect your skin and eyes. Even if the sky is overcast, be sure that everybody uses sunscreen and wears hats and sunglasses.

Center for Wooden Boats

1010 Valley St., Seattle
(206) 382-BOAT (328-2628)
Season: Open year-round; closed Tuesdays
Rentals: $10-$37.50/hour

With interesting marine businesses, a variety of fancy and funky houseboats along its shores, and sea planes from Lake Union Air taking

TIPS

Although boat rental places are required to provide life vests, bring along your child's own life vest when you rent a boat. That way you will know you have the best fit and style for your child's age and size.

off and landing frequently, Lake Union is a fun place to explore. The Center for Wooden Boats, located on the south end of Lake Union, offers skiffs, canoes, sailboats, and kayaks for rental year-round. (Customers' boat-handling skills are checked out before they are allowed to rent sailing craft.) The center also offers sailing lessons.

Greenlake Boat Rentals
7351 E. Green Lake Dr. N., Seattle
(206) 527-0171
Season: Mid-April to Sept.

TIPS

Gas Works Park, on the north side of Lake Union, directly across from the Center for Wooden Boats, has a playground and is a good place to get out and let kids stretch their legs. East of Gas Works Park, just before the University Bridge, is Ivar's Salmon House. Pull up to the dock and send someone up to the outside fish bar for tasty fish and chips.

Rentals: $8-$12/hour

Located near the Green Lake Community Center, this small concession rents out rowboats, paddleboats, canoes, and sailboards. Kids love to navigate their way to Duck Island, though it's better not explored on foot—too wet and muddy. Boat reservations, though not necessary, are recommended during the summer months.

TIPS

There is a reason why Green Lake is so green: algae. During the summer months, when the algae is thickest, swimming is not advised. Therefore, if you go on a really hot day, make sure that the breeze is sufficient to keep you cool and plan to let the kids splash around in Green Lake park's wading pool, located across the street from the Lakeside Plaza (7900 E. Green Lake Dr. N.).

Green Lake Small Craft Center
5900 W. Green Lake Dr. N.
Seattle; (206) 684-4074

Mount Baker Rowing and Sailing Center
3800 Lake Washington Blvd. S.
Seattle; (206) 386-1913

These city-run facilities do not rent boats, but they do offer rowing and sailing lessons for children and adults, as well as youth summer camps. Mount Baker also offers family kayaking and canoeing classes.

Mercer Slough Nature Park

2102 Bellevue Way S.E., Bellevue
(425) 462-2752
Tours: May-Sept., Sat. only
Rates: $6/person, $15/family per

canoe

Three-hour guided canoe trips leave Enatai Beach Park on Lake Washington and paddle up the mouth of Mercer Slough. No experience or equipment is necessary. Call for a current schedule and to register.

Explore the arboretum in a canoe rented from the UW Waterfront Activity Center.

STEPHANIE DUNNEWIND

Northwest Outdoor Center

2100 Westlake Ave. N., Seattle
(206) 281-9694
Rentals: $10/hour single kayak,
$15/hour double

Rent a two-person double kayak
from Northwest Outdoor Center and
see Lake Union from a new perspective. Paddle to Gas Works Park
in 10 minutes, the Ballard Locks in
about 45 minutes. Several different
models are available for rental, seating one, two, or three people. Kids
sit in front, adults in the rear steer-
ing position. Rentals are available
by the hour, half-day, full day, and
longer. No experience is necessary.
The center also offers guided tours.

Pacific Water Sports

16055 Pacific Hwy. S., SeaTac
206-246-9385
Rentals: $30/day single kayak or
canoe, $55/day double kayak

You can take the boats anywhere, but Saltwater State Park is
nearby. A roof rack is required to
transport the boats; these can be
rented as well.

University of Washington
Waterfront Activity Center

Montlake Blvd. N.E. (north of the
Montlake Bridge and southeast of
Husky Stadium), Seattle
(206) 543-9433
Hours: Open Feb.-Oct.,
10 a.m.-dusk
Rentals: $5/hour per boat with
driver's license

Enjoy a leisurely paddle through
the Arboretum in a canoe or rowboat rented at the Canoe House.

The Foster Island area is full of
mysterious waterways and foot
bridges to navigate through and
under, a multitude of interesting
birds to observe, and an unlimited
number of places to hop ashore
and stretch. Canoes seat up to three
people; rowboats seat up to four.
Life vests are available for children
as small as 25 pounds. Boats are
available on a first-come, first-
served basis, so arrive early on
sunny weekends.

OUTDOOR POOLS
(OPEN SUMMERS ONLY)

Colman Pool, 8603 Fauntleroy Way (in Lincoln Park), Seattle; (206) 684-7494. Heated saltwater pool. (See "Tips" for Lincoln Park in Chapter 3.)
Cottage Lake Pool, 18831 N.E. Woodinville-Duvall Road, Woodinville; (206) 296-2999
Lynnwood Recreation Center, 18900 44th Ave. W., Lynnwood; (425) 771-4030. Retractable roof rolls back in the summer.
McCollum Pool, 600 128th St. S.E., Everett; (425) 339-1208
Peter Kirk Pool, 380 Kirkland Ave., Kirkland; (425) 828-1235
Redmond Pool, 17535 N.E. 104th, Redmond; (425) 296-2961
Vashon Pool, 9600 S.W. 204th, Vashon Island; (206) 463-3787

TIPS

Lifeguards are at nine Seattle beaches from 11 a.m.–8 p.m. daily in the summer, weather permitting. Each site offers free swimming lessons for children age 6 and up; preregistration is required. You can get more information at the beaches, or call (206) 684-4075.

Five King County beaches and six Bellevue parks also have summer lifeguards; call (206) 296-4258 and (425) 455-6803, respectively, for more information.

INSIDE SCOOP

Good Swimming Beaches

Clyde Beach, Bellevue
Chism Beach, Bellevue
Chesterfield Beach, Bellevue
Coulon Park, Renton
Enatai Beach, Bellevue
Five Mile Lake, Federal Way
Green Lake, Seattle
Houghton Beach Park, Kirkland
Juanita Beach Park, Kirkland
Lake Ballinger, Mountlake Terrace
Lake Sammamish State Park, Issaquah
Lake Wilderness Park, Maple Valley
Luther Burbank Park, Mercer Island
Madison Park, Seattle
Madrona Beach, Seattle
Magnuson Park, Seattle
Matthew's Beach, Seattle
Meydenbauer Park, Bellevue
Mount Baker Beach, Seattle
Newcastle Beach, Bellevue
Pine Lake Park, Issaquah
Pritchard Beach, Seattle
Seward Park, Seattle
Waverly Park, Kirkland

WADING POOLS

Seattle Wading Pools
Hotline: (206) 684-7796
Hours: Open daily, 11 a.m.-8 p.m.
(weather permitting)
Green Lake, N. 73rd and W. Green Lake Way
Lincoln Park, 8600 Fauntleroy Way
Magnuson, N.E. 65th and Sand Point Way N.E.
Volunteer Park, 1400 E. Galer

Hours: Open most weekdays (call for schedules)
Beacon Hill, 1820 13th Ave. S.
Bitter Lake, 13040 Greenwood Ave. N.
Bobby Morris, 1635 11th Ave.
Dahl, 7700 25th Ave. N.E.
Delridge, 4555 Delridge Way S.W.
E.C. Hughes, 2805 S.W. Holden St.
East Queen Anne, 160 Howe St.
Georgetown, 750 S. Homer
Gilman, 923 N.W. 54th
Hiawatha, 2700 California Ave. S.W.
Highland Park, 1100 S.W. Cloverdale St.
Lower Judkins, 2150 E. Spruce St.
Powell Barnett, 352 Martin Luther King Jr. Way
Pratt, 1800 S. Main St.
Sandel, 9035 Frist Ave. N.W.
South Park, 8319 Eighth Ave. S.
Van Asselt, 2820 S. Myrtle
View Ridge, 4408 N.E. 70th St.
Wallingford, 4219 Wallingford Ave. N.

INSIDE SCOOP

Fountain Fun

International Fountain, Seattle Center, Seattle. Children are now encouraged to play in the giant metal fountain.

Water Fountain, Waterfront Park, Pier 59, Seattle. Near the Seattle Aquarium.

Water Wall, Westlake Park, Fourth Ave. and Pine St., Seattle. Huge fountain arch.

Water Fountain, Bell Street Pier, Pier 66, Seattle. Fish-shaped artwork with pool, spraying fountains, and a globe fountain.

Harbor Steps Park, Western St. and University Ave., Seattle. Cascading fountains and pools flow downhill from near the Seattle Art Museum to the waterfront.

Waterfall Garden, Second Ave. and S. Main St., Seattle. Water bubbles from sculptures and fountains in this Pioneer Square retreat.

Downtown Park, 100th Ave. N.E. and N.E. First St., Bellevue. Fountains, a 1,200-foot canal, a 240-foot-wide waterfall, and a reflecting pond.

FISHING/ GATHERING CLAMS AND MUSSELS

Shellfish

Kids typically like any activity that allows them to play in wet muck, and they quickly catch on to the fun of digging for butter clams and harvesting oysters and mussels off rocks. What's surprising, given the slippery texture of shellfish, is that most kids like eating them, too.

All you'll need for your excursion are a shovel, a bucket, boots (if you don't want wet feet), and a low tide. Seattle's public beaches are open for clamming year-round, unless pollution alerts are posted. Alki Beach is the most popular in-city spot, but digging is better (and the clams are probably healthier) at public beaches in Edmonds and Mukilteo and on Whidbey Island. Children 14 and under don't need a shellfish license, but adults do ($5). This covers shellfish, crab, and even seaweed.

Harvesting mussels is remarkably simple; you just find a large mussel bed (Whidbey Island has many good spots) and pull them off the rocks. Oysters beds are a bit more scarce.

Clamming seasons are sometimes canceled because of shortages; consult the Department of Fish and Wildlife in Olympia (360-902-2200) for up-to-date information. There is also a danger of shell-

---

INSIDE SCOOP

Good Beachcombing

Alki Beach
Discovery Park
Golden Gardens
Lincoln Park

---

fish poisoning from a highly toxic microscopic organism that can turn the ocean water red (called "red tide"). Even cooking cannot eliminate it, so always call the Department of Health's Red Tide Hotline (800-562-5632) before you take the family out to gather shell fish.

Fishing

Kids 14 and under can fish during open season on any public dock in the area, without a license. Teens and adults must obtain licenses. For information on fishing licenses and regulations, call the Washington State Fish and Wildlife Department at (360) 902-2200. Fred Meyer, Kmart and Big 5 stores sell the licenses and offer booklets covering seasonal regulations.

Green Lake

Fish anywhere on the lake or at any of the following three piers: E.

Green Lake Dr. and Latona N.E. (at the foot of 65th Ave. N.E.); W. Green Lake Dr. and Stone N. (at the south end of the Bathhouse Theater); or the southwest corner of the lake by the shell house.

Lake Washington

This lake is home to over 40 species of fish, but most people who dangle a line here are hoping to pull out rainbow and cutthrout trout, salmon, and steelhead. Public fishing access is at the docks listed below.

In Seattle:

Commodore Park, W. Commodore Way and Gilman Ave. W. (on the Lake Washington Ship Canal)

Madison Park, (43rd Ave. E. and E. Madison)

Madrona Beach (south), Lake Washington Blvd. S. near the foot of E. Jefferson

Mount Baker Park, Lake Washington Blvd. S. and S. Horton

North Leschi Moorage, Lakeside S. and Alder E.

Mc Clellan Dock, S. McClellan St. and 35th S.

Seward Park, Lake Washington Blvd. S. and S. Juneau.

Stan Sayres Memorial Park, Lake Washington Blvd. S. and 43rd Ave. S.

In Bellevue:

Enatai (underneath the I-90 East Channel Bridge

Newcastle Beach, 4400 Lake Washington Blvd. S.

In Bothell:

Logboom Park (turn south onto 61st Ave. N.E. from Bothell Way).

In Kirkland:

Waverly Park, 633 Waverly Park Way (on Lake Washington Blvd.)

Marina Park, 25 Lake Shore Plaza (in downtown Kirkland at the foot of Central Way N.E.)

On Mercer Island:

Luther Burbank Park, 2040 84th Ave. S.E.

Puget Sound

Public fishing is popular at Waterfront Park at the end of Pier 57; the public seawall just north of Pier 70; and off Myrtle Edwards Park at Pier 86. Pier 86 is the most user-friendly spt, with covered areas and a bait-and-tackle shop, the Happy Hooker (206-284-0441). It also sells snacks. You can also fish at the Alki breakwater and from the pier at the south end of Golden Gardens Park. The pier at Mukilteo next to the ferry dock is an especially good spot.

Trout Farms

Fishing at a trout farm may not paint the most realistic picture of what this sport is all about, but face it: Your child will have plenty of opportunities later in life to experience fishing and catching nothing. The ponds are so crammed the trout seem to *want* to grab the hooks just to escape the crowded conditions. The only down side of these ventures is that most proud fisherpersons will expect their catch to be eaten, and these warm-water fish aren't very tasty.

Some trout farms are seasonal; others are open year-round on a limited schedule. Visitors are charged only for the fish they catch (either by the inch or the pound); all gear, bait, and cleaning are included. No licenses are required. Groups are welcome by reservation.

Gold Creek Trout Farm, 15844 148th Ave. N.E., Woodinville; (425) 483-1415. Open year-round, Tues.-Sun.

Springbrook Trout Farm, 19225 Talbot Road S., Renton; (253) 852-0360. Open March-Oct.

HORSEBACK RIDING

Does your child sleep with a hobby horse and wear cowboy boots to bed? Do you trip over little plastic horses whenever you enter your daughter's room? Horseback riding is a real thrill for young horse lovers, and all of the places listed below provide trail rides and, in some cases, riding classes, summer day camps, and overnight camps. Call for details on classes and camps.

High Country Outfitters
3020 Issaquah-Pine Lake Road, Suite 544, Issaquah
(425) 392-0111

Rates: Packages start at $70/day; family rates available

This organization offers a variety of trail-ride packages out of the Cle Elum area, varying in length and difficulty, from guided day rides to extended pack trips into the Wenatchee National Forest and Alpine Lakes Wilderness Areas. They also operate Camp Wahoo, an American Camp Association-accredited resident horse camp, and Red Gate Farm Day Camp in Issaquah, a summer day horse camp. Reservations are required.

INSIDE SCOOP

Pony Rides

Forest Park Animal Farm, 802 Mukilteo Blvd., Everett; (425) 257-8300., Free pony rides from 2-3 p.m. daily, June to August, weather permitting.

Farrel-McWhirter Park, 19545 Redmond Road, Redmond; (425) 556-2300. Occasionally offers public pony rides for a fee, as well as pony-riding classes.

Woodland Park Zoo, 5500 Phinney Ave. N., Seattle; (206) 684-4800. Pony rides offered in the northwest corner of the zoo daily during the summer months. The hours are limited, usually 11 a.m.-3 p.m. Cost is $2. Children must be at least 2 years old; the maximum weight is 120 pounds.

INSIDE SCOOP

Good Family Outings on Summer Nights

Camp Long overnight cabins

Discovery Park night walks

Everett AquaSox

Howl-ins at Wolf Haven

Seattle Chamber Music Festival: Under the Stars

Seattle Mariners

University of Washington Observatory

Woodland Park ZooTunes

Horse Country
8507 Hwy. 92, Granite Falls
(360) 691-7509
Season: Rides offered Wed.-Sun., year-round
Rates: $17.50/person for one-hour ride, $25/person for 90 minutes

Horse Country features trail rides for children age 6 and up. Adults must weigh under 200 pounds. Reservations required. Other programs include lessons, summer day camps, and lead-around ponies for little ones.

Little Bit Therapeutic Riding Center
19802 N.E. 148th, Woodinville
(425) 882-1554

This non-profit organization offers therapeutic horseback riding programs for differently abled persons, emphasizing their capabilities, rather than their limitations. The center is always looking for volunteers to help riders.

Tiger Mountain Outfitters
24508 S.E. 133rd, Issaquah
(425) 392-5090
Rates: $40/person for three-hour ride

Tiger Mountain Outfitters offers trail rides year-round for anyone over 10 years of age. Call ahead for reservations, and they will take you on a three-hour guided ride through 14,000 acres on Tiger Mountain.

MINI-GOLF (OUTDOOR)

D ress your children in plaid pants and cardigans, and teach them what the good life is all about.

Green Lake Pitch 'n Putt
5701 W. Green Lake Way N. Seattle
(206) 632-2280
Season: March-Oct.
Rates: $3-$4/person for greens fees, 50 cents/person for club rentals, $1/golf balls

If you want to introduce your older child to the real game of golf, this is the place. Green Lake Pitch 'n Putt is not a mini-golf course; it's a nine-hole, par 3 course on eight acres on Green Lake's south shore. Holes range from 55 to 115 yards. You can bring your own clubs and balls or rent them.

Interbay Family Golf Center
2501 15th Ave. W., Seattle
(206) 285-2200
Hours: Open daily, 7 a.m.-11 p.m.
Rates: $6/adults, $4.50/children age 14 and under

Interbay Family Golf Center, one of Seattle's newer facilities, features an 18-hole putting course with a variety of layouts and challenges set among lush gardens, waterfalls, and ponds.

The center also offers golfing lessons and free clinics, as well as a café serving breakfast and lunch. In spring 1998, the nine-hole The Course at Interbay will open.

Jazwieck's Golf
7828 Broadway, Everett
(425) 355-5646
Season: April-Oct.
Hours: Noon-10 p.m. during the summer; spring and fall operations dependent on weather
Rates: $4/person

INSIDE SCOOP Outdoor Movies

Fremont Outdoor Cinema
3416 Evanston Ave. N., Seattle
(206) 634-2150
Season: Saturdays, June-Labor Day
Tickets: $5/all ages (suggested donation)

Fremont's popular outdoor cinema shows classic movies on the side of a building in a parking lot. Seating starts at 7

p.m.; bring your own lawn chairs. Movies begin at dusk. There is a small concession stand with snacks, and the neighborhood is home to plenty of restaurants.

Puget Park Drive-In, Everett; (425) 338-5957

Valley 6 Outdoor Theaters, S. 277th and Auburn Way N., Auburn; (253) 854-1250.

This 18-hole, outdoor course, built in 1961, was one of the first miniature golf courses in the Seattle area. It has traditional mini-golf obstacles and decorations.

Riverbend Mini Putt-Putt
2020 W. Meeker, Kent
(253) 859-4000
Season: Open year-round
Hours: Mon.-Sat., 8 a.m.-9 p.m.; Sun., 8 a.m.-8 p.m.
Rates: $4/adults, $3/children

Riverbend is an outdoor 18-hole miniature course. Groups and birthday celebrations are welcome with advance reservations.

RIVER RAFTING

With an abundance of beautiful rivers nearby, it is no wonder that river rafting is a popular sport in the Northwest. For families, a guided trip is an expensive but unforgettable experience. There are two types of river rafting: white-water rafting, which plows through rapids and is full of thrills (and potential spills), and serene float trips, when the raft meanders downstream. Both types usually offer magnificent scenery, wildlife viewing, and a fascinating up-close look at the river.

Most rafting companies will not take kids under the age of 6 for safety reasons. School-age kids typically love river rafting, especially if the trip includes both mild rapids and interesting wildlife. The Methow, Skykomish, and Wenatchee rivers are recommended in the late spring and summer; in the winter, Skagit River bald eagle float trips are very popular with families.

There are many good river-rafting companies in this region. Most are very helpful in recommending river runs that will suit the age range in your group. Be sure to ask if they offer discounts for kids or large groups.

Here are some popular rafting companies:

Alpine Adventures, Leavenworth; (800) 926-RAFT or (253) 838-2505; www.alpineadventures.com

River Riders, Woodinville; (206) 448-RAFT (448-7238)

Wildwater River Tours, Federal Way; (800) 522-WILD or (253) 939-2151

SNOW FUN

Seattle families are lucky to be able to jump into their car on a winter weekend and arrive at the mountains within an hour. There are plenty of opportunities for you and your kids to have snow fun without enormous expense. Remember to dress kids well so they stay warm and dry, carry chains at all times, bring plenty of snacks, and call the Washington State Department of Transportation's Pass Report, available November through April, at (888) 766-4636), or visit its Web site, www.wsdot.wa.gov/sno-info, to check on road and weather conditions before you venture forth. Other helpful numbers are Cascade Ski Report, (206) 634-0200, and I-90 Sno-Park Report, (509) 656-2230.

Cross-Country Skiing

Summit Nordic Center
(206) 236-7277

Stevens Pass Nordic Center
(360) 973-2441

Nordic centers at Snoqualmie's Summit Central and at Stevens Pass offer 55 kilometers and 25 kilometers of groomed trails, respectively, for cross-country skiers of all abilities. Trail fees range from $7 to $9.

Skiers who prefer trails other than those at the ski resorts can purchase a Sno-Park permit that entitles them to park at designated lots at local passes. Permits are $7/one day, $10/three days, $20/season; they are available at outdoor retail stores and ranger stations. (For a list of vendors, visit the Washington State Parks Web site at www.parks.wa.gov/vendor1.htm.) Good cross-country trails are also plentiful in the Leavenworth area.

Downhill Skiing

Summit Central and Summit West at the Summit at Snoqualmie are two of the best areas for beginning skiers. They have several bunny hills and lifts that give novices a chance to get steady on their skis before facing steeper slopes. All of the following areas offer family- discount season passes that provide significant savings. Consider skiing on a weekday or at night, when lift tickets are generally cheaper. Two of Washington's major ski resorts, Summit at Snoqualmie and Crystal Mountain, plan $45 million of proposed improvements in the next 10 years, including dozens of new chairlifts. This will make for better skiing, but likely will cause lift ticket prices to jump even higher.

All the areas offer lessons and rental equipment (skis, boots, and poles) for the day.

Crystal Mountain
Hwy. 410, 12 miles northeast of Mount Rainier
(888) SKI-6199 (snow phone), (360) 663-2265 (general information)
www.crystalmt.com.
Tickets: $35/adults, $30/youths ages 11-17, free/children age 10 and under
Terrain: 13% beginner, 57% intermediate, 30% advanced.
Child care: Daily, 8 a.m. -5 p.m., for children age 6 months and older. Reservations recommended; call (360) 663-0221.
Kids' lessons: Kids Club Program for ages 4-11. Children can participate in half- or all-day programs that include a lesson, lift ticket, and supervision while parents ski. Make reservations at (360) 663-2265 or

drop in to see if space is available. **Conveniences:** A family drop-off zone right in front of the ticket plaza allows one parent to unload the kids while the other parks the car.

Stevens Pass
U.S. Hwy. 2 (78 miles east of Seattle)
(360) 973-2441
www.stevenspass.com
Tickets: Mon.-Tues., $20/person; Wed.-Fri., $25/person; weekends and holidays, $35/adults, $26/seniors, $24/children ages 7-12, $5/children age 6 and under and seniors 70 and older
Terrain: 11% beginner, 54% intermediate, 35% advanced
Child care: Open Sat.-Tues. 8:30 a.m.-4:30 a.m. for children ages 30 months-7 years
Kids' lessons: For tots up to age 8

The Summit at Snoqualmie
Interstate 90 (about 50 miles east of Seattle)
(206) 236-1600 (snow phone),
(206) 232-8182 (general information)
www.summit-at-snoqualmie.com.

The recently renamed Summit at Snoqualmie comprises four ski areas: Alpental, Summit Central (formerly Ski Acres), Summit West (Snoqualmie), and Summit East (Hyak). One ticket gives you access to lifts at all four areas.
Tickets: Weekdays, $20/adults, $15/seniors; weekends and holidays, $32/adults, $22/youths ages 7-11, $15/seniors, $8/children age 6 and under.
Terrain: Summit Central, 50% beginner, 20% intermediate, 30% advanced; Summit East, 42% beginner, 40% intermediate, 18% advanced; Summit West, 35% beginner, 45% intermediate, 20% advanced; Alpental, 10% beginner, 40% intermediate, 50% advanced.
Kids' lessons: Summit Learning Centers, which operates at all four areas, offers lessons for children age 4 and up.

Tubing

Summit Tubing Center
Snoqualmie Pass, east corner of Summit Central parking lot
(206) 236-7277, ext. 3377
Season: Dec.-mid-April, weather permitting
Hours: Fri., 11 a.m.-10 p.m.; Sat., 8:30 a.m.-10 p.m.; Sun., 8:30 a.m.-6 p.m.
Rates: $8/person admission, $5/tube rental

The Summit Tubing Center takes the work out of snow play by offering two rope tows to carry sliders up the groomed hill, dubbed Mount Tubemore. Kids can rent or bring their own inner tubes or plastic sliding discs. Hard, steerable devices such as sleds are not allowed. Admission is charged whether or not you bring your own tube.

The new owners of Summit at Snoqualmie plan to eventually expand the tubing facility to offer such winter activities as tobogganing, ice skating, sno-cart racing, and luging.

Chapter 5

INDOOR FUN

The mid-January post holiday crash has hit. Or maybe summer vacation started a week ago and it hasn't stopped raining since the last school bell rang. The kids are swinging from the light fixtures.

You can't face another craft project—so now what? Insist the little critters clean their closets? How about recruiting another family for some sanity-preserving adult company and trying out one of these energy-burning activities.

BUMPER BOWLING

B owling with kids is a lot more fun on a lane with bumpers, gutter pads that at least let the ball make it to the end of the alley. The bumpers will guide your child's bowling ball straight to the Big Ten, ensuring at least one satisfying crash. Beware the other, not-so-good crashes, like Bowling Ball on the Toe, Child and Attached Bowling Ball Bouncing Down the Lane, and Bowling Ball Hurled Backwards Toward Little Sister.

Bumper bowling is popular; the fact it helps parents avoid embarrassment too probably doesn't hurt. Prices vary a bit from alley to alley,

Bumpers mean even little ones can bowl.

and don't forget shoe rental. If you can't find shoes small enough to fit your kids, they can bowl in their socks (adds slippery thrills). Call the bowling alley in advance to make sure bumper bowling is offered; if lanes are full or leagues are playing, they won't get the bumpers out.

Brunswick Majestic Lanes, 1300 164th Ave. S.W., Lynnwood; (425) 743-4422

Cascade Lanes, 17034 116th Ave. S.E., Renton; (425) 226-2035

Imperial Lanes, 2101 22nd Ave. S., Seattle; 206325-2525

Kent Bowl, 1234 N. Central, Kent; (253) 852-3550

Leilani Lanes, 10201 Greenwood N., Seattle; (206) 783-8010

Lewis & Clark Bowl, 15820 Pacific Hwy. S., Seattle; (206) 244-2902

Lynnwood Lanes, 6210 200th Ave. S.W., Lynnwood; (425) 778-3133

Robin Hood Lanes, 9801 Edmonds Way, Edmonds; (425) 776-2101

Roxbury Lanes, 2823 SW Roxbury St., Seattle; (206) 935-7400

Skyway Park Bowl, 11819 Renton Ave. S., Seattle; (206) 772-1220

Sportsworld Lanes, 27403 Pacific Hwy. S., Kent; (253) 941-4700

Sunset Bowl, 1420 N.W. Market, Seattle; (206) 782-7310

Sun Villa Lanes, Eastgate Shopping Center, Bellevue; (425) 455-8155

STEPHANIE DUNNEWIND

ICE SKATING

M ost youngsters more or less crawl around the rink on their first few ice-skating attempts, so be sure to provide mittens and encourage plenty of breaks for hot chocolate. Also, you might mention to the kids that although Olympic skaters make it look really easy, they had to sweat for six hours a day beginning at 4 a.m. for most of their childhood to become so graceful on those skinny blades. It also helps to bring along at least one adult who has enough control on the ice to remain upright despite flailing kids hanging onto her. Lessons are offered for budding Tara Lipinskis and Todd Eldredges. Rinks also host ice hockey leagues.

Highland Ice Arena
18005 Aurora Ave. N., Seattle
(206) 546-2431
Hours: Open daily year-round; public sessions vary
Rates: $4/children ages 6-12, $4.50/ teens and adults, free/children age 5 and under; $2.25/skate rental

Sno-King Ice Arena
19803 68th Ave. W., Lynnwood
(425) 775-7511
Hours: Open daily year-round; public skate sessions vary
Rates: $4.75/person; $2.25/skate rental

INDOOR PLAYGROUNDS

S everal parks departments in the Seattle and Eastside areas offer drop-in indoor playgrounds for toddlers and preschoolers. Some programs are offered year-round, others are held only during the school year or select winter months. Special play equipment is set up for these regularly scheduled programs, including climbing apparatus, mats, balls, trikes, toys, and tunnels. Adults must accompany children at all times. The drop-in fee is usually $1 to $2 per child. The schedules and equipment vary for each location; call the site nearest you for details.

Bellevue: Highline Community Center, Bellevue; (425) 455-7686. Ages up to 4 years. Mon., Wed., Fri., 9 a.m.-noon.

Kids can expend excess energy at indoor playgrounds.

TIPS

Parenting a young child is often a very lonely experience, especially when wet weather keeps everybody inside. The indoor playgrounds for toddlers and preschoolers give parents a chance to get to know other parents in the neighborhood.

Green Lake: Green Lake Community Center, Seattle; (206) 684-0780. Toddlers to age 5. Mon.-Fri., 10 a.m.-9 p.m.; Sat., 9 a.m.-5 p.m.

Everett: Everett Community College, Athletic Building, Everett;. (425) 257-8300. Ages 0-6 years. Sept.-May., Tues. and Thurs., 9:30-11 a.m.

Issaquah: Issaquah Community Center gym, Issaquah; (425) 391-1008. Ages 1-3 years. Mon., Thurs., and Fri., 9:30-11:45 a.m.

Kent: Kent Commons, Kent; (253) 2859-3350. Ages 10 months-4 years. Tues., Wed., and Thurs., 9:30-11 a.m.

Kirkland: North Kirkland Community Center, Kirkland; (425) 828-1217. Ages 1-5 years. Tues. and Thurs., 11-2 p.m.

Loyal Heights: Loyal Heights Community Center, Seattle; (206) 684-4052. Infants to age 3. Three weekday sessions.

Mountlake Terrace: Mountlake Terrace Recreation Pavilion, Mountlake Terrace; (425) 776-9173. Crawlers to age 4. Tues. and Wed., 10 a.m.-7:15 p.m.; Thurs., 10 a.m.-

2 p.m.

Renton: Renton Community Center, Renton; (425) 235-2560. Ages 10 months-3 years. Tues., Thurs., and Fri., 9:30-11 a.m.

Shoreline: Shoreline Center Gym, Shoreline; (206) 546-5041. Toddlers and preschoolers. Tues. and Fri., 10-11:30 a.m.

West Seattle: Delridge Community Center, Seattle; (206) 684-7423. Ages 1-5. Wed. and Fri., 9:30 a.m.-1 p.m.

Educational Play Center
Gilman Village, Issaquah
(425) 392-2095

Eight-week play sessions for children ages 3 months to 5 years and their parents. A free play time is offered Wednesdays, 3-5 p.m.

Playspace
Crossroads Shopping Center, N.E. Eighth St. and 156th Ave. N.E., Bellevue
(425) 644-4500
$6.46/child, free/children under 18 months if accompanied by another paying child
Drop-off care is also available for $8/first hour, $1.50/each additional 15 minutes.

At this brightly colored playground, kids 12 and under can climb, jump, slide, bounce, balance, and more in tubes, tunnels, ball baths, obstacle courses, and slides. Energetic parents can join in the fun for free or sit back and have a cup of coffee and a snack from the snack bar. Every Friday and Saturday night, Playspace offers Parents' Night Out, an evening of child care for ages 3-12 (must be potty-trained) that includes a movie, dinner, craft, story time, playtime in the tunnel tubes, and a pager for the parents. Cost of Parents' Night Out is $18.50/child.

INDOOR FAMILY ENTERTAINMENT CENTERS

The atmosphere is "indoor carnival"—noisy, crowded, and fun. Besides video and redemption games, most offer activities such as laser tag, miniature golf, go-karts, and batting cages. All accommodate birthday parties and offer packages.

Chuck E. Cheese
2239 148th Ave. N.E., Bellevue
(425) 746-5000
3717 196th Ave. S.W., Lynnwood
(425) 778-6566

ESSENTIALS

Admission is not charged in most cases; instead, you buy tickets or tokens for various activities or packaged deals. Expect to spend at least $10 per person, excluding food. All have snack bars or cafes with pizza, hot dogs, popcorn, and other fast food.

Redemption games, kiddie rides, tube and ball play area.

Fun Forest Amusement Park
305 Harrison, Seattle
(206) 728-1585

INSIDE SCOOP

Crying Rooms

A handful of local movie theaters have crying rooms, glassed-in areas where the kids can do some primal therapy without disrupting other movie-goers. Most of these crying rooms are small (the exception being Northgate's). Call to make sure that the feature you wish to see is being shown in the theater equipped with a crying room.

Guild-45th St. Theatre, 2115 N. 45th St., Seattle; (206) 633-3353
Varsity Theatre, 4329 NE University Way, Seattle; (206) 632-3131
Metro Cinemas, 4500 Ninth Ave. NE, Seattle; (206) 633-0055
Northgate Theatre, 10 Northgate Plaza, Seattle; (206) 363-5800

Many places have play areas and games for younger children, but the main audience is older children and teens. Depending on your child's disposition, the noise and activity may cause sensory overload. Chuck E. Cheese is geared to younger kids.

Weekends and school vacations are busiest; try to take kids at a slow time for the most fun. Be warned, however, that even weeknights can be crowded if there is a sports team celebration or a large birthday party.

Laser tag, video and interactive games, mini-golf, indoor amusement ride for small children.

Funtasia Family Sports and Entertainment

7212 220th St. S.W., Edmonds
(206) 774-GAME
Hours: Sun.-Thurs., 10 a.m.-11 p.m.; Fri.-Sat., 10 a.m.-1 a.m.

Go-karts, laser tag, batting cages, mini-golf, video games, play land.

Games

3616 South Road, Mukilteo
(425) 353-6800
Hours: Sun.-Thurs., 10 a.m.-10 p.m.; Fri.-Sat. 10 a.m.-midnight

Miniature golf, video games, batting cages, super slides.

Seattle Funplex Indoor Amusement Park

1541 15th Ave. W., Seattle
(206) 285-7842
Hours: Sun.-Thurs., 11 a.m.-11 p.m.; Fri., 11 a.m.-midnight; Sat. 10 a.m.-midnight.
$2 entrance fee on Friday and Saturday nights after 9 p.m.

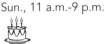

Amusement ride, laser tag, mini-golf, batting cages, play land, video and redemption games.

Zones

2207 Bellevue-Redmond Road, Redmond
(425) 746-9411
Hours: Mon.-Thurs., 11 a.m.-9 p.m.; Fri.-Sat., 11 a.m.-midnight; Sun., 11 a.m.-9 p.m.

Bumper cars, nine-hole mini-golf, batting cages.

ROLLER SKATING

Yes, they still do the Hokey Pokey, and they still play the Top 40. But don't let your warped, disco-days memories stop you from taking the kids roller skating. Not only is it easier than ice skating, it's much warmer. Skaters can bring their own skates (but not in-lines if they have been worn outside) or rent skates at the rink. Rates vary depending on day and time. Activities for families include family skate sessions with special rates, tiny tot skates for children under age 10, teen skates, drop-in skate lessons, and birthday party packages.

Roll-a-Way Skate Center
6210 200th Ave. S.W., Lynnwood
(425) 778-4446
Hours: Skate sessions vary; call for schedule
Rates: $3.75-$5/person.
$1.50/skate rental; $4/inline skates.

Skate King
2301 140th Ave. N.E., Bellevue
(425) 641-2046
Hours: Sessions vary; call for schedule
Rates: $3.50-$5/person, cash only.
$1.50/quad skate rental, $4/inline skates,

Seattle In-Line Arena
The Riverside Mall, 3800 W. Marginal Way S.W., Seattle
(206) 937-2966
Public sessions: Mon., Wed., Fri., and Sat. afternoons; Fri.-Sat. evenings
Rates: $5/person, $4/person for groups of three or more; $5/Rollerblade rentals

West Seattle's full-size indoor rink is for in-line skating only. In addition to public skating sessions, the arena offers lessons, summer kids' camps, and inline hockey leagues.

Southgate Roller Rink
9646 17th Ave. S.W., Seattle
(206) 762-4030
Hours: Public sessions Wed., Fri.-Sun.
Rates: $4-$6/person, including skates; $2 extra for inline skates.

TCL Family Skate Center
10210 S.E. 260th St., Kent
(253) 852-9371
Hours: Open Wed.-Sat.; public skate times vary
Rates: $3-$6/person, cash only; depending on session, skate rental is included in fee or $1.50; $4/inline skates

INDOOR MINIATURE GOLF

Big D's Batting Cage and Mini Golf
1070 Columbia Ave., Marysville
(360) 659-4086
$3/adults, $2.50/children age 12 and under

Eighteen-hole course with mechanical obstacles.

Fun Forest Amusement Park
305 Harrison (Seattle Center)
Seattle
(206) 728-1585
$4/person

Basic 18-hole course.

Skyway Park Bowl features a Carribean theme.

INSIDE SCOOP

Good Family Outings on a Winter Night

Ice skating
Indoor family entertainment center
Roller skating
Swimming
Theater
University of Washington Husky basketball
Seattle Reign basketball

Funtasia Family Fun Park
7212 220th Ave. S.W., Edmonds
(425) 774-GAME
$3.50/adults, $3/children, with unlimited play for an extra $1

Half the 18-hole course is inside and half is outside. Obstacles include a rocket, a Ferris wheel, and statues, including ones that depict a gorilla and Porky Pig.

Games Family Fun Center
3616 South Road, Mukilteo
(425) 745-5033
$3.75/adults, $2.75/children ages 4-12, free/children age 3 and under

The 18-hole course has a Northwest theme, with a volcano, a lighthouse, a wishing well, and a ferry.

Seattle Funplex Indoor Amusement Park

1541 15th Ave. W., Seattle
(206) 285-7842
$3.50/adults, $3/children, with unlimited play for an extra $1/person; Fri.-Sat., $2 cover charge after 9 p.m., free admission the rest of the time

Northwest-themed, 18-hole indoor golf course.

Skyway Park Bowl

11819 Renton Ave. S., Seattle
(206) 772-1220
$5/adults, $4/children, $3.50/person from 9 a.m.-1 p.m.

Lush Caribbean-themed 18-hole course with real water traps.

Zones

2207 Bellevue-Redmond Road., Redmond
(425) 746-9411
$2.50/person

Nine-hole course with a Seattle theme.

ART, CRAFTS, AND PROJECTS

Creation Station

19511 64th Ave. W., Lynnwood
(425) 775-7959
Hours: Mon.-Sat., 10 a.m.-6 p.m.
$3.75/child per project

As any parent knows, stuff that we consider "junk" is often, in the eyes of a child, material for creation. C.C. Leonard, owner of the Creation Station, agrees. "I hate to see anything thrown away," she says, which explains why she was inspired to open a store where kids (and adults) can make anything their imagination allows from assorted odds and ends such as ribbons, binders, film canisters, and juice box straws. Leonard is a born recycler, and a scavenger for things that local businesses consider rubbish.

The store is chock-full of unusual and unused, uncontaminated, recyclable materials, including cones, tubes, fabrics, plastic, paper, foam, and wood. Expert guidance is available, complete with lots of ideas on how to use the various items (although Leonard, a former preschool teacher, is quick to point out that kids don't need any help with ideas).

Creation Station has tables set up with loads of material to spur creativity. If your children would rather work at home, however, the store sells prepackaged kits in a retail area.

Hands of the Hills
3016 78th Ave. S.E., Mercer Island
(206) 232-8121

Drop-in work area where families can make bead jewelry of all sorts. Call for a quarterly schedule of classes. Recommended for ages 8 and up.

Kirkland Arts Center
620 Market St., Kirkland
(425) 822-7161

Art classes and workshops for youths and teens.

Neo Art Schools
4649 Sunnyside Ave. N.,
Suite 121, Seattle
6717 212th Ave. S.W., Brighton
Campus, Edmonds
(206) 632-2530

Classes, Parents' Nights Out, day camps, and Saturday art field trips.

CERAMICS / POTTERY

For a personalized present or keepsake, kids can pick out a ceramic dish, cup or figurine and then paint it with glaze. You pay for the piece and studio time. Expect it to take at least a couple days for it to be fired in the kiln.

All Fired Up, 23814 Bothell-Everett Hwy., Bothell; (425) 547-7249

Bisque It, 107 5th Ave. N., Suite 103, Edmonds; (425) 775-8045

City Ceramics, 413 15th Ave. E., Seattle; (206) 329-1604

Creative Cafe, 8516 Greenwood Ave. N., Seattle; (206) 706-7074

Indigo Crow Ceramics, Gilman Village, Issaquah; (425) 557-4544

Paint Bar, 2020 Bellevue Square, Bellevue; (425) 637-9979

Paint-It-Up Ceramics-U-Design, 3929 Factoria Square Mall S.E., Bellevue; (425) 957-9884

The Paint Patch, 5405 Ballard N.W., Seattle; (206) 789-7160

Paint My Day, 1402 S. Everett Mall Way, Everett; (425) 710-9414

Paint the Town, 4527 University Village Court N.E., Seattle; (206) 527-8554

Paint This, 10101 N.E. Main St., Bothell; (425) 487-9406

Painted Fire, 3601 Fremont N.; (206) 545-2816

The Studio, 851 108th Ave. N.E., Bellevue; (425) 455-0566

INDOOR ROCK CLIMBING

"**I**t's instinctual: Kids want to climb anything," says Rich Johnston, owner of Vertical World, one of several indoor rock-climbing gyms offering classes for children. "Inside, they'll climb furniture; outside, they climb trees."

Most children are naturals at rock climbing because they are so light and nimble, Johnston says. It gives kids a challenge they can control, forcing them to focus their energy. Plus, it's an indoor activity that parents and children can do together, in which neither is just a spectator.

"It blows kids away that their parents are allowing them to climb," says Johnston. "Parents can let them loose instead of saying, 'Hey, get off of there.' "

Cascade Crags Indoor Climbing Gym
2820 Rucker Ave., Everett
(425) 258-3431

More than 10,000 square feet of climbing wall. Kids' programs, classes, family discounts. Age 4 and up.

Kirkland Boys and Girls Club
10805 124th Ave. N.E., Kirkland
(425) 827-0132

A four-part class for children ages 6 to 18 is offered on the club's rock-climbing wall. Cost is $20 plus club membership.

REI
222 Yale Ave. N., Seattle
(206) 223-1944
4200 194th Ave. S.W., Lynnwood
(206) 774-1300
Free/REI co-op members,
$5/non-members

REI doesn't offer climbing classes, but anyone is welcome to try to scale its indoor rock pinnacle. Children must fit into the store's smallest harness (usually age 4 and up). Parents must sign a release waiver for children age 18 and under, and stay in the area with children age 14 and under. You sign up when you arrive at the store; no reservations are taken. The wait can be as long as two hours on the weekend. Rock-climbing footwear is provided. REI belayers will give novices a few pointers and suggest an easy route. No birthday parties.

At the Lynnwood store, a climbing wall is open Wednesday and Thursday, 6-8:30 p.m., and Saturday, 11 a.m.-1 p.m.

Stone Gardens

2839 N.W. Market St., Seattle
(206) 781-9828
www.stonegardens.com

Offers regular kids' climbs Mon.-Fri., 3:30-5:30 p.m., and Saturdays, 10-1 p.m., for children age 6 and up.

Vertical World

15036 N.E. 95th, Redmond
(425) 881-8826
755 N. Northlake Way, Suite 100, Seattle; (206) 283-4497
www.verticalworld.com

Introductory climbing classes for families and children, as well as after-school junior programs and competitive climbing teams.

SWIMMING

An indoor swim in the middle of winter soothes kids and gives parents a chance to sneak in a few laps. The public pools in the area have designated family swim times, and the admission fees are very reasonable.

All the pools listed below are indoors, and all offer family swims and lessons.

Seattle Parks and Recreation Pools

Admission is $2.50/adults and $1.75/children age 18 and under. Punch tickets are available at a discounted rate.

Ballard, 1471 NW 67th; (206) 684-4094

Evans, 7201 E. Green Lake Dr. N.; (206) 684-4961

Madison, 13401 Meridian N.; (206) 684-4979

Meadowbrook, 10515 35th Ave. N.E; (206) 684-4989

Medgar Evers, 500 23rd St.; (206) 684-4766

Queen Anne, 1920 First Ave. W.; (206) 386-4282

TIPS

Green Lake Community Center puts an aquatic twist on Halloween, offering a Haunted Pool and Carnival for all ages each Oct. 31 at Evans Pool.

Swimming at King County pools is even more fun with inflatable toys.

Rainier Beach, 8825 Rainier S.; (206) 386-1944

Southwest, 2801 S.W. Thistle; (206) 684-7440

King County Pools

Family swim admission is $1.40 per person.

Aquatic Center, 650 S.W. Campus Drive, Federal Way; (206) 296-4444

Auburn, 516 Fourth N.E., Auburn; (253) 939-8825

Evergreen (Burien), 606 S.W. 116th St., Seattle; (206) 296-4410

Federal Way, 30421 16th Ave. S., Federal Way; (253) 839-1000

Kent, 25316 101st Ave. S.E., Kent; (206) 296-4275

Mercer Island, 8815 S.E. 40th, Mercer Island; (206) 296-4370

Mount Rainier, 22722 19th Ave. S., Des Moines; (206) 296-4278

Northshore, 9815 N.E. 188th St., Bothell; (206) 296-4333

Redmond, 17535 N.E. 104th St., Redmond; (206) 296-2961

Renton, 16740 128th Ave. S.E., Renton; (206) 296-4335

St. Edward, 14445 Juanita Drive N.E., Bothell; (206) 296-2970

Shoreline, 19030 First Ave. N.E., Seattle; (206) 296-4345

Si View, 41600 S.E. 122nd, North Bend; (425) 889-1447

South Central, 4414 S. 144th, Seattle; (206) 296-4487

Tahoma, 18230 S.E. 240th, Kent; (206) 296-4276

Other city pools

Bellevue Aquatics Center, 601 143rd Ave. N.E., Bellevue; (425) 452-4444

Julius Boehm Pool, 50 S.E. Clark St., Issaquah; (425) 557-3298

Lynnwood Recreation Center, 18900 44th Ave. W., Lynnwood; (425) 771-4030

Mountlake Terrace, 5303 228th St. S.W., Mountlake Terrace; (425) 776-9173

Shoreline, N. 190th St. and First Ave. N.E., Shoreline; (206) 362-1307

Aqua Barn Ranch

15227 S.E. Renton-Maple Hwy.
Renton
(425) 255-4618
Open year-round
Rates: $2.75/children age 12 and under, $3/children ages 14-18, $3.50/adults

    Aqua Barn Ranch is a private facility with a large pool that is well equipped with a slide, diving board, and a good-sized kiddie pool. Family swims are scheduled most afternoons, with lifeguarded public swims Thursday through Saturday evenings and Sunday afternoons. Call for specific times.

Downtown YMCA Family Swim

909 Fourth Ave., Seattle
(206) 382-5000
Public hours: Sat., 5:30-8 p.m.; Sun., 7:30 am.-5 p.m.
Rates: $12/adults, $1/children.

COMMUNITY CENTERS

Most community centers offer a variety of activities, from art classes to fitness programs to preschool activities to teen nights.

Seattle

    Alki, 5817 S.W. Stevens St.; (206) 684-7430

    Delridge, 4501 Delridge Way S.W.; (206) 684-7423

    Garfield, 2323 E. Cherry St.; (206) 684-4788

    Green Lake, 7201 E. Green Lake Dr. N.; (206) 684-0780

    Hiawatha, 2700 California S.W.; (206) 684-7441

    High Point, 6920 34th Ave. S.W.; (206) 684-7422

    Loyal Heights, 2101 N.W. 77th St.; (206) 684-4052

    Magnolia, 2550 34th Ave. W.; (206) 386-4235

    Montlake, 1618 E. Calhoun St.; (206) 684-4736

    Queen Anne, 1920 First Ave. W.; (206) 386-4240

    South Park, 8319 Eighth Ave. S.; (206) 684-7451

    Yesler, 825 Yesler Way; (206) 396-1245

Eastside

    Crossroads, 16000 N.E. 10th, Bellevue; (425) 455-4874

    Gracie Hansen, 27132 S.E. Ravensdale Way, Ravensdale; (425) 432-2158

    Highland, 14224 Bellevue-Redmond Road, Bellevue; (425) 455-7686

Issaquah, 301 Rainier Blvd. S., Issaquah; (425) 391-1008

Lake Wilderness, 23601 S.E. 248th, Maple Valley; (425) 296-4298

Mercer View, 8236 S.E. 24th, Mercer Island; (206) 236-3537

North Kirkland, 12421 103rd Ave. N.E., Kirkland; (425) 828-1105

Northwest, 9825 N.E. 24th, Bellevue; (425) 462-6046

Si View, 41600 S.E. 122nd, North Bend; (425) 888-1442

South

Kent Commons, 525 Fourth Ave. N., Kent; (253) 859-3350

North SeaTac Park, 13735 24th Ave. S., SeaTac; (206) 439-9273

Renton, 1715 Maple Valley Hwy., Renton; (425) 235-2560

North

Frances Anderson Cultural and Leisure Center, 700 Main St., Edmonds; (425) 771-0230

Lynnwood, 18900 44th Ave. W., Lynnwood; (425) 771-4030

Mountlake Terrace, 5303 228th St. S.W., Mountlake Terrace; (425) 776-9173

YMCA

The YMCA offers programs for children and youths. For more information, call the facility in your area.

Auburn, (253) 833-2770; **Bellevue/Eastside**, (425) 746-9900; **Seattle** (downtown), (206) 382-5000; **Fauntleroy**, (206) 937-1000; **Federal Way**, (253) 838-4708; **High Point**, (206) 937-1936; **Highline**, (206) 244-5880; **Lake Heights**, (425) 644-8417; **East Madison**, (206) 322-6969; **University Family**, (206) 524-1400; **Northshore**, (425) 485-9797; **Sammamish**, (425) 391-4840; **Shoreline**, (206) 364-1700; **West Seattle**, (206) 935-6000.

- -

TIPS

The East Madison YMCA offers a drop-in progrm for youths ages 7 to 13. The program runs Mon.-Fri., 3-7 p.m., and Sat., noon-4 p.m. Activities include games, computer time, field trips, bike rides, swimming and gym play. Cost is $1/day or $5/month, plus a $10 annual fee. Some trips require an additional fee.

PUBLIC LIBRARIES

Bellevue Regional Library
(425) 462-9600; children's services, (425) 450-1775

King County Public Libraries
Information, (206) 462-9600 or (800) 462-9600; children's services, (206) 684-6619; www.kcls.org

Mercer Island Public Library
(206) 236-3537

Pierce County Public Libraries
(253) 536-6500

Renton Library: (425) 235-2610

TIPS

If your child wants a story and you just can't oblige, let her "Dial a Story," at (206) 386-4656.

The King County Library System offers dozens of kits with books, videocassettes, and puppets centered on different themes. "Books to Grow On," designed for preschoolers, cover topics such as animals, babies, feelings, and trains. A list of kits is available at all branch libraries. "Discovery Kits" are for older students, hitting such topics as dinosaurs, aviation, birding, and horses. You can find a complete list by using any branch library computer and typing in "Discovery Kit" as the title.

In addition to videos and books, you can check out educational CD-ROMs and access the Internet at many libraries.

Seattle Public Libraries
(206) 386-4636 or www.spl.lib.wa.us
Sno-Isle (Snohomish/Island County) Libraries
(800) 342-1936
Tacoma Public Libraries
(253) 591-5666
Hours vary

Your local public library is not just a place for research and study; it's a family resource, with events and activities for every member of your family. In addition to loaning out books, audio cassettes, and videos, these library systems offer a wide variety of programs, including preschool story times and parenting programs, hands-on science programs, craft activities, concerts, author appearances, used book sales, and family movies. (Contact your local library for a complete schedule of events.) Most libraries have a children's librarian available to answer questions about the programs and to help children in their reading selections.

SHOPPING WITHOUT SPENDING

Whatever their attitude toward consumerism, parents of young children have to love shopping malls. Big, indoors, and inexpensive (as long as you stay out of actual stores), malls are a great place to kill an afternoon. If parents are willing, toddlers will spend hours just riding up and down escalators! Fortunately, many malls and individual stores also offer other diversions.

Bellevue Square
N.E. Eighth and Bellevue Way N.E., Bellevue
Administration, (452) 454-2431; information booth, (425) 454-2431

This is a great mall for kids with

excess energy on a rainy day. First, it's huge. Second, it has not one, but *two* play boats—one for each level. Third, it has glass elevators in the middle of the mall so you don't have to seek out hidden elevators inside stores to get a stroller between levels (and kids like looking out as they go up and down).

The best-known boat is on the first level across from Eddie Bauer (from the Center Court, head toward Nordstrom.) The second-level boat is right outside J.C. Penney. The padded tugboats are completely encircled by a carpeted bench where parents can sit, relax, and scheme about how they are going to get their kids off the thing and back to shopping. The boats are restricted to

children age 6 and under.

Stores to visit with children include Turn Off the TV, The Paint Bar, The Disney Store, Imaginarium, The Right Start, Store of Knowledge, and Warner Bros. Studio Store. You can't miss The Great Train Store, which has a train whistle that serves as a beacon to all small children in the vicinity and a model train that runs around the top of the store. FAO Schwarz is also a fun place to visit, with dozens of stuffed animals and a talking tree. The mall also harbors several upscale children's clothing stores, including Baby Guess, Gap Kids, and Gymboree.

Bell Square doesn't have a food court; instead, restaurants are scattered around the mall. For a tasty

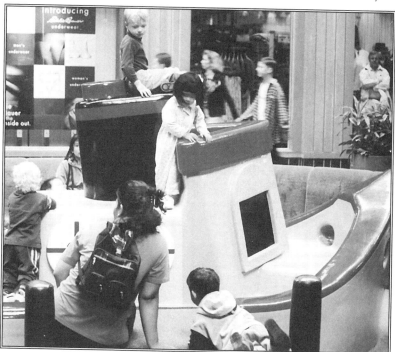

STEPHANIE DUNNEWIND

The Bellevue Square boat is always a hit with young kids.

buffet, try Zoopa (see Chapter 11 for a review).

Until 2000, the Bellevue Art Museum will be located on the third floor of the mall. See "Museums" in Chapter 7.

Strollers are available for rent.

Country Village
23730 Bothell-Everett Hwy., Bothell
(425) 483-2250

This outdoor mall charms children, with a merry-go-round, gazebo, walking paths, bridges, and a pond. A quarter buys food to feed the ducks; rabbits and doves have special homes where children can watch them. One store is housed in a train, another in a tug boat. A couple of stores sell children's books and toys, but most are craft and antique stores. It's a good place to come with another adult, so one person can play outside with the kids while the other browses. Country Village hosts special Halloween and Christmas events (which includes Santa's arrival by sleigh and a tree lighting), as well as a farmers market from June through September on Fridays, 10 a.m.-2 p.m.

Factoria Square Mall
128th Ave. S.E. and S.E. 38th, Bellevue
(425) 747-7344

A play boat is located near Dream Tree Toys and the Ice Cream Palace, which are both near the Target mall entrance. Other stores to visit include Game Plays, a video arcade; Paint It Up Ceramics; and Sweet ReTreat.

IKEA
600 S.W. 43rd, Renton
(425) 656-2980 or (800) 570-4532

Depending on how crowded it is, you can leave children ages 3 to 9 at IKEA's free child-care area for 45 minutes to an hour, which is barely enough time to walk through this giant furniture store. And kids probably won't want to leave, either. Not your standard in-store child-care place, IKEA has a large ball room with a slide, a small theater with movies playing, and plenty of toys.

Redmond Town Center
16495 N.E. 74th St., Redmond
(425) 867-0808

This outdoor mall has covered walkways between stores, with a small, covered play area for children age 6 and under tucked under an escalator. Stores to visit with children include Dream Tree Kids, Kay-Bee Toys, Rubber Soul Stamps, Paint the Town, and Borders Books. Two stores are combination toy stores and haircut parlors: Kids Cuts 'N Play and Brat Pack Toys. A park and a trail are nearby if children need to burn off some energy.

SuperMall of the Great Northwest
1101 SuperMall Way, Auburn
(253) 833-9500 or (800) SAY-VALU

The highlight at this discount store mall is a carousel; rides are $1. A unique feature is a nursing lounge located near the food court. Strollers are available for rent. Stores to check out with kids include Foozles, a bookstore; Kay-Bee Toys; and Toy Works. The food court offers a variety of fast-food options.

University Village
25th Ave. N.E. and N.E. 45th St.
Seattle
(206) 523-0622

The small, covered open-air playground in the middle of University Village features a climbing structure, but the real draws are several cars and trikes that kids can pedal around on rubber mats. The fenced area is open to kids age 6 and under and is closed from 9:30-10:30 a.m. and 3-4 p.m. while a day care uses it. The playground is strategically located by Teri's Toybox, Kids Club, and Shoe Zoo. The Barnes & Noble Bookstore nearby has a large children's section and often has story times. You can entice kids to walk through the mall by showing them two fountains and a couple of bronze statues that kids will appreciate—one is of a cow and calf; the other, a calf looking down at a turtle. For lunch, munch on a burrito-style meal from World Wrapps ($4-$6), then walk over to the giant QFC and snack on a Cinnabon while warming up next to a fireplace. The QFC also has a salad bar and deli, as well as several small food stores, including a bagel shop and an upscale gelato bar. If you have any grocery shopping to do, QFC has a free child-care area or child-sized shopping carts for them to push if they would rather stay with you.

INSIDE SCOOP

Free Fun

Bellevue Art Museum
 (Tuesdays)
Boeing Tour Center
Capitol tours
Center for Wooden Boats
Concerts in the Park
Daybreak Star Center
Farmers Markets
Farrel-McWhirter Park (and
 farm)
Frye Art Museum
Henry Art Gallery (Thursdays)
The Herbfarm
Hiram M. Chittenden
 Government Locks
Issaquah Alps Trail Club hikes
Kelsey Creek Community
 Park/Farm
Klondike Gold Rush National
 Historical Park
Library programs
Museum of Flight (first Thurs-
 day of the month, 5-9 p.m.)
Nordic Heritage Museum (first
 Tuesday of the month)
Seattle Art Museum (first
 Thursday of the month)
Seattle Asian Art Museum
 (first Thursday and first Sat-
 urday of the month)
Seattle Chamber Music
 Festival (outside on lawn)
Snoqualmie Falls Park
Tacoma Art Museum
 (Tuesdays)
Wing Luke Asian Museum
 (Thursdays)

REI

222 Yale Ave. N., Seattle
(206) 223-1944
4200 194th Ave. S.W., Lynnwood
(206) 774-1300

You can see the giant glass building encasing the world's tallest freestanding indoor climbing structure from Interstate 5. The 65-foot pinnacle can be climbed by anyone on a first-come, first-served basis. The wait on weekends can be as long as two hours. (See "Indoor Rock Climbing" elsewhere in this chapter for more information.) Besides the rock, REI delights kids with animal tracks stamped into the floor, the Gore-Tex Rain Room (where kids can stand and get sprayed), and a great little play area with a mini-climbing wall, tunnels, and play gear. The play area is, of course, located next to the kids' clothing section on the second floor. The store also rents a variety of outdoor gear.

At the Lynnwood store, a climbing wall is open Wednesday and Thursday, 6-8:30 p.m., and Saturday, 11 a.m.-1 p.m..

FOR TEENS

Teen Centers

Ground Zero

257 100th Ave. N.E., Bellevue
(425) 452-6118
Hours: Daily, 3-9 p.m.

Live concerts, pool table, air hockey, computers, homework center, and classes.

Issaquah Youth Center

301 Rainier Blvd. S., Issaquah
(425) 557-3283
Hours: Mon.-Thurs., 2-6:30 p.m.;
Fri., until 10 p.m.

Special Friday-night activities, classes, teen discussion group, and outings.

Old Fire House Teen Center

Downtown Redmond
(425) 556-2370
Hours: Mon.-Tues., 3-6 p.m.; Wed.-Thurs., 3-9 p.m.; Fri., 3-11 p.m.; Sat., 6-11 p.m.

Pool tables, free video games, computer, outdoor cafe, art room, and games court. Open to teens ages 13 to 19. Structured programs include workshops, adventure trips, and band concerts. Most activities are free.

Kirkland/Redmond Boys and Girls Club

10805 124th Ave. N.E., Kirkland
(425) 827-0132

Indoor climbing wall, plus art classes and basketball and volleyball leagues. A late-night program for

Live bands often play at the Old Fire House Teen Center in Redmond.

grades 7 to 12 is held Fridays, 7-10 p.m., with sports, computers, music, and dancing. $1/person fee for late-night program.

Renton Teen Nights
Highlands Neighborhood Center
800 Edmonds Ave. N.E., Renton
(425) 277-4432 or (425) 235-2560
Basketball, games, and free refreshments.

Shoreline Youth and Teen Program
Richmond Highlands Community Center
16554 Fremont Ave. N., Shoreline
(206) 542-6511
After-school program for youths and teenagers. Pool and Ping-Pong tables.

Tuesday Nite Live
Lynnwood Recreation Center,
18900 44th Ave. W., Lynnwood
(425) 771-4030

Meets second, fourth, and fifth Tuesday, 6:30-8:30 p.m. Free drop-in for teens ages 13-18. Movie nights, games, and pizza feeds.

King County Programs
(206) 296-2956 or (800) 325-6165, ext. 2956
Gracie Hansen Community Center, 27132 S.E. Ravensdale Way, Ravensdale. Teen Nights on Fridays, 7:30-9:30 p.m., for ages 13-18; teen open gyms Mon. and Wed., 3:30-5:30 p.m. Basketball, Ping-Pong, and indoor baseball.
Si View Teen Center, 400 S.E. Orchard, North Bend. Teen programs on Saturdays, 6-11 p.m. Movies, basketball, cooking, and crafts for ages 13-19. Si View Community Center also offers Family Night activities on selected Friday nights; call (206) 296-2964 for more information.
White Center Park Teen Program, 1321 S.W. 102nd, White Cen-

ter. Teen programs: Tues.-Thurs., 3-9 p.m.; Fri.-Sat., 4-10 p.m. Classes, gym, games room, field trips, and leadership opportunities.

Information
   Bellevue Youth Link, (425) 637-5254
   Kirkland Youth Line, (425) 803-2848
   Kent Youth/Teen Activities, (253) 859-3599
   Seattle LateNight and Teen Programs, (206) 684-7136

Skate Parks

Bellevue Skate Park
14224 Bellevue-Redmond Road (near Highland Community Center), Bellevue
(425) 452-2722
Hours: Mon.-Fri., 3-9 p.m.; Sat.-Sun., noon-1:30 p.m. (age 12 and under

only); 1:30-5 p.m. and 5:30-9 p.m.
   Indoors; open to skateboards and in-line skaters. Full protective gear required, including helmet and knee pads; parent or guardian must sign waivers on first visit. $2 per session.

Des Moines Skate Park
Des Moines Field House Park, 1000 S. 220th St., Des Moines
(253) 870-6527
Hours: 8 a.m.-dusk
   Outdoors, unsupervised.

Issaquah Skate Park
301 Rainier Blvd. (southeast side of Issaquah Community Center), Issaquah
Hours: Daily, 8 a.m.-dusk
   Outdoors, unsupervised.

Kirkland Skate Park
Peter Kirk Park, 202 Third St. Kirkland
Hours: Open daily
   Outdoors, unsupervised.

Several cities, including Kirkland, have outdoor skate parks.

STEPHANIE DUNNEWIND

Mercer Island Skate Park
Mercerdale Park, 78th Ave. S.E.
and S.E. 32nd St., Mercer Island
Outdoors, unsupervised.

Skate Boarding Park
Sixth Ave. N. at Republican (east of
Seattle Center grounds), Seattle
Hours: Open daily April-October
Outdoors, unsupervised.

Batting Cages and Ranges

Batter Up Batting Cages, 23609
104th S.E., Kent; (253) 859-6499
Bleacher Reachers, 18466
Eighth St., SeaTac; (206) 439-0779
Dave Henderson's Ballyard,
13414 N.E. 16th, Bellevue; (425)
644-2255
**Fat Bat Batting Range and
Fun Center**, 1008 N. Central, Kent;
(253) 854-6783
MiniMountain, 1900 132nd N.E.,
Bldg. A-3, Bellevue; (425) 746-7547

Game Centers

Command Center's Video Arcade
Renton Shopping Center, Renton
(425) 255-1405
Video arcade.

Entros
823 Yale Ave. N., Seattle
(206) 624-0057
"Amusement park" with interac-

tive mind and body games. Activities include a game show, scavenger hunt, and ball maze. For
older teens.

Fun-N-Games
Northgate Mall, Seattle
(206) 367-0680
Alderwood Mall, Lynnwood
(425) 771-8009
Video arcades.

Gametown Family Fun Center
14822 Pacific Hwy. S., Tukwila
(206) 241-9108
Video arcade.

GameWorks
1511 Seventh Ave., Seattle
(206) 521-0952
See "Downtown" in Chapter 8
for more information.

Oblivian Entertainment Center
15 Lake St., Kirkland
(425) 889-9239
Computer network gaming center and Internet access.

Quarters
206 Main St., Kirkland
(425) 889-2555
Video arcade.

Shorty's
2222 Second Ave., Seattle
(206) 441-5449
Vintage video arcade and pinball.

WhirlyBall Center
23401 Hwy. 99, Edmonds
(425) 672-3332
www.whirlyball.com
Rates: $65/half-hour game, for group of 10 or more people

Ball game played while driving bumper cars.

Wizards of the Coast Game Center
4518 University Way, Seattle
(206) 675-1608; www.wizards.com

More than 250 games, including arcade games, sports simulations, BattleTech simulation pods, a library of board games, and Internet access.

(See Chapter 5 for more amusement centers.)

Paintball

AWOL/Splat Mountain Paintball
7018 N.E. Bothell Way, Bothell
(425) 487-9158

Private outdoor games for groups.

Bill & Jim's Excellent Adventure
13425 S.E. 30th, Suite D, Bellevue
(425) 643-7785
Rates: $15/person includes rental and 90-minute session; paint pellets, $1/10 shots

Indoor games; public sessions vary.

KC's Paintball Sports
South Prairie; six miles east of Puyallup
(360) 897-6267
Rates: $25/person for game fee, gun rental, and 200 rounds of ammunition

Ongoing open play. Groups who want a private field need to make reservations.

Paintball Playground
17307 N.E. Woodinville-Duvall Road, Woodinville
(425) 483-6611
Hours: Sat.-Sun., 9 a.m.-4 p.m.; weekdays by reservation
Rates: $25/person for a three-hour session, including rentals and 100 rounds of ammunition

Outdoor field. Players must be age 13 or older.

Laser Tag

Q-Zar
18905 33rd Ave. W., Lynnwood
(425) 712-9000
Rates: $7/game

Laser tag in huge arena.

(See Chapter 5 for more amusement centers.)

Chapter 6

SPECTATOR SPORTS

For many parents, sharing the thrill of an exciting sports event is one of the first opportunities for common ground with their child. Although it is easy to get cynical about the corrupting influence of money and politics on professional sports, lessons in fair play, team cooperation, and the agony of losing and the glory of winning still abound at all levels of team sports.

The cost of a family outing to a professional sporting event can be prohibitive, especially when you add parking and snack expenses to the cost of the tickets. Keep in mind that professional teams don't necessarily provide the best entertainment. Don't forget to think of smaller arenas, such as local high schools and colleges, when you're hankering for a sports night out. You'll spend less, still see good games, and avoid the traffic hassles of the larger events.

THE BIG GUYS

Seattle Mariners

Games at the Kingdome until 1999
New stadium opens July 1999
(206) 346-4000; TicketMaster,
(206) 622-HITS
www.mariners.org
Season: April-September
Tickets: $6-$25; $2 discount for
kids on some seats

With several of baseball's most
famous and beloved players, including Ken Griffey Jr. and Alex
Rodriguez, and two recent trips to
the playoffs, the Mariners have been
hot both on the field and in attracting fans. Even preschoolers can usually tell you their favorite Mariner.

The Mariners have made a special effort to keep America's pastime
affordable and fun for families.
Many special promotional events are
offered throughout the season, featuring a variety of souvenir giveaways and incentives such as free
bats, T-shirts, or caps for the first
several thousand kids in the Kingdome. On Picture Day, fans can
crowd onto the field to take pictures

ESSENTIALS

Food at the Kingdome is no
bargain, but the hot dogs are
yummy and the foil bags of aro-
matic hot peanuts are enough to
make most grownups nostalgic.
Peanut vendors will throw bags of
peanuts from several rows away for
fans to catch, to the delight of any
nearby children. If you want to
save money, you can bring in your
own food. Cans and glass bottles
are prohibited, but juice boxes and
plastic water bottles are allowed.
Food will also be permitted in the
new stadium.

TIPS

If you want a little different
perspective on a Mariners game at the
Kingdome, get seats overlooking third
base. You'll get a surprisingly good
view of the game, plus an interesting
sideshow, because the Mariners' pitch-
ers warm up on this side of the field.

If your kids want to acquire a
baseball the hard way (rather than
just buying one), come to batting
practice, which starts two hours
before the game. Bring mitts and sit
in the outfield section. Fewer people
are in the stands, and easier pitches
are thrown to the batters, meaning
kids have a better chance at catching
those would-be home runs.

The new ballpark, with a capacity
of 46,621, will be located south of
Royal Brougham Ave., site of Kingdome
parking lot C. A retractable roof will
allow covered play in the rain or an
open-air experience when it's sunny.
Tickets will be as cheap as $5, but
there will be fewer inexpensive outfield seats (6,591 in the new stadium
compared to 18,378 in the Kingdome.)

of the players. Several games are designated as Family Nights, offering half-price tickets for adults. To keep the game interesting during those inevitable slow points, the Kingdome's giant screen flashes bloopers, amazing plays, a hat trick, mini-hydro races, and baseball trivia. And if the M's hit a home run, the audience is rewarded with a fireworks display. Most younger kids will actually sit through all nine innings in anticipation of this event (and given Griffey's affinity for the long ball, it usually does). The corny stunts of the Mariner Moose will entertain the smaller fries.

Seattle Reign, a professional women's basketball team, targets families.

COURTESY OF SEATTLE REIGN

Seattle Reign
Games at the Mercer Arena,
Seattle Center
(206) 285-5225
www.seattlereign.com
Season: October-February
Tickets: $11-$35

While you won't see the showy slam dunks and high jumps found in men's basketball, supporters of professional women's basketball say that the women's games are truer to the sport. These fast-paced, intimate games emphasize defense and ball handling. The Reign, who go into their third American Basketball League season in fall 1998, target families as their main audience. Mascots throw giveaways such as T-shirts into the crowd during the game, and two players are available for autograph signing after every home game. Family Nights offer a ticket package and prizes.

No outside food is permitted.

Seattle Seahawks
Games at the Kingdome
New stadium opens in 2002
(206) 827-9766 (tickets)
Season: August-December
Tickets: $10-$48

With a new local owner (billionaire Paul Allen) and a new stadium on the way, the Seahawks are on the upswing. But football can be a difficult game to watch if you don't understand all the various rules, so families might be best off taking only kids who are into football and can follow the complexity of the sport. Depending on the game, between 10,000 to 15,000 tickets are available to the general public; about 7,000 are in the $10 range. A free tailgate party before each home game (10 a.m. until kickoff) features games, face painting, and bands in the Kingdome Pavilion.

TIPS

The new stadium, which will be built on the Kingdome site after that building is demolished, will seat 72,000. It will be open air, but 70 percent of fans will be protected by a roof (guess which seats will be the cheapest!) It will have twice as many toilets per person as the Kingdome, and twice as many concession areas.

Seattle Sounders

Games at Memorial Stadium
Seattle Center
(800) 796-KICK
Season: Mid-April to mid-October
Tickets: $10-$12/adults, $8-$10/children age 15 and under, free/children age 2 and under

The Sounders, a professional soccer team, have won two of the last three A-League (the division below the major leagues) championships for North America. The team, which started in 1994, plays on artificial turf in an outdoor arena. Games always feature lots of giveaways. A couple of times a season players are available before home games for autographs; players can also easily be approached after the game. Picnic food is allowed in Memorial Stadium; concession stands sell the usual fare.

Seattle SuperSonics

Games at the KeyArena
Seattle Center
(206) 281-5800; (206) 628-0888 (tickets)
www.nba.com/sonics
Season: September-May
Tickets: $7-$100

Many NBA players seem to have achieved cult status, so school-age kids will probably beg more for Sonics tickets than for other professional sports. It does gets pricey to take kids to a Sonics game and finding a place to park can entail more time or money than you might expect. But if you can swing it, basketball is exciting and easy enough to understand to hold most children's attention.

Aside from providing a noisy,

Seattle's professional soccer team, the Sounders, often win their championship.

> ## ESSENTIALS
>
> No outside food is allowed. The Sonics store sells a wide variety of souvenirs at a range of prices.

spirited atmosphere, the SuperSonics do a good job of providing diversions with their Sasquatch mascot, dance team, entertainment at timeouts, a toy blimp that cruises around inside the arena dropping prizes, and other treats. The level of play is high, with the Sonics perennially at or near the top of their division. The first Saturday of each month is Family Night, with $7 tickets for children under 18.

Seattle Thunderbirds
Games at KeyArena, Seattle Center
(206) 448-PUCK
Season: Sept.-March
Tickets: $10-$20/adults,
$8-$12/children

Since Old Man Winter doesn't freeze the ponds around here very often, it's easy to forget about hockey and other ice sports. But Seattle does have a Western Hockey League team, the Thunderbirds, and if you think your child would enjoy the fast-paced action, it's a fun and easily comprehensible sport to watch. Many of the players are teenagers or just barely older.

The downside of hockey is usually the raucous atmosphere, obnoxious crowds, and sometimes bloody fights. If you can tolerate those negatives, the Thunderbirds promise some competitive, exciting entertainment. Alcohol is not permitted in the family seating section (tickets $10-$12).

THE LITTLE GUYS

Emerald Downs
2300 Emerald Downs Dr., Auburn
(253) 288-700 or (888) 931-8400
www.emdowns.com
Season: April-Sept., Thurs.-Sun.;
June-Aug., Wed.-Sun.
Admission: $3/adults, free/children age 10 and under.
$2/reserved grandstand seats,
$2.50/reserved clubhouse seats,
free/festival seating.

Though some people might not find gambling at a racetrack an appropriate outing for children, fans disagree. Of course, you don't have to bet; you can go just to give kids an upclose view of the horses and get into the excitement of the races. The 166-acre facility, which opened in 1996, features a six-level stadium and special events throughout the summer. Family Sundays (June-Aug.) include face-painting clowns, games, and pony rides. There are also grassy areas where children can run around. Live music is played Friday nights July-Aug. The first race begins at 6 p.m. weekdays and 1 p.m. weekends and holidays. Children age 13 and under must be accompanied by an adult at all times.

Everett AquaSox

Everett Memorial Stadium, 38th and Broadway, Everett (I-5 exit 192)
(425) 258-3673
Season: Mid-June to Labor Day
Tickets: $5-$10/adults, $4-$5/children ages 3-12, free/children age 2 and under

The AquaSox are the Class A farm team of the Seattle Mariners. Former Everett players include Matt Williams (he played when Everett was an affiliate of the San Francisco Giants) and Jose Cruz Jr. Everett Memorial Stadium was renovated for the 1998 season. It's one of the coziest ballparks in baseball, featuring a children's playfield where kids can play catch with their parents or wait for a foul ball. Homer Porch allows fans to stroll behind the right field fence to wait for and try to catch a home run. Players enter and exit the field through public areas, making it easy to get autographs before or after the game. The team also stages contests between innings.

Tacoma Rainiers

Cheney Stadium, Tacoma
(253) 752-7707; (800) 281-3834 (tickets)
Season: April-Sept.
Tickets: $5-$10/adults, $3-$8/children age 14 and under, seniors, and military personnel

The Tacoma Rainiers are the Mariners' AAA affiliate, just one step away from major league baseball. Games are played outdoors at Cheney Stadium in Tacoma. The season features several promotional activities, including souvenir giveaways and a special fireworks show July 3.

University of Washington Huskies
(206) 543-2200

At UW sporting events, you will find highly talented athletes and great competition at a fraction of the cost of the professional games. Many have fun half-time events with entertainment or free T-shirt giveaways.

Husky football (Sept.-Nov., at Husky Stadium) tickets are $30 for reserved seats and $15/adults, $13/kids for general admission, which is sold the Monday before the game. Games usually sell out, not only because the team is outstanding, but because alumni are fervently dedicated and often reluctant to give up their season tickets before they die. A football family plan costs $90/two adults and up to three children, and includes admission to three games against lesser teams.

Men's basketball (Nov.-March, at Hec Ed Pavilion) tickets are $14-$16 for reserved seating and $6/adults,

$3/children for general admission. Women's basketball tickets are $9-$11 for reserved seating and $6/adults, $3/children for general admission. A basketball family plan costs $13 and includes five general admission tickets for two adults and three children.

For Olympic sports, which include baseball, softball, gymnastics, soccer, and volleyball, admission is $4/adults, $2/children, $10/family. An annual family pass costs $35 and allows two adults and three children admission to any of the Olympic sports (not basketball or football).

The baseball team (Feb.-June) will have a new stadium with lights in 1999 so they can play at night. Games will still be played outdoors on real grass. Softball (Feb.-June) is played on a field near the football stadium. Gymnastics (Jan.-March, at Hec Ed Pavilion) is a fun winter diversion. Both the men's and women's soccer teams (Sept.-Nov.) are rated among the top in the country. They play on a new soccer field near the baseball stadium. The volleyball team, also one of the best in the country, plays August-November in Hec Ed.

Tickets are sold at the ticket office just north of Hec Edmundson Pavilion, adjacent to Husky Stadium.

Velodrome Bike Racing

Marymoor Park, Redmond
(206) 527-9345
www.iscn.com/marymoor

One of only 19 velodromes in the United States, the velodrome at Marymoor Park is home to a full sea-

> ## ESSENTIALS
> Food and thermoses of two quarts or less are allowed in Husky Stadium. No alcohol, glass containers or ice chests are allowed.

son of bicycle racing and events. From mid-May until early September, cyclists compete on Wednesdays at 7 p.m. and Fridays at 7:30 p.m. Admission is free on Wednesday nights, when races are open to beginners, juniors, masters, and women. (Call for more information about the youth racing program for teens ages 14-18.) Friday night is probably the best night to go as a spectator, with mass-start racing. Spectator admission is $3/adults, $5/families, free/children under 12. Families can enjoy a picnic and watch the races while children play on the grassy berm. The third Friday of every month from May to August, children age 10 and under can ride their own bikes in a free Kiddie Kilo race; helmets are required. The steep slope of the track can be intimidating.

TIPS

Bring cushions to sit on—the bleachers at the Velodrome aren't exactly comfortable. Marymoor is a wonderful park, so if you or your children get restless, take advantage of the nearby playground, surrounding lawns and open spaces. (See Chapter 3 for more information.)

Chapter 7
KID CULTURE

Give your kids some culture? Yeah, right. It's hard enough to get them to take a bath, let alone drag them into a museum. And at least with a bath you can see results. Visiting the art world involves a much more subtle cleansing, sort of a polishing of the senses.

The fact of the matter is that museum exhibits, theater performances, and concerts can be intimidating even for adults, and taking your kids to such events can be like taking them to a remote land where no one speaks your language. What you might not know is how many of our local arts organizations have programs designed especially for kids, to help them learn to appreciate art on their level.

MUSEUMS

Bellevue Art Museum

Bellevue Square, third floor
Bellevue
(425) 454-3322;
www.bellevueart.org
Hours: Mon.-Sat., 10 a.m.-6 p.m.;
Tues. and Fri., until 8 p.m.; Sun, 11
a.m.-5 p.m.
Admission: $3/adults, $2/seniors
and students, free/children age 12,
free/all ages on Tuesdays
Annual membership: $40/family

The art museum offers special classes for
kids on some Saturdays

It's natural to be skeptical about
having a cultural experience in a
shopping mall, but don't let that
stop you from visiting the Bellevue
Art Museum on the third floor of
Bellevue Square. BAM is accessible
by elevator or stairs from the main
retail shop area and is easily negoti-
ated by strollers. The museum,
which has no permanent collection,
showcases five or six different
exhibits each year and is small and
intimate—a good size that won't
overwhelm kids.

By July 2000, BAM hopes to
have its own 40,000-square-foot
museum located across from Bellevue Square at N.E. Sixth Street and
Bellevue Way. The facility will feature three galleries to showcase
Northwest art, an artist-in-residence
program so the public can see artists
at work, interactive learning stations,
an electronic library, classrooms,
lecture halls, and artists' studios.

Burke Museum of Natural History and Culture

University of Washington campus,
near the entrance at N.E. 45th St.
and 17th Ave. N.E., Seattle
(206) 543-5590
www.washington.edu/burkemuseum
Hours: Open daily, 10 am-5 p.m.;
Thurs., until 8 p.m.
Admission: $5/adults, $4/seniors
and students, $2.50/students,
free/children age 5 and under
Annual membership: $35/family

Kids will quickly shorten the
name of the Burke Museum of Natural History and Culture to "the
dinosaur museum." After the museum was renovated in late 1997,
curators pulled out some of the
more exciting aspects of Washington's history—dinosaurs, volcanoes,
woolly mammoths—and tried to
make them accessible and under-
standable for children.

The first floor is devoted to a
permanent exhibit, "Life and Times
of Washington State." Here you'll

TIPS

The best time to visit the Bellevue Art Museum is in November and December, when the museum stages its "Celebration Entirely for Children." As the name says, the whole gallery is devoted to artwork that children will enjoy, with related hands-on activities. In a previous year, for example, an exhibit centered around Leonardo da Vinci featured dry erase boards next to mirrors so kids could try imitating Leonardo's famous mirror script. During this exhibit, the museum also offers workshops and classes for children to complement the artwork on display.

The rest of the year, the museum offers "Super Saturday" classes for children in grades 1 to 6 that focus on BAM's current exhibit. It also offers summer and winter day camps for elementary-school-age children in conjunction with the Pacific Science Center.

The museum's Gallery Shop, which is open during Bellevue Square's hours, has a special section especially for kids.

The boat play areas on the first and second floors of Bellevue Square are a good place for young kids to release some extra energy. (See "Shopping Without Spending" in Chapter 5.)

find the mostly real remains of a 40-foot-long allosaurus threatening a stegosaurus, which, despite the pointed plates down its back, looks like it might lose the battle. An elasmosaur, a sleek marine reptile bearing a fair resemblance to the Loch Ness Monster, hangs overhead. Children can measure themselves against the thigh bone of a 140-million-year-old sauropod, check out a clutch of real dinosaur eggs, and view the skull of a triceratops. (Forget, in your enthusiasm, that dinosaur remains have never actually been found in Washington.)

The Burke has tried to make history something kids can experi-ence, rather than just read about or look at. Children can walk through a volcano for an inside glimpse into the state's not-so-peaceful mountains or crawl inside a replica of the impression made by the decayed body of a 15-million-year-old two-

TIPS

Special events at the Burke include Dinosaur Day in February and Be an Archaeologist for the Day in October.

STEPHANIE DUNNEWIND

The Burke Museum will catch kids' attention with dinosaurs inside and these totems outside.

horned dinosaur trapped in lava.

The Ice Age portion of "Life and Times" features more skeletons, including an enormous mastodon

and a vicious-looking saber-toothed cat. The exhibit's final section highlights some of the natural resources that our present-day state offers. A 9-foot-long transparent bug wall shows off 1,000 insects.

"Life and Times" is broken up into sections, each with a kiosk where kids can punch a time card that explains the various epochs. The kiosks also have video screens with educational "newscasts."

The other permanent exhibit, "Pacific Voices," doesn't have as much kid appeal as "Life and Times" since most artifacts are in no-touch display cases. Still, the bright masks, outrigger canoe models, and puppets will hold their attention for a while, as will the video screens telling tales and explaining oral traditions. A few pull-out drawers allow children to discover such things as costumes, masks, and puppets to play with.

The museum store is full of items for kids, including books, puppets, dinosaurs, toys, and games.

Center for Wooden Boats
1010 Valley St., Seattle
(206) 382-2628
www.eskimo.com/~cwboats
Hours: Open daily year-round; June-Sept., 12-6 p.m.; Oct.-May, 11 a.m.-5 p.m.
Admission: Free, but donations are gladly accepted
Annual membership: $40/family

It is difficult to be a resident of the "Boating Capital of the World" without catching at least a little boating fever. The Center for Wooden Boats at the south end of Lake Union is a great place to show your kids some of the most beautiful boats ever built. This floating museum and shop features a collection of approximately 70 small wooden boats, including rowing, sailing, and power crafts. Many of them are moored along the docks, where you can stroll and enjoy the floating collection. (Parents can stop by the Oar House or the Boat House and borrow life vests for the little ones.) Children will love climbing aboard the Panesano, a Monterey fishing

NEIGHBORHOOD NOTES

UNIVERSITY OF WASHINGTON

If it's a nice day, take time after your museum visit to stroll through the campus. **Red Square** is a bricked expanse that offers running space (when student traffic is low), beautiful architecture, and a spectacular view of Mount Rainier and the campus's Drumheller Fountain. You can reach Red Square from the Burke by walking down Memorial Way. Red Square is right next to the **Henry Art Gallery** (see later this chapter). **Suzzallo Library,** the graduate library, is the architectural highlight of the campus, and if your kids are well behaved it deserves a quick tour for its architecture and sheer immensity.

Northeast of Red Square is the grassy **Quad,** which is stunning in the early spring when the cherry trees are blossoming. If you had an aerial view, you would see that the trees are planted in the shape of a "W." Make sure you point out the gargoyles decorating the old buildings.

Stay until dark and visit the **UW Observatory,** located at 17th Ave. N.E. and N.E. 45th St. (across from the Burke Museum). The observatory is open to the public Monday and Thursday nights (it's also open during UW school breaks, except on major holidays). Hours are 9-11 p.m. in the summer, 7-9 p.m. in the winter.

On clear nights, visitors can look at the sky through a 6-inch refractor telescope; on cloudy nights, a slide show on astronomy is presented. Guides are on site to answer questions and help operate the telescope. Admission is free; all ages are welcome. Children should be accompanied by an adult. Call (206) 543-0126 for more details.

Down at the southern end of campus, past Husky Stadium, is the **Waterfront Activity Center**, where you can rent canoes from spring to fall or just watch boats from the dock. Nearby is a climbing rock that kids will enjoy trying to scale (the lower part, anyway!). A large grassy area is perfect for a picnic, and a trail runs along the Ship Canal. This area is a popular viewing place on Boating Day, which features a parade of decorated boats and crew races on the first Saturday in May (see Chapter 10). Be warned it's quite a hike to here from the main campus.

On the other side of the Montlake Bridge are the **Museum of History and Industry** and the **Washington Arboretum**. (See later this chapter for the museum and Chapter 5 for the arboretum.) On-campus dining options include the **HUB** (the student union building) cafeteria, located east of Red Square, past Suzzallo and the Allen Library. If you're adventurous, head for "the Ave," as University Way N.E. is known. You'll find all sorts of ethnic restaurants, as well as pizza and other fast-food options. One possibility is **Flowers** (University Way N.E. and N.E. 43rd St.; 206-633-1903), located in a former flower shop. It features a large vegetari-

an lunch buffet, but isn't for picky eaters.

While you're on the Ave, visit the **University Book Store** (4326 University Way; 206-634-3400), which has a large children's section. Another store kids might enjoy is **Dollar$** (4231 University Way N.E.; 206-545-0724), which, as the name suggests, has lots of items available for $1. **The Wizards of the Coast Game Center** (4518 University Way N.E.; 206-675-1608) features a video-game and pinball arcade, a virtual reality center, computer network games, and a tournament center.

The **University District Farmers Market** (University Heights Community Center playground, N.E. 50th and University Way N.E.) is open Saturday mornings from spring to fall and often has special activities, such as cooking deomonstrations.

The Ave also hosts the **University District Street Fair** (206-527-2567) in May. This granddaddy of Northwest street fairs features 500 booths, music, a children's festival area, an ethnic dance stage, and plenty of good people-watching and food.

Be warned that the Ave can be pretty seedy, and your kids will likely ask why someone's hair is blue or why a particular body part is pierced. It's best avoided at night.

For more information, stop by the **visitors information center** at 4014 University Way, or call (206) 543-9198. The University of Washington's Web site is www.washington.edu.

TIPS

Skiffs, canoes, sailboats, and kayaks are available for hourly rental from the Oar House year-round (closed Tuesdays). Rentals range from $10 to $37.50 per hour. Life jackets are supplied for everyone. The center also offers sailing lessons; call (206) 382-BOAT for information.

The annual Wooden Boat Festival is a fun diversion over Fourth of July weekend. Activities include small boat races, toy boat building, face painting, music, food, contests, and maritime crafts. Admission is free.

a shelf of children's books and a comfortable couch.

➤ *Nearby attractions:* Gas Works Park, Northwest Outdoor Center.

ESSENTIALS

Parking is free. Quite a few restaurants are within walking distance of the center, including Burger King, Benjamin's, and Cucina!Cucina!, a good, inexpensive Italian spot.

boat, where they can work the wheel and imagine they're the captain of their own ship!

The staff at the center builds and restores small water craft using a variety of tools from the past and the present, so there is always some boat-building or restoration activity going on in the shop. You might even get an impromptu lesson on varnishing, knot tying, or woodworking during your visit. Periodically, the center holds toy boat building workshops.

Inside the Boat House, you'll find old photos, canoes and shells hanging from the ceiling, and an old binnacle (a housing for the large compass on a big ship), which children can examine. There are also several model boats, as well as

Children's Museum

Seattle Center, Center House,
lower level, Seattle
(206) 441-1768
www.seattle.net/museums/kidmuse.html
Hours: Mon.-Fri., 10 a.m.-5 p.m.;
Sat.-Sun., 10 a.m.- 6 p.m. (open
one hour later June 15-Labor Day)
Admission: $5.50/children ages
1-12, $4/adults, free/babies under
1 year
Annual membership: $48/family

Shrink the world down to a child's size and you have the experience offered by the Children's Museum. With room after room of hands-on activities, this place will keep your kids amused (and painlessly educated about physics, foreign cultures, medicine, and history) for hours.

A trail climbs up Mountain Forest, a simulated mountain with rocks kids can look under, a cave, a hollow log, animal costumes, a camping tent, and a rock slide. There is even a small climbing wall

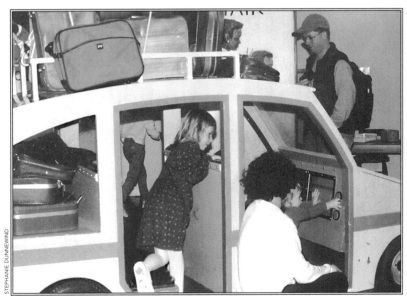

STEPHANIE DUNNEWIND

Global Village shows what it's like to live in another country.

they can try to inch across. Cog City is always chaotic, with kids pulling levers and pipes to move balls around various mazes. Outside Cog City is a collection of thousands of Legos. The Global Village shows children what it's like to live in different countries; places are rotated into the exhibit every five years. Children can sit in a car and watch a video about life in Ghana, catch a Japanese subway train, and take off their shoes before entering a Japanese home. Time Trek will interest older children more than little ones as it introduces the cultures of the Shang Dynasty of China, classical Greece, and the Mayan civilization in South America. The Neighborhood will likely be most kids' favorite area as it includes a supermarket for grocery shopping, a Metro bus and a fire truck to drive, a restaurant with tables to serve,

and a doctor's office equipped with instruments to check vital signs. Bijou Theatre has an actual stage where kids can control the lighting and sound effects to tell two stories or make up their own.

Admission to the museum also includes daily hands-on workshops in which children create their own special crafts, as well as entry to Imagination Station, the museum's

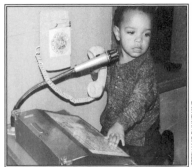

STEPHANIE DUNNEWIND

Even young kids get into the fun at a play restaurant.

drop-in art studio, where kids can work with professional artists to create a variety of masterpieces.

TIPS

The Children's Museum is a good outing for an active toddler. The special toddler play area features a foam playground with an under-the-sea motif. Kids under age 2 1/2 can climb over a padded whale and a ferryboat.

If you need to bring along older children who might be bored by most of the exhibits, steer them to Mindscape, a technology room where kids can explore virtual reality and the Internet, as well as make music in a recording studio.

The museum can get crowded, especially on weekends. There is a stroller parking area. The excellent gift shop is filled with quality educational toys.

Special events include Festival of Lights, a celebration of holiday rituals from different cultures featuring musicians, dancers, and community guests. It runs from November through early January.

"If I Had a Hammer," a two-hour workshop, lets participants construct a small house by putting up prefabricated wall frames, roof trusses, and siding. Preregistration is required.

Both the hands-on workshops and activities at Imagination Station are excellent, featuring quick and interesting creative activities.

ESSENTIALS

Food choices are abundant in the Center House, just up the stairs from the Children's Museum. Recommendations include Cafe Loc's Vietnamese noodles and The Frankfurter's hot dogs. A free play area is on the third floor. (See "Seattle Center" in Chapter 8.)

➤ *Nearby attractions:* Located within the Seattle Center grounds are the Pacific Science Center, the Space Needle, the Pacific Arts Center, the Fun Forest, and ample room to picnic and roam. A short Monorail ride from the Seattle Center takes you to the retail district of downtown Seattle, including Westlake Mall. From there, a walk of a few blocks takes you to Pike Place Market.

Experience Music Project
Fifth Ave., between Thomas St. and Harrison St., Seattle
(425) 450-1997
www.experience.org

Your kids will likely drag you to this museum dedicated to rock and roll. Scheduled to open in 1999, the Experience Music Project will be the newest addition to the Seattle Center campus. Besides traditional museum displays of such items as musicians' costumes and sheet music, EMP will offer live performances and educational programs.

Expect plenty of items belonging to Jimi Hendrix and other Northwest musicians. (See the "Seattle Center" entry in Chapter 8 for more details.)

Frye Art Museum

704 Terry Ave., Seattle (in the First Hill neighborhood)
(206) 622-9250
Hours: Tues.-Sat., 10 a.m.-5 p.m.; Thurs., until 9 p.m.; Sun., 12-5 p.m.
Admission: Free

The Frye Art Museum is good for kids' first exposure to art because it's small but worthwhile, all on one floor, and if they hate it you haven't shelled out anything since admission and parking are free. The recently remodeled museum feels much like a European art gallery since the private collection of 1,200 paintings includes one of the country's most extensive collections of 19th-century German art, as well as works by early 19th- and 20th-century American artists and French Impressionists. The American paintings include pieces by such artists as Mary Cassatt, John Singer Sargent and Andrew Wyeth.

Admission is free to the Frye Art Museum.

COURTESY OF THE FRYE ART MUSEUM

Like most art museums, the tone is quiet and reverent, so it's probably best for either kids who will sit in strollers or elementary-school children who know not to run and yell.

The museum, which features three permanent galleries and three changing exhibition galleries, opened to the public in 1952 after Charles Frye left his fortune and collection in trust to create a free public art museum.

TIPS

The museum offers art education workshops for children year-round in basic drawing, painting, and ceramics. Guided public tours are offered on Sundays at 12:30 and 2:30 p.m. Group tours are by reservation. Also, this is mostly European art, so be prepared for some bare bosoms.

The Henry offers popular art classes for children.

Henry Art Gallery

University of Washington campus, 15th Ave. N.E. at N.E. 41st St., Seattle

(206) 543-2280; www.henryart.org

Hours: Tues.-Sun., 11 a.m.-5 p.m.; Thurs. until 8 p.m.

Admission: $5/adults, $3.50/seniors, free/high school and college students with ID and children under age 13, free/all ages every Thursday, 5-8 p.m.

Annual membership: $50/family

The Henry opens new exhibits of modern and contemporary art about every six to 12 weeks, showcasing a variety of artists and artistic mediums. A 1997 expansion quadrupled the museum's size, offering a light, airy new space for its permanent collection and educational programs. The Henry has one of the most successful and well-designed educational programs in the city, offering lectures, workshops, classes, and tours. The children's workshops, led by professional artists, bring even the most esoteric of exhibits within

ESSENTIALS

Parking is available in the underground Central Parking Garage at N.E. 41st Street. Cost is $6 for the whole day; part of the fee will be reimbursed if you stay less time (an hour is $2). Parking is free on Sundays.

The café serves snacks and beverages. Food can be eaten out in the Sculpture Court on nice days.

The museum store has a children's section with games, books, and art-related toys.

reach of kids' creativity and understanding, and are highly participatory. (Be sure to preregister your child
for any workshops or events as they
are quite popular.)

The Henry was the first public
art museum in Washington state,
donated to the people of Washington in 1927 by Horace C. Henry, a
local tycoon. Included in this donation was his personal collection of
early-20th-century works

TIPS

On designated Saturday afternoons during each exhibition, free
docent-led tours are scheduled for
families with children age 5 and
older. Special age-appropriate docent-
led school and group tours are also
offered Tuesday through Sunday; cost
is $20 for groups with 10 to 20 peo-
ple. Teachers and parents are encouraged to contact the Education
Department at (206) 616-8782 to
receive information on tours and curriculum guides.

Klondike Gold Rush National Historical Park

117 S. Main, Seattle
(206) 553-7220; www.nps.gov/klgo
Hours: Daily, 9 a.m.-5 p.m.
Admission: Free

You and your kids have probably
passed by this little museum in Pio-

neer Square dozens of times and
never thought about going in. But
consider this: Everyone can relate to
wanting to strike it rich, and because
of this age-old desire, Seattle was
able to prosper in its early years. This
museum actually tells a pretty good
story, which makes it fun for all ages.

The National Park Service, which
set up this historical park, has done
a thorough job in using a variety of
media, including maps, photos,
slides, and films, to document the
Gold Rush and its enormous effect
on the city of Seattle. Your kids will
enjoy seeing the shovels, picks, and
other tools used by the prospectors,
and watching the rangers demonstrate how they panned for gold. A
visit through this interesting park is
a quick and easy stop, and once
you do it, you and your kids will
know at least two things: Learning
history can be painless, and finding
gold is easier dreamed than done.

TIPS

During the summer, rangers
organize a variety of educational
programs and lead Pioneer Square
walking tours.

ESSENTIALS

See the "Pioneer Square" entry
in Chapter 8. Nearby attractions:
Pioneer Square and the Seattle
Waterfront. Catch the Waterfront
Trolley for a scenic ride along the
waterfront to Pier 70.

Museum of Flight

9404 E. Marginal Way S. (next to
Boeing Field), Seattle
(206) 764-5720
www.museumofflight.org
Hours: Daily, 10 a.m.-5 p.m.;
Thurs., until 9 p.m.
Admission: $8/adults, $4/children
ages 6-15, free/children age 5 and
under, free/all ages the first Thursday of the month, 5-9 p.m.
Annual membership: $35/family

In most cities, an airplane museum would have a couple of old
planes, a bunch of models, and
maybe some historical displays. But
in Seattle, home of one of the largest
airplane manufacturers, the real
planes outnumber the models.
Dozens of airplanes, ranging from
simple gliders to fighter jets, hang
from the ceiling of the vast steel-and-
glass Great Gallery. Others are modeled on the floor for a closer look.

The large, airy museum is very
kid friendly, with plenty to do as
well as look at. Older enthusiasts
can learn about the history of flight
from the earliest aircraft to the
space stations of the future.
Younger folks will be impressed
with all the gadgets and machinery.

When kids get tired of gazing at
the different aircraft, they can climb
into the cockpit of a full-size replica
of a Northrop F/A 18 jet fighter,
which measures 56 feet long with a
wing span of 40.5 feet. It features a
moveable joystick, control panels,
and radar screens. Since only one
person can get in at a time, expect
a wait in line.

The Great Gallery displays dozens of airplanes from early aircraft to military jets.

TIPS

The Challenger Learning Center features mock-ups of a 21st-century space station and a mission control facility. Mostly used by elementary and middle school groups, the museum occasionally offers Family Missions that let families and small groups take on the roles of space station specialists and mission controllers; there is a fee for these activities. The center is the only one of its kind in the Northwest.

The museum presents FlyerWorks, an aerial show, during the Fourth of Jul-Ivar's celebration each July 4 at Myrtle Edwards Park in downtown Seattle. The flying parade features antique flying machines, World War II-era aircraft, and modern military planes. Down on the ground, the museum hosts the Fun Zone, with entertainment, games, and workshops. The event is free.

Throughout the year, special drop-in programs are held in the Hangar to teach young people about the skills needed to design, build, and maintain aircraft. Weekend hands-on family workshops allow youngsters to design gliders, learn about hot-air balloons, and much more. Most of these workshops are appropriate for children age 5 and up and their parents.

Upstairs, the Hangar has a collection of small but real planes that kids can sit in and pretend to drive. There are even levers that move the wings. Kids should also enjoy the Apollo exhibit, with space suits and a mock-up of a Lunar Roving Vehicle on display. Bring a camera to snap a picture of your child posing as an astronaut.

On the top level of the three-floor museum, visitors can pretend to be air traffic controllers. Older children will appreciate the science and technology; younger kids will have a ball listening to telephones and pushing buttons. In the museum's control tower, which looks out over Boeing Field, speakers relay the actual "tower chatter" between pilots and the real control tower. Binoculars and more buttons and gauges add to the fun.

The Red Barn features historical displays and models; videos play old film footage of the flying

ESSENTIALS

Metro Bus Route 174 takes you right to the museum from Sea-Tac or downtown Seattle. If driving, take exit 158 from I-5 and follow the signs along E. Marginal Way for about a quarter mile. Parking is abundant and free. Strollers are not available for rent, although you can easily negotiate one throughout the exhibit. Wings Cafe offers a deli menu with sandwiches, soup, and hot dogs.

The museum shop has dozens of models, books, clothes, and aircraft-related toys.

machines. Free hands-on workshops are held on most weekends throughout the year; kids work on crafts and projects to learn about flight dynamics.

Outside the museum, you'll find more airplanes, including the original Air Force One. This is the only big airplane you can actually go inside, which kids will like. Parents should enjoy walking on the plane that carried former Presidents Eisenhower and Kennedy on historic missions.

Museum of History and Industry
2700 24th Ave. E. (just south of Husky Stadium), Seattle
(206) 324-1126
www.historymuse-nw.org
Hours: Tues.-Fri., 11 a.m.-5 p.m.; Sat.-Sun., 10 a.m.-5 p.m.; closed Mondays except holidays
Admission: $5.50/adults, $3/youth ages 6-12, $1/children ages 2-5, free/children under 2
Annual membership: $40/family

Despite its ho-hum name, the Museum of History and Industry is very kid-oriented, with wooden boats to play with and a water table where kids can test paper boats. Most exhibits feature some hands-on activities.

The exhibit "Seattle in the 1880s" re-creates a section of First Avenue, with a barber shop, general store, and other shops visitors can peek into to see actual machines, tools, and products used by settlers.

In "Salmon Stakes," children can climb aboard a boat to haul in play

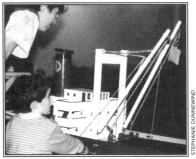

Kids can maneuver cranes in the "Work Boats" exhibit at the Museum of History and Industry.

STEPHANIE DUNNEWIND

salmon, walk through an early-20th-century cannery, and visit a hatchery. "The Great Seattle Fire" educates children about the fire that ravaged the city in 1889, using pictures and interactive computer kiosks. It also shows some of the antiquated equipment used to battle the flames. "Seattle Roots" offers a historical timeline of Seattle from 1850 to the present. Two galleries provide changing exhibits.

"Work Boats" is the place to head so kids can maneuver cranes to load a model container ship with wooden blocks and learn how to

ESSENTIALS

MOHAI's layout is open and spacious with ample room to maneuver wheelchairs and strollers. Free parking is available on the grounds. The downstairs women's bathroom has a changing table. Except for snack machines, food is not available in the immediate area, but you can bring a lunch to enjoy outside the museum while the kids climb on the giant cannon that sits next to the lower parking lot. The museum sets out tables during the summer.

make paper boats. In addition, the museum offers special events for families throughout the year, designed to complement and enhance the temporary exhibits.

The gift shop at the entrance to the museum has many interesting items for sale.

➤ **Nearby attractions:** *Arboretum, Henry Art Gallery, University Book Store, UW Waterfront Activity Center.*

TIPS

Family Fest, which runs from Thanksgiving to New Year's, celebrates winter holiday customs from around the world with crafts, games, artist workshops, dance, music, and storytelling.

The museum's auditorium hosts visiting children's productions, such as plays and concerts, throughout the year.

Adjacent to the museum's parking lot is a waterfront pathway that leads to nearby Foster Island. This is a great walk for kids; they enjoy negotiating the little bridges along the way and watching the boat action at the Montlake Cut.

Nordic Heritage Museum

3014 N.W. 67th St. (in Ballard), Seattle

(206) 789-5707

Hours: Tues.-Sat., 10 a.m.-4 p.m.; Sun., 12-4 p.m.

Admission: $4/adults, $3/seniors and college students, $2/children in grades K-12, free/children under age 5, free/first Tuesday of every month

Annual membership: $50/family

The Nordic Heritage Museum, located in Ballard, Seattle's Scandinavian neighborhood, shows how immigrants from Denmark, Finland, Iceland, Norway, and Sweden shaped the Pacific Northwest. Take a journey back in time and follow the path of a Scandinavian immigrant from the old country to Ellis Island and on to the American frontier in the interactive exhibit "Dream of America." Children can explore the realistic logging and fishing rooms that are part of the "Promise of the

► ESSENTIALS

► The museum is located in a renovated school, with plenty of free parking and an adjacent playground. If you get in the spirit of things, Scandies and the Troll Café on Market Street in downtown Ballard offer tasty and authentic Scandinavian food. (Be warned it's a good 12-block walk to downtown Ballard from the museum.) Another good food spot (near the Hiram M. Chittenden Locks) is the Totem House, which serves some of the best fish and chips in town.

TIPS

The Nordic Heritage Museum hosts annual special events for families, including Tivoli—Viking Days, which transforms the museum's grounds into a Viking marketplace in July; Yulefest, a Nordic pre—Christmas holiday event held in November; First of Advent, with a gingerbread house workshop; and Children's Christmas in Scandinavia, featuring a St. Lucia pageant. All events include music, food, and children's activities.

Northwest" exhibit, then check out the Scandinavian customs and traditions highlighted in the museum's five ethnic galleries. Monthly children's programs offer hands-on activities such as weaving, celebrations, and even a dress-alike birthday party for Pippi Longstocking.

➤ *Nearby attractions: Golden Gardens, Hiram M. Chittenden Government Locks.*

Odyssey: The Maritime Discovery Center
Pier 66, 2205 Alaskan Way, Seattle
(206) 374-4001
www.discoverodyssey.org

Scheduled to open in July 1998, the new maritime center will edu-

cate visitors with its three galleries, "Harvesting the Sea," "Ocean Trade," and "Sharing the Sound." Children can paddle Puget Sound in a virtual kayak or try guiding a freighter through the Strait of Juan de Fuca. In the gallery dedicated to commercial fishing, children can examine different fish, face the difficulties of a fisheries manager, and skipper a commercial fishing boat, "Kid Skiff II." Other interactive exhibits include loading huge containers on a ship and following shipping routes on colorful, animated maps. There is also an observation deck so visitors can watch ships out on Elliott Bay.

TIPS

The Skippers Club, for students in grades K—8, allows members to take part in maritime, fishing, trade, and transportation experiences.

Pacific Science Center
200 Second Ave. N. (in the Seattle Center), Seattle
(206) 443-2001; www.pacsci.org
IMAX Theatre: (206) 443-IMAX
Laser Theatre: (206) 433-2850
Hours: Mon.-Fri., 10 a.m.-5 p.m.; Sat., Sun., and holidays, 10 a.m.-6 p.m.
Admission: $7.50/adults, $5.50/children ages 6-13 and seniors, $3.50/children ages 2-5. With Science Center admission, laser or IMAX matinees cost $2/person.

Pacific Science Center appeals to all ages.

Annual membership: $52/family

The Pacific Science Center is a fantastic place to take kids because the fun (and educational) exhibits appeal to all ages, including adults. With the center's interactive displays, there is no question science is cool. Young children will enjoy pushing buttons and meeting small animals; teens will be thrilled to watch themselves deliver a weather report on TV or climb a rock wall.

The center is expanding its already huge campus with an $18.5 million project in 1998, which will include a new IMAX theater and additional gallery space. The theater will open in October 1998 with a six-story-high screen, 3-D capability, and digital sound. It will be located in an orb-shaped building on the southeast side of the museum.

In the center's current facility, one of the larger theme exhibits explores the era of dinosaurs and features five moving, roaring, robotic dinosaurs. (Many preschoolers choose to stand outside the door to this exhibit and just peek inside.) Kids can stand in a gigantic footprint of a duckbill dinosaur or operate the controls of a dinosaur model.

Another section, the "Kids Works" area, features an indoor playground for young kids called "Just for Tots" (persons over 48 inches tall can't get in unless accompanied by a tot). Kids can also freeze their shadow, take off in a star ship, and meet rats and snakes in "Animal Attractions." In "Body Works," children can test their eyesight, weight, strength, and eating habits.

"Tech Zone," at the far end of the museum in Building 3, features virtual reality games and robots that move and speak (attention all "Star

The museum rotates special exhibits.

Wars" fanatics).

After all the energetic exploration, the IMAX Theatre is an excellent place to relax and have a truly unforgettable experience watching movies shot on 70mm film. Tickets may be purchased as you enter the Science Center, or you can go to just IMAX. Cost is $5.50/adults, $4.50/children ages 6-13, $3.50/children ages 2-5. (Ticket prices for the new theater were not set at press time.) Popular movies fill up early on busy days.

The Ackerley Family Exhibit Gallery, which will be located near the new theater, will add 12,500 square feet of exhibit space. Slated to open in late 1998, the gallery will include a permanent butterfly exhibit and perhaps traveling exhibits or special events.

Laser Fantasy is another theater inside the Science Center that is well worth experiencing. (It is also one of the few places in town that provides good evening entertainment for teenagers.) Viewers can lie back in comfy chairs or stretch out on the carpeted floor to watch a laser light show accompanied by music. Evening shows feature music popular with teens. Matinee shows are set to such music as the Beatles or *The Wizard of Oz* and provide a soothing break. Cost is $2/person for matinees, $6.75/person for evening shows (Tuesday discount nights, $3/person).

The Willard W. Smith Planetarium shows the wonders of the universe to children age 4 and up. A special program for children ages 4

to 7 is offered at certain times. The planetarium is free with admission.

TIPS

The Pacific Science Center is one of those rare places that everyone in the family will enjoy. There is no certain order in which you should see the exhibits. With more than 200 hands-on exhibits, it really is a science playground; allow at least a full afternoon.

Popular annual events not to miss are the Model Railroad Show in November, a special holiday break show with different themes held between Christmas and New Year's, and the Bubble Festival, held each August.

The gift shop is outstanding, offering one of the best places in town to find creative, educational toys and children's books. Save time for browsing.

With all the cool stuff inside, don't miss fun displays outdoors in the area between the center's buildings. All ages will enjoy the interactive water fountains, where visitors can spray water cannons to make metal sculptures spin.

ESSENTIALS

All exhibits at the center are stroller and wheelchair accessible. A stroller is recommended rather than a backpack so you can easily let loose a curious child who wants to explore. (The Science Center is meant to be a completely hands-on experience, so you might want to skip carrying equipment altogether.) The food at Fountains Café is good, with a selection of made-to-order deli sandwiches, soups, and salads, as well as cookies, coffee, and juices.

The closest parking lot is at Second Avenue N. and John Street. Expect to pay $6 for the day.

► *Nearby attractions: See the Seattle Center entry in Chapter 8.*

Rosalie Whyel Museum of Doll Art
1116 108th Ave. N.E., Bellevue
(425) 455-1116
Hours: Mon.-Sat., 10 a.m.-5 p.m.; Sun, 1-5 p.m.
Admission: $6/adults, $5.50/seniors, $4/children ages 5-17, free/children under 5
Annual pass: $30/family

This 13,000-square-foot, peach-and-cream Victorian-style mansion is home to more than 1,200 dolls collected by Rosalie Whyel. The

The Rosalie Whyel Museum of Doll Art houses more than 1,200 dolls.

museum, which cost her $3.5 million to build, opened in 1992 to celebrate the history, technology, and artistry of doll making. The collection appeals to all ages, from preschool to seniors, and includes everything from antique dolls dating back to 1650 to Barbie, as well as toys, miniatures, teddy bears, and other childhood memorabilia. The collection even includes two ancient Egyptian tomb dolls. All the displays are housed within glass cases, safe from little hands.

ESSENTIALS

A store sells dolls, toys, and gift items.

► *Nearby attractions: Bellevue Art Museum, Bellevue Square, Meydenbauer Park.*

Seattle Art Museum
100 University St., Seattle
(206) 654-3100 (recorded information); (206) 654-3255 (information desk)
www.sam.tripl.org
Hours: Tues.-Sun., 10 a.m.-5 p.m.; Thurs., 10 a.m.-9 p.m.; open select Mon. holidays
Admission: $6/adults, $4/seniors, disabled persons, and students, free/children age 12 and under when accompanied by an adult, free/all ages on the first Thursday of each month. If used within a week, your ticket is good for free admission to the Seattle Asian Art Museum.

Annual membership: $50/family

The best time to visit the Seattle Art Museum with children is during one its family days, when hands-on activities help children learn about the museum's current featured exhibit. SAM's marvelous education program truly encourages children and families to experience art on a level comfortable to them. The museum has been applauded for making the art world less intimidating for everyone.

The Seattle Art Museum has had some diehard fans through the years, perhaps most notably its founder and primary benefactor, Dr. Richard E. Fuller. His collections of Japanese and Chinese art and other works formed a small but important holding for the Seattle Art Museum, which he and his family financed and opened in 1933 in Volunteer Park.

SAM opened its downtown location in late 1991. The kids will recognize the Seattle Art Museum by the famous 48-foot-tall *Hammering Man*, weighing in at over 20,000 pounds, located just outside the building. The building itself is spacious and bright, and the collection, which has grown to include early European works; art from Asia, Africa and the Near East; modern art; and photography, is exquisitely exhibited.

The fourth floor, which houses the modern European and American art collection, is always fun to explore with kids, mostly to watch their reactions to the abstract

ESSENTIALS

Several public parking garages and lots are located within walking distance of the museum, including one adjacent to SAM (prices vary); however, several Metro bus routes stop right outside the museum, so that may be more convenient. (Call 206-553-3000 for information on how to take the bus to SAM from anywhere in King County.) SAM is fully accessible to strollers and wheelchairs.

The museum has a good café located off the main stairwell. If it's too crowded, walk a couple of blocks to the Pike Place Market (First Avenue. and Pike Street), and grab a snack at one of the many restaurants there. (See the Downtown and Pike Place Market sections of Chapter 8 for a detailed look at this area.)

pieces. (Hint: Don't take any child who is in that stage of asking "Why?" every five seconds.).

On the first floor, visitors will find View Point, a user-friendly interactive touch-screen computer that offers loads of information and a close-up look at the artwork housed within the museum. Special exhibitions are presented several times per year, showcasing traveling exhibits or special selections from the museum's permanent collection.

➤ *Nearby attractions: Pike Place Market; a free ride aboard a Metro bus takes you to Pioneer Square and the waterfront.*

STEPHANIE DUNNEWIND

These replicas stand at the entrance of the Seattle Asian Art Museum.

Seattle Asian Art Museum

1400 E. Prospect St. (in Volunteer
Park), Seattle
(206) 654-3100
Hours: Tues.-Sun., 10 a.m.-5 p.m.;
Thurs. until 9 p.m.
Admission: $6/adults, $4/students
and seniors, free/children age 12
and under, free/all ages the first
Saturday and first Thursday of the
month. If used within a week, your
ticket is good for one free visit to
the Seattle Art Museum.

Large statues of Buddha, delicate
Japanese wall hangings, and intri-
cate jade carvings are highlights of
the Seattle Asian Art Museum,
housed in the Seattle Art Museum's
former home in Volunteer Park.
Most of the art is in display cases,

though an educational resource
room offers hands-on activities such
as kids' books, clothes to try on,
and an educational video. Older
children will find the art an interesting introduction to Asian religions
and philosophies.

TIPS

Pick up a "Self-Guided Tour"
brochure, which has educational information and activities for children.

The museum hosts regular concerts as part of its Performances in
the Park series. The series runs year-
round and has a different theme
each season.

ESSENTIALS

Parking is free and right next to the museum.

The Kado Tea Garden features dozens of kinds of teas, tea accessories, tea sandwiches, salads, and sweets such as scones and cookies. Take-out containers are available for anyone who wants to have a picnic in the park.

Visit the wonderful conservatory nearby, especially during the winter, when colorful, blooming tropical plants will momentarily transport you from Seattle's rainy gloom. There is also a nice playground. (See the Volunteer Park entry in Chapter 3.)

The best day to visit is the first Saturday of the month, when admission is free and the museum sometimes stages free family acitivities and programs, including a series of family films.

The museum store has a small children's section with games and toys.

Wing Luke Asian Museum
407 Seventh Ave. S., Seattle
(206) 623-5124; www.wingluke.org
Hours: Tues.-Fri., 11 a.m.-4:30 p.m.; Sat.-Sun., 12-4 p.m.
Admission: $2.50/adults, $1.50/seniors and students, 75 cents/children ages 5-12, free/all ages on Thursdays
Annual membership: $50/family

The Wing Luke Asian Museum, located in Seattle's historic International District, showcases the many contributions of Seattle's Asian communities. In addition to three to four changing exhibits yearly, the museum has two permanent exhibits. "One Song, Many Voices" tells the 200-year story of the Asians and Pacific Islanders who settled in Washington state. Visitors can see 85 photos and over 200 artifacts—many of which were donated by individuals from different communities—illustrating immigration, employment, community life, discrimination, and cultural traditions. "International District: Portrait of a Community" shows

INSIDE SCOOP

Museums aren't always about serious stuff. If you want to add some levity to your cultural outings, try the **Banana Museum**. Curator "Anna Banana" has collected some 3,500-4,000 banana-related items, from salt-and-pepper shakers to telephones to earrings. Located in Anna's Auburn home, the museum is not open for drop-in visitors, but the curious can leave a message to schedule an appointment (253-833-8043). And let the collection be a warning to parents who give cute nicknames to their kids: Anna insists she wouldn't have gotten started on yellow fruit if her family hadn't called her Anna Banana.

the history and contributions of the neighborhood through visual displays, pictures, and video interviews. An annual exhibit on Asian New Year celebrations usually opens in January and runs until early spring. School and community groups are welcome; tours and craft sessions complement the featured exhibits. Once a month, a Saturday program for kids is offered.

> ## ESSENTIALS
> One of Metro's underground stations is located in the heart of the International District, at Fifth and Jackson, where you can catch buses to and from Pioneer Square, University Street, Westlake Mall, and Convention Place, free of charge. (See the International District section of Chapter 8.)

➤ *Nearby attractions: Pioneer Square, Seattle Waterfront.*

MUSIC

Concerts in the Park
Auburn, (253) 931-3043
Concerts at the Locks, (206) 783-7059
Bellevue Parks and Recreation, (425) 452-4106
Downtown Seattle Association, (206) 623-0340
Edmonds Parks and Recreation, (425) 771-0228
Everett Parks and Recreation, (425) 257-8300

Federal Way Arts Commission, (253) 661-4050
Kent Parks and Recreation and Arts Commission, (253) 859-3991
King County Parks, (206) 296-4258
Kirkland Parks and Recreation, (425) 828-1217
Lynnwood Arts Commission and Parks and Recreation, (425) 670-6254
Mercer Island Arts Council, (206) 236-3545
Redmond Arts Commission and Parks and Recreation, (425) 556-2350
Renton Parks and Recreation, (425) 235-2560
Seattle Center Mural Concert Series, (206) 684-7200
Shoreline Summer Concerts, (206) 361-7133
Woodland Park ZooTunes and ZooTunes Jr., (206) 684-4800

Outdoor concerts are what easy summer living is all about: slowing down the pace and letting the hours drift. The price is free for most, the sound is first-rate, and the atmosphere is perfect for kids—they can shake, wiggle, and roll all they want. These regularly scheduled events feature a wide variety of music, from folk to soft rock, and all are family affairs. Some concerts are held at noon on weekdays, but most are on weekend evenings or Sunday afternoons. Go early, bring a blanket and a picnic, then kick back and let the music surround you.

Bellevue Philharmonic Orchestra
(425) 455-4171
Season: October-May
Tickets: $10-$15/person

The Philharmonic designates Tuesdays as Family Nights during its Westminster concert series. Children 10 and under are free with an adult, and dress is casual for audiences and musicians alike. Performances begin with an informal talk by the conductor. The orchestra also performs several holiday concerts in December. Concerts are held at the Westminster Chapel and at several outreach locations in the community.

Chamber Music Play-In
Music Center of the Northwest
(206) 526-8443
Season: Throughout the year
Tickets: Free

Music Center of the Northwest seeks to provide enjoyable musical activities for all ages at no cost. Two to three times per year, in the fall, winter, and summer, the center hosts an evening of informal chamber music performances by ensembles of varied experience and ages. The public is invited to drop in to listen or participate—wind, vocal, and youth ensembles are especially encouraged to perform. The fall and winter concerts are held at a church at N. 96th Street and Linden Avenue N., Seattle; the summer play-in usually takes place outdoors in a park with an informal potluck. The Music Center also offers music lessons for children and adults at reasonable cost.

Discover Music!
Seattle Symphony
(206) 443-4747
www.seattlesymphony.org
Season: October-June
Tickets: $11/adults, $8/children

Each year, the Seattle Symphony Orchestra presents a very popular series of concerts designed to introduce children ages 6 to 10 to the world of classical music. The one-hour concerts are held at 11 a.m. Saturdays at the Seattle Center's Opera House (spring 1998); starting in fall 1998, all performances will be at the new Benaroya Hall, located at the corner of University Street and Second Avenue in downtown Seattle.

Discover Music performers are expert at captivating young audiences with entertainment that is cleverly laced with lessons in music basics. Families can also come an hour early and participate in a vari-

TIPS

All seats for Discover Music! are general admission, but purchase tickets early because some shows sell out. Dress is comfortable despite the Opera House setting. A public parking garage is located across the street, accessible by a covered walkway over Mercer Street.

Parking for Benaroya Hall will be a two-level, 430-space underground garage on Second Avenue near Union Street.

ety of hands-on activities, such as making instruments and learning new tunes. Season or individual tickets may be purchased.

Musical Experiences
(206) 367-6106
Tickets: $14/adults, $10/students (suggested donation)

Musical Experiences was formed in 1991 to "further the appreciation and knowledge of music to a broad audience." By presenting a series of short recitals, along with talks about the composers and music being performed, the organization hopes to educate and entertain Seattle audiences in an intimate setting that encourages discussion between the musicians and the audience. It is recommended for children age 8 and up.

Northwest Chamber Orchestra
Performances in Kane Hall on the UW campus, Seattle Art Museum, and Seattle Asian Art Museum
(206) 343-0445
Season: September-May
Ticket prices vary by venue:
$15-$21/adults at Kane Hall, $21-$22/adults at Seattle Art Museum, $12.50/adults at Seattle Asian Art Museum. At all venues, children under 17 are admitted free when accompanied by an adult.

The Northwest Chamber Orchestra's series of concerts at the Seattle Asian Art Museum is geared toward families, with one-hour afternoon performances and lower ticket prices. NWCO also gives several performances and presents a chamber music series at the SAM auditorium. In contrast to many arts organizations

Northwest Chamber Orchestra Music Director Adam Stern performs on the keyboard at the Madrona Middle School as part of "Taking It to the Streets," Northwest Chamber Orchestra's Music Education program.

in town, NWCO does more than just talk about getting children culturally involved: It offers free admission to anyone under 17 attending its performances with an adult.

Philadelphia String Quartet
Olympic Music Festival
(206) 527-8839
Season: Late June-early September
Tickets: $10-$20/person
Directions: The farm is located 11 miles west of the Hood Canal Bridge, half a mile south of Hwy. 104, on Center Road.

The Olympic Music Festival in the Barn series is held on Saturday and Sunday afternoons beginning the last weekend in June and running through the first weekend in September. Concerts take place on a picturesque 40-acre farm on the Olympic Peninsula. Concert-goers can opt to either sit in the turn-of-the-century barn ($15-$20/adults, $11/children age 5 and older; children age 5 and under are not permitted) or outside on the lawn ($10/person, free/children age 5 and under). Each concert starts at 2 p.m.; gates open at 11 a.m.

RAF Foundation
(206) 654-4498
Tickets: Free

Musician Tracey Waring, sometimes backed by an orchestra (in past years the Northwest Chamber Orchestra), presents 17 themed programs that teach kids about music with hands-on, interactive activities. The free programs are held periodically at libraries and community

TIPS

Even though children age 5 and up are allowed to sit in the barn at the Olympic Music Festival, most families prefer to bring blankets and relax on the grass outside the barn. Everyone can still enjoy the music, and the kids are free to frolic and pet the animals. You can bring your own picnic, or buy sandwiches, pop, espresso, wine, and cookies in the milking shed.

centers, as well as schools. The sessions are geared for children as young as age 4. In "The Life and Times of Mozart," for example, Waring has children act out stories about Mozart and teaches them to dance the minuet. She tells stories set to music and lets children try out all the instruments she brings. Call for a schedule of public events.

Rainier Chamber Winds
(206) 780-1021 or (800) 956-WIND
www.nwartist.org/rcw/index.htm
Tickets: Free children's concerts

The only professional wind ensemble in the Northwest, the Rainier Chamber Winds perform a children's concert in the fall or spring, each year alternating two commissioned compositions that narrate a story, similiar in style to "Peter and the Wolf." The location for the public performances vary, but often take place at community center or libraries.

Seattle Chamber Music Festival
Music Under the Stars
Lakeside School, 14050 First Ave. N.E., Seattle
(206) 283-8808
Season: July, every Mon., Wed., and Fri., 8 p.m.
Ticket prices: $28/adults inside St. Nicholas Hall; free/sitting outside on the grounds

This popular month-long series, started by UW cello professor Toby Saks, is well known for its top-notch performances by local and international talent and for the charming ambiance of the Lakeside School grounds. Music-loving families can enjoy the concert without paying to sit inside St. Nicholas Hall, thanks to a stereo system that pipes music out of the hall onto the pastoral campus grounds. Weather permitting, anyone can bring a blanket and picnic and enjoy the music for free, while children play and dance "under the stars." Come early if you'd like to hear a free recital inside the hall at 7 p.m.

INSIDE SCOOP

Benaroya Hall

The new $109 million facility will be owned by the city of Seattle but managed by the Seattle Symphony. Designed as a state-of-the-art concert hall, it will host other classical music groups, as well as jazz, country, popular and folk musicians. A half-acre of open space along Second Avenue will include a Garden of Remembrance commemorating state residents who died in World War II and the Korean and Vietnam conflicts.

A 38-foot-wide, 26-foot-high concert organ with 4,154 pipes will be installed in the hall; the instrument will debut in July 2000.

TIPS

The Seattle Chamber Music Festival is an extraordinary opportunity to hear fine music for free. Ticket holders have the option of purchasing catered dinners in advance. Desserts can be purchased, and complimentary coffee and lemonade are available prior to the concert.

Children under age 6 are not allowed in the concert hall, but they are probably better off outside anyway. Concerts last about two hours, so be sure to bring plenty of blankets and sweaters if you sit outside.

The Seattle Conservatory of Music
(206) 632-6715
Tickets: $10/adults, $5/students

The conservatory trains more than 70 students, ages 9 to 19, in classical music. Concerts are held in various Seattle venues.

University of Washington School of Music
Musicfest
(206) 543-4880
Season: October-June
Tickets: Prices vary; some concerts are free

The University of Washington School of Music presents a complete season of musical entertainment performed by students, faculty, and guest artists. Concerts are held at Meany Theatre and other sites on campus. The series includes vocal, instrumental, group, and solo performances, including pieces by contemporary artists as well as the masters.

Youth Symphonies

Bellevue Eastside Youth Symphonies
(425) 821-9880

Three graded orchestras consist of children ages 8 to 20. They give four main performances: a dessert social in November, a holiday concert in December, a winter concert in mid-March, and a spring performance at the Meydenbauer Theater in June.

Renton Youth Symphony Orchestras
Carco Theater, 1715 Maple Valley Hwy., Renton
(425) 277-5536

The orchestra, composed of students ages 12 to 18, performs for the public three times a year: in March, May, and December.

Seattle Youth Symphony Orchestra
11065 Fifth Ave. N.E., Suite E, Seattle
(206) 362-2300
Season: November-May
Tickets: $5-$25/person

The Seattle Youth Symphony Orchestra, the largest youth symphony organization in the country, comprises more than 600 young musicians ages 8 to 21 in five orchestras: the Symphonette (ages 7-11), the Seattle Debut Symphony (ages 8-14), the Seattle Junior Symphony and the Classical Orchestra (both ages 12-16), and the Seattle Youth Symphony (ages 15-21). Each orchestra performs three weekend concerts a year. Tickets are $5 to $25 for the Youth Symphony at the Seattle Opera House, and a $5 donation for the training symphonies, which play in venues such as high school auditoriums and the UW's Meany Hall. Overseen by musical director Jonathan Shamese, the young performers invariably give first-rate concerts and provide fine role models to inspire the

The Seattle Youth Symphony is the largest in the country.

young musician in your family. The company runs summer music festivals in Seattle and Port Townsend.

Youth Philharmonic Northwest
Orchestras
(425) 869-9757

Children ages 7 to 21 perform in three orchestras and two harp ensembles. Two concerts are held at the end of each term, in December, March, and May, at the Eastlake Performing Arts Center at Eastlake High School in Redmond.

Vocals

Columbia Choirs
Boys Choir, Girls Choir, and Youth Choir of East King County

(425) 869-0320 (tickets),
(425) 486-1987 (information)

The Boys Choir is composed of children in kindergarten to "voice change," usually around 14 years; the Girls Choir includes girls in kindergarten through 12th grade; and the Youth Choir is a co-ed group made up of young people from ninth grade through freshman year in college. Annual public concerts include several holiday concerts in December, as well as concerts in March and June.

Mercer Island Children's Choir
(206) 232-8007

The Mercer Island Children's Choir puts a Broadway slant to its two public performances in June and December. The 85 members, boys and girls in grades 4 to 6, do a classical segment moving to the music, then perform small group vignettes with choreographed dances, costumes, and sets. Performances are recommended for children age 4 and up. The group's usual performance hall is the Mercer Island High School auditorium.

Northwest Girlchoir
728 21st Ave. E., Seattle
(206) 329-6225

The 290-member Northwest Girlchoir has been performing for Seattle family audiences for nearly 20 years. Annual public performances include three holiday concerts in December and two spring concerts in April.

Pacifica Children's Chorus and Pacifica Youth Choir

(206) 527-9095

Tickets: $9/adults, $7/children

The 85 members of Pacifica's coed choir range from preschoolers to high-schoolers. Five levels are based on age and ability. The group performs two weekend concerts, one in December and the other in May, at two Seattle churches.

Seattle Children's Chorus

(206) 542-5998 or (888) 561-7139

The coed chorus has two branches in Shoreline and Everett, with a training chorus for children ages 7 to 11 and a performing chorus for ages 11 to 18. Formal performances for both choirs are given in December and May.

Seattle Girls' Choir

Veterans Hall, 7220 Woodlawn Ave. N.E., Seattle

(425) 656-9229

The internationally renowned Seattle Girls' Choir and its affiliate choir, the Highline-area Girls' Choir, have a total membership of almost 200 girls ages 6 to 18. The Choir comprises five levels, from junior preparatory to advanced. Prime Voci, the Seattle Girls' Advanced Choir, is regarded as one of the best in the world. The Girls' Choir is a resident ensemble at St. James Cathedral.

Annual public performances include holiday concerts in December, a winter concert in February or March, and a spring concert in May. Some concerts feature sing-alongs.

STORYTELLING

Seattle Storytellers Guild

(206) 621-8646

The guild, one of the strongest of its kind in the country, holds frequent workshops throughout the year. Participants can either tell or listen to stories at monthly get-togethers in private homes. Seattle Story and Snack is held the last Thursday of the month; Eastside Story and Snack the third Thursday.

Third Sunday Storytelling is held each month at 1 p.m. at the All for Kids Bookshop (2900 N.E. Blakely St., Seattle; 206-526-2768). Admission is $3. Call for information about local storytelling events.

There are many other places in town to take your child to hear a good story. Almost any bookstore that has a strong children's book section offers storytelling sessions, including Barnes & Noble, Borders and Secret Garden. (See "Shopping List" in Chapter 11 for a bookstore near you.) Most libraries also offer storytelling sessions on a regular basis. Check your local branch for details. (See "Public Libraries" in Chapter 5.)

THEATER

The Auburn Ave. Dinner Theater

10 Auburn Ave., Auburn
(253) 833-5678
Season: Year-round
Hours: Fri.-Sat., dinner seating at
6:15 p.m. with the show at 8 p.m.;
Sun., meal at 2:30 p.m. with the
show at 4 p.m.
Tickets: Dinner and show,
$29/adults, $14.50/children age 6
or under; show only, $18.40/adults,
$9.20/children age 6 or under. (Dis-
counted general admission tickets
are available at the door on night of
show based on space availability.)

The dinner theater presents a
season of five musical productions
plus a holiday show in December.
Recent shows included "My Fair
Lady," "Sound of Music," and "Fiddler on the Roof." The theater also
offers free family shows periodically
on Saturday mornings. Tickets must
be picked up in advance.

Bainbridge Performing Arts

Cultural Arts Center, 200 Madison
Ave., Bainbridge Island
(206) 842-8569
Tickets: Prices vary

For 41 years, Bainbridge Performing Arts has been an integral
part of the Bainbridge Island community, presenting a wide variety of
theater productions, including dramas, musicals, and children's
favorites. In its home at the Cultural
Arts Center (a short walk from the
Winslow ferry), BPA hosts a theater
school, monthly improvisational

INSIDE SCOOP

Radio Shows

KING 98.1 FM (206-448-
3981; www.king.org) presents
two radio programs geared to
children. During the **Classic
Kids** hour (Sat., 9-10 a.m.)
host Miss Marta encourages
children to dance, read, and
draw pictures as they listen to
classical music. **Starwin Studios** (Thursdays during the
school year, 1:30-2 p.m.)
focuses on a certain instrument and discusses basic
music theory.

Bellevue Community Col-
lege's noncommercial radio
station, KBCS 91.3 FM. The
program plays childrens programs at 11:30 a.m. on Fridays.

comedy, concerts, and performances
by the Bainbridge Orchestra.

Bathhouse Theatre

7312 W. Green Lake Dr. N., Seattle
(206) 524-9108
Season: February-December
Tickets: $10-$28/person

Productions by the Bathhouse
Theatre appeal to a broad range of
audiences, young and old, with special emphasis on the classics. Two
productions each year feature out-

reach programs for middle school and high school students, including special student matinees, workshops, and classes, and special curriculum materials for teachers to enhance the theater experience. The productions are most suitable for older children; the theater asks people not to bring infants or young kids who might be disruptive.

Civic Light Opera
Jane Addams Theatre, 11051 34th Ave. NE, Seattle
(206) 363-2809
Season: September-May
Tickets: $18/person; $14/person on Sundays with festival seating

Don't be turned off by the word "opera": Instead of traditional operas in foreign languages, the Light Opera does four Broadway-style musical productions each season. Recent performances included "Mame" and "Seven Brides for Seven Brothers."

Group Theater
305 Harrison St. (Seattle Center House, lower level), Seattle
(206) 441-1299
Season: Fall to spring
Tickets: $20-$22/person

Some of the Group Theater's performances are appropriate for older children, and it offers Family Fridays for younger ones: While parents enjoy a show, children can play at the Children's Museum. Cost is $10/child, $5/each additional child. Family Fridays are the first Friday of the regular run of each of its four to five main-stage performances. Parents must register two weeks in advance. The Group Theater also puts on an annual holiday show, "Voices of Christmas."

IKEA Family Stage
The Theater at Meydenbauer Center, Bellevue
(425) 450-3801
Season: January-May
Tickets: $12.50-$15/adults, $6-$7.50/children

Designed to provide quality family entertainment on the Eastside, the Family Stage brings nationally recognized performers to Bellevue's Meydenbauer Center. Recent shows on its main stage included "Frogs, Lizards, Orbs, and Slinkys" by Imago Theater and "Schoolhouse Rock Live!" A series of "Wiggle" musical performances are geared for younger children, ages 3 to 6. Public performances are held on weekends; there are also shows for school groups during the week.

Langston Hughes Cultural Arts Center
104 17th Ave. S., Seattle
(206) 684-4757

The Langston Hughes Cultural Arts Center runs DCM, a theater-arts education program for middle school students, who give at least one free public performance a year. In late August, students in the center's summer arts program put on a free production. Occasionally the center works with ACT, the Seattle Rep, and Intiman to offer a Family Theater series with discounted tickets. Call to be added to the center's mailing list for more information.

The Northwest Puppet Center features companies from around the world.

Northwest Puppet Center

9123 15th Ave. N.E., Seattle
(206) 523-2599
Season: October-April
Tickets: $6.50/adults, $4.50/children

Northwest Puppet Center, Seattle's only permanent puppet theater, offers seven productions for the entire family each year. Puppet companies from around the world are featured, as are performances by the award-winning resident company, the Carter Family Marionettes. The center, which is housed in a former church in a residential neighborhood, strives to present different styles of puppetry. Recent shows included "Babar and Father Christmas," "Thumbelina," and "Mrs. Twig and the Stupid Machine." The center has a small picnic area and playground.

Parks and Recreation Department Family Theater Series

Bellevue Parks and Recreation,
(425) 452-4106
Lynnwood Arts Commission
and Parks and Recreation,
(425) 670-6254
Kent Parks and Recreation and Arts
Commission, (253) 859-3991
King County Parks, (206) 296-4258
Redmond Parks and Recreation and
Redmond Arts Commission
(425) 556-2300
Renton Parks and Recreation
(425) 235-2560
Shoreline Summer Concerts
(206) 361-7133

Several parks and recreation departments organize family performing-art series. Productions include everything from stage plays to musical performances by popular local talents. Tickets may be purchased as a series or for individual shows. Prices vary from free to $7.

Pied Piper Productions
Mount Baker Community Club, 2811 Mount Rainier Dr. S., Seattle (206) 722-7209
Season: Fall-spring
Tickets: $3/person (suggested donation)

Pied Piper Productions offers low-cost, high-quality performing arts for young children and families. This nonprofit organization is devoted to presenting quality entertainment for children ages 2 to 7 and their families. Programs are held on selected Saturday mornings during the fall, winter, and spring, and include popular local puppet shows, storytellers, music, dance, and sing-alongs. Recent performers included a Latin American folkloric musical group and Charles the Clown.

Renton Civic Theatre
507 S. Third St., Renton (425) 226-5529
Season: September-May, plus a summer production
Tickets: $18/adults, $14/children, students, and seniors

Renton Civic Theatre, a professional theater located in downtown Renton, offers a full season of musicals, dramas, and comedies, most of which are suitable for families. Recent productions included "The Secret Garden" and "Godspell." The theater is large and completely handicapped accessible. Productions are most suitable for older

children; the theater asks people not to bring infants or young kids who might be disruptive.

Seattle Children's Theatre
Charlotte Martin Theatre
Seattle Center, Seattle
(206) 443-0807, (206) 441-3322 (tickets)
Season: October-May
Tickets: $18/adults, $12/children

Rated one of the top children's theater companies in the United States, Seattle Children's Theatre offers some of the very best in family entertainment. Most seasons offer several world premieres, with productions targeted at younger and older children. Recent shows included "Stellaluna," "Mr. Popper's Penguins," "Frog and Toad," and "The Tempest." Performances run one to two hours, including a question-and-answer period with the actors after the show—always a big hit.

In addition to its theater productions, the SCT Drama School offers year-round theater arts classes and workshops for students ages 3 1/2 to 19. It also has a Deaf Youth Drama Program, one of only a few in the country.

Seattle Puppetory Theatre
13002 10th Ave. N.W., Seattle (206) 365-0100
Tickets: Prices vary

Seattle Puppetory Theatre is a touring company that offers performances for children as well as adults. Although its primary focus is

Seattle Children's Theatre, here performing "Stelluna," is rated one of the top in the country.

performing at schools, libraries, and birthday parties, the theater has also been involved in bringing international puppet companies, especially ones from Japan, to Seattle. In addition, the theater hosts occasional workshops and performances for the general public.

Seattle Shakespeare Festival

Performances at the UW Ethnic Cultural Theatre, 3940 Brooklyn Ave. N.E., Seattle
(206) 467-1382
www.seanet.com/~ssf
Season: Fall and spring, plus summer Shakespeare in the Parks
Tickets: $18/adults, $12/children, free/summer performances

The Shakespeare Festival, Washington's only professional classical theater, designates its Sunday matinees as Family Days. Intended for

children age 8 and up, the matinees include a pre-show presentation on the play to be presented, then a question-and-answer period with actors following the performance.

The festival also presents free Shakespeare in the Parks performances each summer in King County parks.

Snoqualmie Falls Forest Theatre

36800 S.E. David Powell Road
Fall City
(425) 222-7044
Season: June-August
Tickets: $13/adults, $12/students and seniors, $5/ ages 6-12; optional salmon or steak dinner, $12 additional.

Located just east of Issaquah in Fall City, the Snoqualmie Falls Forest Theatre offers two or three productions each summer. Visitors to this outdoor theater, set within 100 acres of natural forest, will also enjoy a view of Snoqualmie Falls. The Mainstage productions are presented at 8 p.m. on Friday and Saturday evenings, 3 p.m. on Sunday afternoons. Optional steak or salmon barbecue dinners are served prior to the Friday and Saturday performances and after the Sunday

matinee. Reservations are required for dinner and are recommended for all performances. The theater is a five-minute walk from the free parking area and is accessible for the handicapped.

INSIDE SCOOP Cheap Seats

■ Oh Dear! . . . Not Shakespeare! adapts the Bard and classic literature for children. (206) 368-7007.
■ Pied Piper Productions; (206) 722-7209.
■ Studio East; (425) 827-3123.
■ Productions sponsored by parks and recreation departments.
■ Auburn Ave. Dinner Theater free family shows. (253) 833-5678.
■ Seattle Shakespeare Festival has pay-what-you-will performances. Also watch for free summer performances in King County parks. (206) 467-1382.
■ The Seattle Children's Theatre Drama School presents a free performance at the end of each quarter of classes. (206) 443-0807.
■ Performances of the four training orchestras of the Seattle Youth Symphony. (206) 362-2300.
■ Seattle's Shorecrest High School has an award-winning drama department that stages a family-oriented play each spring. Reserved-seat tickets are $6-$7/person. (206) 361-4286.

■ The Seattle Department of Parks and Recreation sponsors The Bard in the Park, free performances of plays by Shakespeare at various Seattle parks from mid-July to August. (206) 684-4075.
■ At the Seattle Repertory Theatre, tickets are $10 for anyone under age 25, for any performance. The Rep also offers a pay-what-you-can night on the first Thursday of some of its productions. (The lowest suggested ticket price is $10.) (206) 443-2222.
■ The Bathhouse Theatre at Green Lake offers $10 seats for people under age 25, as well as pay-what-you-can performances. (206) 524-9108.
■ Seattle Chamber Music Festival: Music Under the Stars
■ Ticket/Ticket booths, located at the Broadway and Pike Place markets, sell half-price day-of-show tickets for theater, dance, music, and comedy productions. Tickets must be purchased at the booths with cash only. (206) 324-2744.

Studio East
402 Sixth St. S., Kirkland
(425) 827-3123; www.studio-east.org
Season: October-May
Tickets: $6-$9/person

Studio East's theater students present six shows a season, mostly musicals. Recent productions included "Animal Farm," "The Wizard of Oz," "West Side Story," and "The Magic of Mrs. Piggle Wiggle." The theater also hosts Sprouts productions, one-hour shows by adults appropriate for young children. A family improv comedy night is held most months.

Thistle Theatre
(206) 524-3388
Season: October-February
Tickets: $7/adults, $5/children and seniors

Though it hopes to have a permanent home at some point, Thistle Theatre performs its puppet shows in two locations, Burien Little Theatre (425 S.W. 144th, Burien) and Moore Theatre at Sacred Heart School (9442 N.E. 14th, Bellevue). The shows run about 45 minutes and are appropriate for preschoolers and up. The theater has adapted a Japanese style of puppetry, bunraku, where puppeteers wear black costumes and visibly move puppets on stage. Most productions feature original music. Recent shows included "Winnie the Pooh" and "Welcome to Candyland."

UW Ethnic Cultural Theatre
3940 Brooklyn Ave. N.E., Seattle
(206) 543-4635
Season: November-May
Tickets: $10/adults, $5/students

The University of Washington's Office of Minority Affairs Ethnic Cultural Center organizes a series of plays, concerts, lectures, readings, and forums that feature performances by people of color. Recent productions included "Faces of America" and "I Ain't Yo' Uncle."

Variety Plus
223 N.E. 175th, Shoreline
(206) 368-8386

Variety Plus, founded by a husband and wife team, produces an annual children's musical using a cast of children, teens, and adults. The 1997 show, "Pinocchio," was staged at the Museum of History and Industry's auditorium.

Village Theatre/Kidstage
303 Front St. N., Issaquah
(425) 392-2202; www.vt.org
Season: September-June
Tickets: $18-$28/person; discounts for students and Family Room seating

Village Theatre presents quality family theater and provides a Family Room so even parents with infants and small children can enjoy the shows. The season features four musicals and a comedy. Recent productions included "Little Shop of Horrors," "Fiddler on the Roof," and "The Miser." Performances are

Wednesday through Saturday evenings, with matinees on Sundays.

Kidstage, a theater-arts education program, offers classes for children age 5 and up. It presents a musical production that is directed, designed, and performed by young people each July and August.

West Seattle KidsTheatre
(206) 935-9782
Most performances at Sealth High Little Theatre, 2600 S.W. Thistle, Seattle
Season: Fall, winter, spring
Tickets: $10/adults, $8/seniors, $5/children

The theater stages three productions a year, including one musical. Every other year it produces a Christmas show (most recently, "The Best Christmas Pageant Ever"). The shows, which feature child actors except for adult roles, are both classics ("Alice in Wonderland") and original plays by Northwest authors. The staff is all professional; adult actors are community or semi-professional performers.

Youth Theatre Northwest
88th Ave. S.E. and S.E. 40th St., Mercer Island
(206) 232-2202
Season: August-May
Tickets: $9/person

Youth Theatre Northwest on Mercer Island presents six productions, with three designed especially for younger children and three targeted at ages 7 and up. The pro-

ductions include old favorites as well as original works, dramas, and musicals. Recent shows included "Cinderella," "Winnie the Pooh," and "The Wind in the Willows." Young people are involved in all aspects of the productions, including the design and creation of the sets, acting, and directing. Following each performance, the young actors return to the stage for a question-and-answer period with the audience. Youth Theatre also offers an array of theater-arts classes throughout the year for children preschool age and older.

DANCE

Cameo Dance Theatre
(206) 528-8183
Tickets: $7-$15/person

Cameo Dance Theatre, which includes hundreds of students from age 2 to adults, performs three public performances: an all-studio production in November, "The Nutcracker" in January, and "Festival of Dance," an all-school show in June. Performances are held at the Museum of History and Industry and Civic Light Opera.

Cornish College of the Arts
710 E. Roy, Seattle
(206) 726-5066
Tickets: Prices vary

The Cornish Junior Dance Company performs a spring concert for the public in May. The dancers, ages 4 to 17, present a repertory of original choreography and classical pieces in modern dance as well as ballet. Also in May, different dance classes do an end-of-the-year presentation, which is open to the public. Junior company apprentices perform "The Nutcracker" in December.

Cornish students present Shakespeare in the Park at Volunteer Park one week each spring, which families may enjoy.

Emily's Dance Arts
(425) 746-3659
Tickets: $11-$14/person

The Bellevue-based dance studio presents an annual performance of "The Nutcracker" in December at Bellevue Community College and a June recital at the UW's Meany Hall.

Kaleidoscope Dance Company
(206) 363-7281

The Northwest's only professional modern dance company of young people presents an annual spring series of four performances over Mother's Day weekend at the Broadway Performance Hall (1625 Broadway, Seattle). The 17-year-old company also performs the second week of December at Roosevelt High School and gives an informal recital in March. In addition, it often dances at schools, community events, and Bumbershoot.

COURTESY OF THE OLYMPIC BALLET

Olympic Ballet performs a family production each year.

Olympic Ballet
(425) 774-7570
Tickets: Price varies

The Edmonds-based ballet school, which includes students age 3 and up, performs "The Nutcracker" each December in Bellevue, Everett, and Edmonds. It also presents a late-winter family production, such as "Peter and the Wolf," in Everett, Seattle, and Bellevue.

Pacific Northwest Ballet
Seattle Opera House
Seattle Center, Seattle
(206) 441-9411
Season: September-June
Tickets: Prices vary

The 50-member ballet company, which celebrated its 25th anniversary during the 1997-1998 season, presents 100 performances of classic and contemporary works at the Opera House and on tour. PNB stages "The Nutcracker" each November and December, with sets and costumes designed by Maurice Sendak.

Chapter 8

EXPLORING DOWNTOWN

Familiarity with a city as an
adult and as a parent are two
entirely different things.
Sometimes it is difficult to pull back
and see a neighborhood in terms of
what might appeal to children—the
sights, shops, and snack spots that
hold a certain charm for them.

This section is meant to help
you discover some of Seattle's most
interesting areas with your child.
You'll discover why visiting an Asian
grocery store can be so exciting for
a kid. You'll learn how to explore
the waterfront without wearing
out little legs and where to sit
down and have a juice box in Pioneer Square. In short, you'll see
Seattle in a new light, and realize
that though your old haunts are
not necessarily ideal for kids, this
city has plenty of good alterna-
tives to offer.

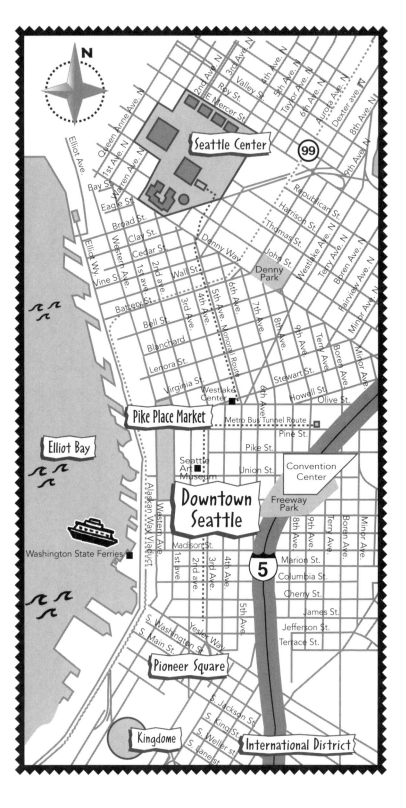

PIKE PLACE PUBLIC MARKET

The Pike Place Public Market, located at Pike Street and First Avenue in downtown Seattle, doesn't attract over 9 million shoppers a year for its farm-fresh goods alone, though these are certainly a main attraction. What does draw people—both residents and tourists—is its lively atmosphere. Smack in the midst of downtown, it is one of the least glitzy, most diverse areas of Seattle, a place where even the most tight-collared urbanite rubs shoulders with the greenest of earth mothers, without any friction.

Officially opened in 1907, the Market has grown to encompass a wide variety of merchants and wares, plus over a dozen ethnic groceries and bakeries, several restaurants, and an assortment of novelty shops. Though its existence has been threatened twice, once by developers in the early 1970s, and again in the 1980s by investors who wanted to make it more commercial, it has survived and been labeled a Historic District, character intact.

The Market is open daily year-round, Mon.-Sat., 9 a.m.-6 p.m. and Sun., 11 a.m.-5 p.m. Most food places are open at 8 a.m. Come early for the best pick of produce.

The following highlights of the Market are meant to be happened upon rather than sought out. Only by strolling the Market and exploring its many nooks and crannies will your family gain a sense of its offerings and its significance to the community.

TIPS

- Trying to negotiate a stroller through the Market is virtually impossible because it gets so crowded. Use a front or backpack instead—the kids will be able to see the action more clearly, and you'll be able to move swiftly when the "I want, I want" chants begin.

- The Market hosts the Pike Place Market Festival each year in May, featuring a full weekend of entertainment, special events, and hands-on activities for kids (see Season by Season).

- Most Market locations offer the Pike Place Market News, a complimentary newspaper that contains a map of the nine-acre Market area.

- The Market Information Booth, located on First Avenue and Pike Street, offers shopping and restaurant brochures, maps, and tour information. It is open daily from 10 a.m.-6 p.m. Make sure to ask for a Kids' Market Walk guide, which suggests items for kids to watch for and gives them space to note their observations. Also at the booth is Ticket/Ticket, open noon-6 p.m., with half-price, day-of-show tick-

continued ➡

ets to local theater, music, and comedy productions.

■ If your kids need to run off some energy, take them to Victor Steinbrueck Park, a small grassy area at the north end of the market. There are plenty of benches, two totem poles, and views of the Olympic Mountains. It's a popular place for an outside picnic (and, often, the homeless.)

➤ **Nearby Attractions:** Seattle Art Museum, Waterfront.

Pike Place Market Preservation and Development Authority
(206) 682-7453

The Preservation and Development Authority offers tours to Seattle school children that include the rich history and lore of the Market as well as interesting behind-the-scenes facts and figures.

Main and North Arcades
The west side of the market, on Pike Place between Pike St. and Virginia St.

The Pike Place Market is a spectacle in and of itself, but it does have two distinguishing characteristics: a big, red neon clock and "Rachel," the fat bronze piggy bank that kids love to sit on, pet, and stuff with spare change (money collected goes to social service programs at the Market). The clock and the pig are located where Pike Street meets Pike Place.

The Main Arcade is easy to find: Just listen for the hollering fish mongers and the wet slap of fish being tossed among them. It's an amusing spectacle that always attracts a crowd. The Pike Place

ESSENTIALS

■ Parking can be frustrating in the Market area, especially on sunny summer days. Whatever you do, don't get stuck driving on Pike Place (the road that goes through the Market): Though you might find a parking space, you will surely lose your sanity. Opt for parking in one of the many garages or lots located along Western Avenue; the Public Market Parking Garage (1531 Western Ave.; (206) 621-0469) has a skybridge elevator that provides direct access to the North Arcade. Some merchants offer parking discounts with purchases, so be sure to ask. The Public Market Parking Garage offers free parking with validation before 10 a.m. on Saturday.

■ Rest rooms in the Market are located at the southern and northern points of the Main Arcade, on the First Floor Down Under.
■ If you need to get down to the waterfront from the Market, you can take the elevator from the parking garage mentioned above, or take the elevator or stairs located at the southern end of the Market, to Western Avenue. Cross the street and follow the stairs down to the waterfront. (See the Pike Place Hillclimb). The stairs do pose a problem for wheelchairs, strollers, and cranky kids, so if you just need to get to the waterfront, opt for taking the elevator in the Public garage, just north on Western.

Fish Co. warns: "Caution: Low flying fish." And they mean it.

There's much more to be seen, however, including colorful rows of fruits and veggies, handmade children's clothing and toys, homemade jams and honeys, seasonal fresh-cut flowers, dried flower arrangements, handcrafted silver jewelry, pottery, photographs and pictures, unidentifiable junk, and lots of action. Many farmers offer samples of their latest products and produce, as well as recipes and information about the locations of their U-pick farms.

This bustling scene, including a variety of musicians, balloon sculptors, and other entertainers, is exciting for kids. The man who plays the spoons (forks, spatulas, you name it) is a favorite around the Market.

If you can find enough space to stand still and look down at the floor, you will see the names of various patrons who gave donations to help replace the Market's old wooden floor in the mid-1980s. There are 46,500 tiles in all. (One bears the names of Ronald and Nancy Reagan; another is designated as The Very First Tile.)

First Floor Down Under

(In the Main Arcade)

Craft Emporium
(206) 622-2219

Inside your kids will find trays and trays of beads—metal, glass, porcelain, clay—of all shapes and sizes. Craft Emporium also features different craft materials, such as sequins, glitters, feathers, and trimmings, as well as glues and wires. For obvious reasons, this is not a good place to take a very young child.

Golden Age Collectables
(206) 622-9799

Golden Age Collectables is stuffed full of comic books, modern and old, for children and adults (be forewarned that some of the material is not at all appropriate for kids). Also featured are baseball and other sports cards, signed baseballs, models, books, and "Star Trek" memorabilia.

Market Coins
(206) 624-9681

Lots of old baseball cards, stamps, and coins will attract the serious and amateur collectors in the family.

Market Magic Shop
(206) MAGIC-71 (624-4271)

This authentic magic shop sells a wide variety of supplies for magicians of every level. You'll find everything from gags to juggling supplies, rubber chickens to ventriloquist dummies, puzzles to books and videos. Performances by professional musicians, mimes, and jugglers are a regular occurrence at this store, and the staff are more than willing to show what's up their own sleeves.

MisterE Books
(206) 622-5182

A small but well-stocked book-store, MisterE has a good children's book section located at the back on the right.

Old Seattle Paper Works and Giant Shoe Museum
(206) 623-2870

Besides selling old posters, mag-azines, and newspapers, the store features an old-fashioned peep-show type of "museum" where you pay a quarter and a curtain lifts to reveal, yes, big shoes. Outside on the store's wall is a painting of the world's tallest man.

Pike Place Gift Gallery
(206) 223-9430

Seattle T-shirts, baseball caps, mugs, and other tourist parapherna-lia are crammed in here.

Raven's Nest Treasures
(206) 343-0890

The curio shop offers fossils (including petrified dinosaur poop), Native art, and antique jewelry.

Sweetie's
(206) 467-4587

Get your sugar fix with a bag of candy you can munch as you walk along.

Second Floor Down Under

Charlotte's Web
(206) 292-9849

The place to go for miniature dolls, doll houses, and collectible figurines.

Grandma's Attic
(206) 682-9281

This is an ideal stop for decorat-ing a doll house, with a nice selec-tion of reasonably priced miniatures.

Silly Old Bear
(206) 623-2325

Aptly named, this charming little store carries all sorts of stuffed bears and bear stuff. Other mer-chandise includes gnomes, minia-tures, little books, tea sets, blocks, and stickers.

Tabula Rasa
(206) 682-2935

The antique and handmade miniature books will enchant kids.

Mezzanine Level

The Candy Store
(206) 625-0420

This place looks more like a junk shop than a candy store. A quick sampling, however, verified that the candy is as fresh and sweet as ever. A good place to get cotton candy.

Seattle Parrot Market
1500 Western Ave.
(206) 467-6133
www.speakeasy.org/parrots

This small and crowded bird store at the base of Pike Place Market should not be missed, despite the 50-cent browsing fee for non-member browsers (money collected goes to feeding the birds and critters and will be refunded if you make a purchase). Upstairs you will be greeted by the screaming caws and cheeps of a variety of different birds, including parrots and macaws. For a quarter you can buy seeds to feed to the birds, who, despite their menacing beaks, accept food very politely.

Economy Arcade
Just south of Main Arcade, running east-west from Pike Place to First Avenue.

Stamp Happy
(206) 682-8575

This tiny stand sells personalized stamps and rubber stamps.

Daily Dozen Doughnuts
(206) 467-7769

Kids will be charmed by these miniature doughnuts, which you can buy by the half-dozen. They'll also love watching the automatic machine, dubbed the "Donut Robot," making the treats.

Economy Market Atrium
Just south of Pike Street, accessible from First Avenue or Economy Row.

The Great Wind-Up
(206) 621-9370

The employees of The Great Wind-Up do more than ring up the sales—they keep about a dozen toys flipping, barking, walking, and hopping. The store claims to have the largest collection of wind-up and animated toys in the Northwest, a number of which can be tested on a counter exclusively for this purpose. The only problem is that the counter is high, even for an adult, so young kids will have to be lifted up to play (a clever ploy to make sure that patrons supervise their kids). The rest of the store has very specific signs posted, stating what kids can and cannot touch.

Post Alley Market
Opposite the Main Arcade, across Pike Place, Post Alley starts mid-block and cuts toward Pine Street.

Puzzletts
(206) 223-2340

Look for puzzles of all sorts and sizes.

Biringer Farm, Bakery, and Country Store
Post Alley Market
(206) 467-0383

If anyone in the family likes berries, you should know that this place has the best cobblers around. Biringer Farms also sells muffins, scones, soups, and treats, as well as scone mix, teas, sauces, and syrups.

Cinnamon Works
Triangle Building on Pike Place
(206) 583-0085

Who can resist fragrant cinnamon rolls, sticky buns, or cookies?

Chocolate and Ice Cream Delight
Soames-Dunn Building (opposite the North Arcade, midway between Stewart and Virginia Streets on Pike Place)
(206) 441-8877

This ice cream fountain offers all the rich traditional treats, as well as delicious frozen yogurt.

The Crumpet Shop
Corner Market Building
(northwest corner of First Avenue and Pike Street)
(206) 682-1598

The Crumpet Shop features a selection of teas, crumpets, scones, preserves, and other treats. With over 40 different crumpet toppings from which to choose (from jam to green eggs), everyone in the family should be sated. Two outdoor tables are available. A crumpet with butter and jam and a cup of tea run about $2.35.

Cucina Fresca
Stewart House (near the corner of Stewart and Pike Place)
(206) 448-4758

The take-out pastas, lasagna, cannelloni, breads, and foccaccia pizza are fresh and delicious.

Danny's Wonder Freeze
Economy Arcade
(206) 382-0932

Kids will enjoy the amusement-park-style fast food, including hot dogs and milkshakes.

DeLaurenti's Pizza Window
Economy Row and First Avenue, across from the Read All About It newsstand
(206) 622-0141

The delicious to-go pizza slices start at $1.25. Stop by their adjoining store if you need any Italian delicacies; the wonderful deli counter is replete with fresh Tuscan baguettes, cheeses, and meats, and the shelves bulge with a fine selection of olive oils and other specialties.

El Puerco Lloron
Hillclimb
(206) 624-0541

This little spot serves some of the most authentic, tasty, and reasonably priced Mexican food in the city. Finding a place to sit is a trick; send someone to grab a table while you stand in the cafeteria line to get the food.

La Vaca
First Avenue, just south of Economy Row
(206) 467-9262

There's always a long line at this take-out lunch spot that makes yummy fresh burritos "from scratch" and without lard.

Pike Place Bakery
Main Arcade
(206) 682-2829

Dieters beware: The bakery's enormous Texas doughnuts are

about the size of a tricycle wheel.

Pike Pub and Brewery
Economy Building
(206) 622-6044

INSIDE SCOOP Pike Place

Scott Davies, the Market's Public Information Specialist and school tour guide, offers these often-missed spots of interest and quirky facts:

■ Read All About It, in the Economy Arcade, sells magazines and newspapers from more than 35 states and 15 countries. A world map lights up the cities that the newspapers come from.

■ When you're in the Economy, Main, and North Arcades, look up. Hundreds of light bulbs line the ceiling. There are also different signs hanging up there.

■ "Rachel" the pig statue was modeled after a real pig from Whidbey Island. The real pig's hoofprint is in the cement next to the piggy bank.

■ At the very north end of the North Arcade, a map on the wall designates the spot where "Roll Call" is held at 9 a.m. daily. The Market Master tells farmers and craftspeople where they can sell that day.

■ More than 500 people live in the Market neighborhood, many of whom are low-income, elderly, or disabled.

■ In the Stewart House, stop in and say hello to Viola, the current owner of Trudy and Leno-

ra's Barber Shop, which has been run by women in her family for five generations. The window display shows photographs of the business's 60-year history in the Market.

■ The red musical notes painted on the walls at a dozen locations around the market have numbers inside telling how many performers are allowed to play in that spot at one time.

■ The Giving Tree, located on Flower Row, sells wooden toys handmade by homeless senior citizens.

■ The benches in seating areas around the Market were made by the same artist, who used recycled materials such as old tractor seats.

■ In the Post Alley seating area (across from Seattle's Best Coffee), check out the cement on the ground. When the concrete was poured, the workers incorporated plates, mugs, and cups. Portions can be seen sticking out.

■ In Upper Post Alley, at the south end of the Market in the alley near Il Bistro, you can see where the cobblestones of the old street (1910) meet the new road (1980), an interesting juxtaposition. This is the southern boundary of the Market Historic District.

Even if they can't drink beer, kids will probably be fascinated by all the equipment required to make it. The shiny metallic vats, pipes, nozzles, and gauges should keep them interested until the food arrives. The gourmet food isn't cheap: Sandwiches are $6.95 and up; salads begin at $7.95. The pizza dough is made from spent grain and features such toppings as artichoke hearts, shrimp, and goat cheese. Most meals come with a bread basket. Kids' meals (crayons provided, of course) are $2.95 for a hot dog, etc. Be warned: They don't have French fries. Guided tours of the brewery production cellars are also offered.

Piroshky-Piroshky
Stewart House
(206) 441-6068

The pastries are stuffed with 15 different fillings, from cabbage to smoked salmon. The Moscow breakfast roll is good (just don't tell kids it has Cream of Wheat in it).

Rasa Malaysia
Sanitary Market (opposite the Main Arcade, north of the Corner Market Building)
(206) 624-8388

Rasa Malaysia's take-out counter serves up delicious noodle and vegetable dishes, as well as tasty barbecued pork and chicken. Prices are $3 to $4.50 per dish.

Shy Giant Frozen Yogurt and Ice Cream
Corner Market Building
(206) 622-1988

Shy Giant was one of the West Coast's first frozen yogurt shops.

Three Girls Bakery
Sanitary Market
(206) 622-1045
Hours: Mon.-Sat., 7 a.m.-6 p.m.

Three Girls Bakery, one of the oldest businesses in the Market, bakes its own breads and other goodies and makes some of the biggest and best sandwiches in town. Don't bother trying to get a counter seat with the kids—it is much too popular, especially at lunch time. Soups are also delicious.

Pike Place Hillclimb
The long set of stairs connects the Market and the waterfront.

THE WATERFRONT

On the downtown Seattle water-front you'll find the good, the bad, and the ugly. Stand on Pier 62 facing Elliott Bay and feast your eyes on the sparkling waters and the glorious Olympic Mountains beyond. Remind your kids that over one hundred years ago Native Americans used this very spot for landing their boats. Notice the bustling seagoing traffic and the picturesque ferries.

Now turn around and behold the ugly—the Alaskan Way Viaduct, a dinosaur of a freeway that crudely interrupts downtown's graceful slope to the water and serves as a hideous and noisy testimony to the price of urban nonplanning.

The bad side of this strip that marries land to sea is the endless assortment of shops filled with mounds of schlock. But don't be discouraged; despite this area's hel-ter-skelter development, or perhaps because of it, there is plenty to see and do here with kids. The Seattle waterfront is a splendid place to spend an afternoon, and if being close to the water just isn't enough, you can extend your adventure by hopping on a ferry or one of the other boats taking off from various piers.

TIPS

Watch kids extra carefully when walking the Seattle waterfront: The guardrails next to the water are not childproof.

You may view the endless tourist shops as pure torment, but many school-age kids are thrilled to putter around a store full of cute and useless items. Be sure to clearly spell out the shopping budget before you get inside the first store. If you have a young child, skip the shops and go straight to the carousel (Pier 57), the aquarium, or the ferry dock.

The half-mile walk between Pier 48 and Pier 59 covers the most interesting and entertaining segment of this area. If you decide to head farther north to Pier 70's shops or Myrtle Edwards Park, either prepare yourself and the kids for a rather boring walk, or jump aboard the trolley.

STEPHANIE DUNNEWIND

The Waterfront Trolley is an easy and fun way to transport kids.

If you think your fellow explorers have the stamina, the best way to see the waterfront is to walk. Ride the Waterfront Streetcar (commonly called the trolley) in one direction and then stroll back, or if you're not sure how far little ones will go, walk first and then take the trolley back.. On your promenade you'll find public art, countless shops, maritime traffic to distract and entertain you, and plenty of tasty food and invigorating salt air.

The most interesting segment of the waterfront extends from the south end at Pier 48 (at the base of Washington Street) to the north end at Pier 70 (at the base of Broad Street). One suggestion is to park near the base of the Pike Place Hillclimb, across the street from the Seattle Aquarium (Pier 59), and then climb aboard the southbound trolley at the Pike station. Disembark at the Washington Street station and cross the road to Pier 48, about a half-mile walk from your car. If you prefer, you can park at the north end at Pier 70, by Myrtle Edwards Park, ride the trolley the length of the waterfront, and extend your walk back by another half mile.

Though you're sure to occasionally sink deep into touristville on your waterfront tour, you will just as often be charmed by the beauty and rich history of this area and amazed at its outstanding offerings: a first-rate aquarium, several charming parks, and countless stunning vistas.

ESSENTIALS

Metro's bright green Waterfront Streetcar offers connections between Pier 70 and the International District, with nine stops along the way. You can ride along the waterfront on Alaskan Way to Main Street, then through Pioneer Square to the edge of the International District at Fifth Avenue and S. Jackson. The kids will love the noise and commotion of the ride. A transfer allows you to hop back on for free if you ride within two hours. The conductors are very helpful with information on what sites are located at each stop and directing you to your destination. The Waterfront Streetcar operates daily year-round, every 20 to 30 minutes; seasonal hours vary. Fares are: $1/adults non-rush hour, $1.25 rush hour; 75 cents/children ages 5-17 at all times; free/children age 4 and under.

If fatigue sets in on your outing, you can hitch a ride on Casual Cabs, bicycle cabs that cover the waterfront and Pioneer Square area. Cost averages about $10 for a 10-minute ride. Horse-drawn carriages also run up and down here.

Parking is available at the meters that run along under the Alaskan Way Viaduct, but have your quarters handy: They cost $1/hour, and take only quarters. Sundays are free. There are also several parking lots on Western Avenue, one block off the waterfront, and a parking garage across the street from the Aquarium is handy if you plan to use the Hillclimb stairs to extend your tour to the Pike Place Market.

Pier 48

At the Washington Street Public Boat Landing, take the time to look over the fine totem pole that sits inside the park and to read the historical plaques on the guard railings.

Pier 50–Pier 53

Pier 50 marks the beginning of Colman Dock, the terminal for ferries heading to Bremerton on the Kitsap Peninsula, Bainbridge Island, and Vashon Island (passenger only).

Just north of the terminal, on Pier 53, sits Fire Station No. 5, home of two magnificent fireboats,

the "Alki" and the "Chief Seattle." On summer days you might see the fireboats out in the bay spraying their hoses up toward the sky in a majestic waterworks display.

Washington State Ferries
(206) 464-6400 or (800) 843-3779
Season: Operates year-round
Tickets: $2.30-$3.50/walk-on passengers, $4.80-$7.10/vehicle and driver; schedules and rates vary for each route

Operating the largest ferry system in the United States, the Washington State Ferries connect island and peninsula communities throughout the Puget Sound region. Colman Dock at Pier 52 is the Seattle terminus for the Bainbridge, Bremerton, and Vashon routes. Passengers can ride aboard a variety of boats within the fleet, from the smallest passenger-only ferry, which carries 250 people, to the jumbo ferry, which carries 2,000 people and 206 cars! The shortest Seattle-based ride is the 15-minute run between Fauntleroy (in West Seattle) and Vashon Island. The longest is the Seattle-to-Bremerton run, which lasts just about one hour.

TIPS

Parking the car and walking onto the Seattle–to–Bainbridge ferry is a great outing with a kid (and a fine way to show off Seattle to out–of–town visitors). The ride is an easy 30 minutes, and the town of Winslow is a short stroll from the ferry dock. Take a morning ferry and enjoy a scrumptious breakfast at the Stream–liner Diner (397 Winslow Way E., 206–842–8595). Winslow hosts a farmers market every Saturday from May through October.

ESSENTIALS

Passengers are welcome to bring their own food on board or enjoy something from the cafeteria (the food is quite good and reasonably priced). There is even a children's meal packaged in a "ferry box" to take home.

Pier 54–Pier 57

At Pier 54 the tourist shops begin in earnest. If you are determined not to shop, either walk briskly or jump on a tour boat. Otherwise, summon up your patience and take the kids in for some fun browsing.

Argosy Cruises

Departs from Piers 55 and 57, AGC Marina (on Lake Union), and Marina Park (Kirkland)
(206) 623-4252
www.seattleonline.com/argosy
Tickets: Cruise the Locks, $11-$22/person; One-Hour Harbor Tour, $6.50-$13.50/person; Lake Washington Cruise, $8.75-$17/person
Children under 5 are free for all tours
Group rates available
Call to confirm seasonal departure times

You don't need out-of-town guests to embark on a boat tour of the city. Kids will delight in going under, rather than over, familiar bridges and picking out landmarks they have grown accustomed to viewing from a different angle. The narratives are lively and informative—even native Seattleites will probably learn something new about their hometown.

The two-and-one-half-hour Cruise the Locks tour is the most interesting of the three excursions offered by Argosy Cruises, the highlight being a trip through the Hiram M. Chittenden Locks. You'll also cruise through Lake Union, the Fremont cut, Shilshole Bay, around West Point, and along Elliott Bay to Pier 57 on the Seattle waterfront, plus take a 15-minute ride aboard a motor coach between Chandler's Cove on Lake Union and Pier 57. Tours depart daily year-round from Pier 57.

The Harbor Tour is a one-hour trip along the Seattle waterfront around Elliott Bay, including the shipyards and Duwamish Waterway. This tour offers a fascinating look at the downtown waterfront, a central part of Seattle's identity that is easily overlooked when traveling by land. Tours depart daily year-round from Pier 55.

The two-hour Lake Washington Cruise from Seattle covers the historic houseboat district of Lake Union, Portage Bay, and the huge homes that line the lake. Tours depart from AGC Marina on Lake Union daily year-round. For a look from the Eastside, take the one-and-one-half-hour tour that departs from Kirkland's Marina Park year-round and offers a look at the affluent residential developments on the east side of the lake along the Kirkland shoreline, Yarrow Point, Medina (where Bill Gates' new home is located), and Meydenbauer Bay. A quick crossing to the western shore gives a water view of Husky Stadium at the University of Washington, along with some interesting narrative about the two floating bridges that cross the lake.

Tillicum Village Tour

Departs from Piers 55 and 56
(206) 443-1244

Season: Operates year-round; seasonal departure times vary
Tickets: $50.25/adults, $32.50/teens ages 13-19, $20/children ages 6-12, $10/children ages 4-5, free/children age 3 and under

Just eight miles from Seattle in Puget Sound lies Blake Island, a Washington state park featuring nearly 500 acres of natural forest and beaches that is accessible only by boat. It is also home to Tillicum Village, where guests can enjoy a baked salmon dinner, a Native American stage production, and arts and crafts demonstrations. Some adults are put off by the "touristy" style of the tour, but most school-age children consider the trip a fun and memorable treat.

The four-hour Tillicum Village tour departs from the Seattle waterfront, featuring a narrated tour of Elliott Bay and the city's busy port facilities on the way to Blake.

Once you reach the island, you head for Tillicum Village's huge cedar longhouse, where a complete salmon dinner (baked over an alderwood fire) awaits you. Following dinner, you and your family are treated to music, dances, and legends of the Northwest Coast Indians.

On select days between June and September, Tillicum Village offers a Hiker Special, featuring an additional two and one-half hours of time on the island to explore its 16 miles of hiking trails. Wildlife is abundant on Blake Island, with over 50 deer as well as eagles and mink. Additional attractions include a gift shop, five miles of beaches,

cultural displays, and arts and crafts. Reservations are recommended.

Let's Go Sailing
Emerald City Charters
(206) 624-3931
Cost: $20-$35/adults, $15-$28/children under age 12
Season: Spring-fall

Take a one-and-a-half-hour harbor sailing excursion or a two-and-a-half-hour sunset sail on a 70-foot performance yacht. Passengers can help sail or just sit and enjoy the trip.

Pier 54 Adventures
(206) 623-6364
Cost: $7-$35/person

The "Seattle Rocket" speed boat takes passengers on a 30- minute high-speed tour of the bay. For a more leisurely pace, two-hour day sails and three-hour sunset cruises are offered on the "Spray," a 60-foot replica of the ship used in the first solo circumnavigation of the world. The company also offers kayak and bike rentals, seaplane rides, and salmon fishing trips.

Ye Olde Curiosity Shop
Pier 54
(206) 682-5844

You can give your child a glimpse of the bizarre and mysterious side of the world with a visit to Ye Olde Curiosity Shop. Since 1899, this one-of-a-kind place has fascinated waterfront visitors, and your child will probably be talking about it long after you go home. Don't be put off by all the souvenir stuff; instead, head to the back of the store to see the weird attractions that make this a place for the curious indeed. You'll find fully dressed fleas, two shrunken heads, two mummies, and a bean that will hold 10 ivory elephants.

Waterfront Landmark
Pier 55
(206) 622-3939

For $1, your kids can take home a scoop of tiny shells at the front of this shop. Delicious fudge is made and sold at the rear of the store, so depending on your parental position on candy, either head for or steer clear of this area.

Elliott's Oyster House and Seafood Restaurant
Pier 56
(206) 623-4340

Elliott's offers seasonal outdoor dining on the pier.

Ivar feeds the seagulls outside the restaurant.

Ivar's Acres of Clams
Pier 54
(206) 624-6852

Enjoy tasty fish and chips and creamy clam chowder outside under cover (be ready to share with the seagulls) or go inside for a delicious salmon meal (see "Restaurants" in Chapter 11). The kids will like the sculpture of Ivar and his friends, the seagulls, that sits just outside the take-out fish bar.

Red Robin Express
Pier 55
(206) 624-3969

Buy an exceptionally good burger to take outside and enjoy at a table on the pier. If you want a wider selection, dine inside; the restaurant has a very good children's menu.

Steamers Seafood Cafe
Pier 56
(206) 623-2066

Steamers purveys fish and chips, plus ice cream for dessert.

The Frankfurter
Pier 55
(206) 622-1748

The hot dogs and thirst-quenching fresh-squeezed lemonade are the best in the city. Take-out only.

Pier 57–Pier 59

The Bay Pavilion on Pier 57 is home to several shops, the Seattle Sourdough Baking Company (which sells delicious breads), and a hidden delight, a grand old carousel. Merry-go-round rides are $1; popcorn, cookies, and drinks are sold nearby. Be warned you'll probably get hit up for quarters for the surrounding video and skill games.

Waterfront Park on Pier 59 has ample space to run (no grass) and plenty of places to sit. With an unparalleled view of the water and mountains, it is a fine place to rest and revive before visiting the outstanding Seattle Aquarium, located just to the north. Note the plaque on the railing above the park commemorating the landing of the "Portland" in 1897. It was loaded with about two tons of gold from the Klondike and lit the fuse for the gold rush that was to blast Seattle out of its early economic slump.

Access to the Pike Place Market via the stairs (called the Pike Place Hillclimb) is across the street from the north end of the Aquarium. There's also an elevator in the parking garage near the stairs that will take you to the Market.

The Seattle Aquarium and the Omnidome Theatre
Pier 59
(206) 386-4320 (aquarium); 206-622-1868 (Omnidome)
See Chapter 1 for details.

The Bay Pavilion holds several shops and eateries, in addition to a bakery, cafe with ice cream, and Seattle Fudge.

The Crab Pot
(206) 624-1890
The menu lists burgers and seafood for $5 and up; kids' meals are $3.

The Fisherman's Restaurant
(206) 623-3500
Come here for seafood dining with a view of the water. Lunches are in the $6 to $14 range, dinners are $13 and up.

Michelanglo's
Pasta, pizza, and sandwiches here go for $6 to $8.

Pavilion Food Court
A collection of take-out restaurants sits on top of the Pavilion. Open seasonally.

Steamers
Pier 59
(206) 624-0312
Steamers is a good place to grab fish and chips before you go into the Aquarium or the Omnidome.

Pier 62–Pier 63

Piers 62 and 63 are designated as "open space." They are the site of the popular "Concerts on the Dock" series held every summer. Call Ticketmaster, (206) 628-0888, for information.

This is a good place to end your walking tour if your group is running out of steam.

Pier 66

The Bell Street Pier houses the international conference center, retail shops, and several small restaurants, including **Bell Street Deli** (206-441-6907), **Anthony's Fish Bar**, **Bell Street Diner**, and the upscale **Pier 66** (all but the deli are operated by the Anthony's restaurant chain; 206-448-6688).

Odyssey: The Maritime Discovery Center

Pier 66
(206) 374-4001
www.discoverodyssey.org

Scheduled to open in July 1998, the new maritime center will feature interactive exhibits to educate visitors about the sea and its economic importance to Seattle and Puget Sound. (See the "Museums" section in Chapter 7 for more details.) Even if you don't visit the museum, check out the "Sea Totems," whimsical kinetic sculptures, through Odyssey's 40-foot-tall front window.

Pier 70

(206) 441-4668

At Pier 70 the shopping and snacking may be resumed. This lovely old building, which was built in 1910 as a terminal for ocean liners, is being renovated. Work should be finished by 1999 and will include new restaurants and shops. If you are at all up for it, and the kids aren't too crabby, browse through Pier 1 Imports. Then head over to Myrtle Edwards Park for a refreshing stroll to complete your waterfront tour.

Victoria Clipper

Pier 69
(206) 448-5000
Tickets: $89-$109/round-trip adults (fares vary according to the season), children's fares are half the adult's. Packages that include hotel are available.

Victoria, B.C., is a fabulous place to visit with a school-age child, either for a day or overnight. The trip takes two to three hours each way, and there is plenty to see and do within easy walking distance of the Inner Harbour, where the "Clipper" docks.

It is worth going to Victoria for a day just to visit the outstanding Royal British Columbia Museum (675 Belleville St.; 250-387-3014) located a half block away from the Clipper terminal. It is one of the finest natural and historical museums in the world. On the second floor you can walk through spectacular dioramas with authentic sounds and smells of such places as the seashore and a coastal rain forest. A history section features full-scale working models of a sawmill, coal mine, and gold-sluicing operation, as well as a full-scale Victorian town. The reconstructed hull of Captain George Vancouver's H.M.S. "Discovery" is astonishing in its realism. In an outstanding exhibit on Native Canadian history and culture, visitors can sit in a longhouse and hear the sounds of the village. If kids are at all claustrophobic, skip the underwater simulation. The museum is open daily, 10 a.m.-5:30 p.m. Cost is $5.35/adults, $2.14/children ages 6-18, free/children age 5 and under.

The Royal London Wax Museum (205-388-4461) is also located near the harbor; watch out for the truly gruesome Chamber of Horrors.

Other Clipper trips include a day excursion to the San Juan Islands, visiting Friday Harbor and traveling through Deception Pass. Cost is $59/adults, $29.50/children.

Old Spaghetti Factory

2801 Elliott

(206) 441-7724

See the "Restaurants" section in Chapter 11.

PIONEER SQUARE

The history of Pioneer Square is one of the more interesting tales of Seattle, one that will likely prompt even the most distracted youngster to stand still and listen, for at least 30 seconds. From the city's incorporation in 1869 to the late 1880s, it was a thriving business district, where most of Seattle's 40,000 residents lived and worked. But on June 6, 1889, a furniture maker in the area left a pot of glue on a hot stove unattended, resulting in a huge fire that burned the young city to ashes in mere hours.

The real capper of the story (sure to keep your child's attention for an additional 15 seconds) is that you and your family can still visit the Seattle of the late 1800s—at least what remains of it! Because of the Great Fire, and a poorly planned sewage system, the community decided to rebuild the city atop the old one, and, in effect, raised the street level by one story. The old city is still accessible by guided tour and can be seen through some of the

ESSENTIALS

Pioneer Square has plenty of parking meters and parking lots, but they fill up if there's an event at the Kingdome. Probably the easiest place to park is under the Alaskan Way viaduct. If you leave your car along the waterfront, you can catch the Waterfront Streetcar to Pioneer Square from as far north as Pier 70. The stop is between Occidental Mall and Occidental Park.

sidewalk grates in the area.

Today, Pioneer Square is one of Seattle's most diverse and architecturally impressive areas, a neighborhood full of landmarks, galleries, funky shops, and restaurants. It extends north from the Kingdome to Cherry Street, and from Alaskan Way east to Second Avenue, encompassing some of the most exquisite architecture of stone and brick in the city. Don't forget to look up when walking around Pioneer Square, as the art extends far above eye level.

Around Occidental Park

This is where you'll be if you take the trolley. If you park under the viaduct, walk up S. Main or S. Washington to Occidental. (To make things confusing, the street order from west to east is First Avenue, Occidental, and then Second Avenue.) Or walk up S. Main to First Avenue and head north to James Street. Check out Pioneer Place (see next section for more information), then head east on Yesler Way to Occidental, then walk south on Occidental to the park.

Occidental Park
Between S. Main and S. Washington on Occidental

Situated in the center of historic

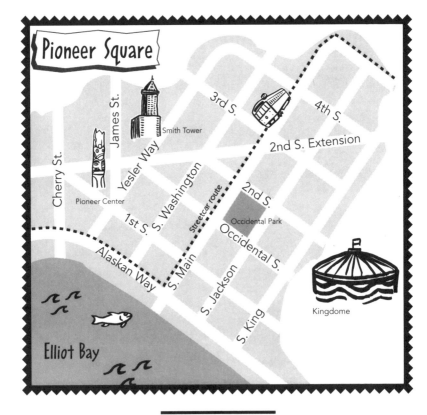

Pioneer Square, this cobblestoned area is the site of summer concerts and the Seattle Fire Festival in June (see Chapter 10). Central to its decor are a pergola, several benches, and four totem carvings, including "Tsonqua" (a welcoming spirit) and the tall, thick "Sun and Raven" pole. The transient population here may be intimidating on some days.

Next to Occidental Park is **Grand Central Arcade** (214 First Ave. S.), which you enter through two big doors. (There are also side entrances on Main Street and First Avenue S.) The two-story complex houses a few shops and restaurants, as well as a sitting area with a fireplace and scattered tables.

Food options include delicious breads and sandwiches from **The Grand Central Bakery and Deli**

STEPHANIE DUNNEWIND

Totem poles mark Occidental Park.

TIPS

■ During the summer months, an information booth in Pioneer Square at Occidental S. and S. Main is open from 10 a.m.–6 p.m. daily, offering directions, suggestions, and literature about the area.

■ Even if the booth is closed, you can pick up a free "Discovering Pioneer Square" guide and map at most stores.

■ Don't be caught off-guard by the number of panhandlers in Pioneer Square. Seattle's bicycle police keep an eye out for any trouble, so you shouldn't feel intimidated. Local businesses ask the community not to give money to these transients. You'll likely support a bad habit instead of a worthy cause. Give instead to charities or missions that help the homeless.

■ If you and the little ones are exploring on foot, note that First Avenue gets pretty boring south of Jackson, and the scene gets slightly scary between Second Avenue and the International District.

■ Two annual events are the Fat Tuesday celebration in February and the Fire Festival in June, which features clowns, antique fire trucks, and children's activities.

(206-622-3644). During the summer you can eat outside in the park. Downstairs you can watch the bakers at work through large glass windows.

Shops include **Paper Cat** (206-623-3636), with hundreds of stamps and stickers, plus one of the best assortments of stationery items. **Underdog Sports Cards** (206-682-6610) features all sorts of collector's cards. **Tom Foolery Pottery**

School (206-343-9879) offers pottery classes and workshops for adults and children.

Occidental Mall
Between S. Main and S. Jackson on Occidental

Across the street from Occidental Park is a red-bricked pedestrian mall lined with galleries, restaurants, and trees. A seasonal information booth is located at the north

TIPS

Pioneer Square is the hub of gallery activity in Seattle. If you want to explore the galleries with your child, avoid First Thursday, the monthly event when new exhibits open and galleries don't close until late evening, attracting throngs of Black Turtleneck People. Don't feel too intimidated, however, to go during the week; just be sure to keep the following recommendations in mind.

The first, of course, is to use common sense. If your child does not respond to the words "Don't touch," he is not ready for the gallery experience, unless you want to start an expensive collection of damaged art. Best to teach your child to regard the entire gallery as a piece of art. That means no hands on the walls and no climbing around on ledges or stairs.

Second, if you have more than one child in the 2- to 8-year-old range, arrange to take only one.

Third, don't take your child to more galleries than his creative intellect can swallow. Choose a weekday, or weekend day, when the galleries aren't apt to be too crowded, and go through two or three. There are a lot of shops in between galleries that have fun, brightly decorated windows to peer into, and several areas to share a snack and discuss what you've seen.

Finally, realize that most of the gallery owners in Pioneer Square agree that "well-behaved" children are welcome guests and that part of a gallery's function is educational. Check the local paper for reviews of current exhibits after the first of each month.

end of the mall.

Check out **Glasshouse Studio and Gallery** (311 Occidental; 206-682-9939) to watch glassblowers in action. Though this may seem like the last place you'd want to venture into with your kids, the studio is one of the more kid-friendly galleries in this area. Glass-blowing hours are Mon.-Sat., 10 a.m.-3 p.m.; Sun., 11 a.m.-3 p.m. The staff always takes the time to answer any questions, and occasionally the glassblowers themselves take a break to talk with visitors.

Farther down, past S. Jackson Street, you'll find the **Great Winds Kite Shop** (402 Occidental S.; 206-624-6886) tucked between galleries and boasting a good selection of high flyers, big and small, simple and elaborate. Sports fans will be impressed by the wide selection of team T-shirts, hats, and related items at **The Seattle Sport** (901 Occidental; 206-624-9569).

Klondike Gold Rush National Historical Park

117 S. Main
(206) 553-7220
Hours: Open daily, 9 a.m.-5 p.m.
Admission: Free

Just a little way down from the Occidental Park trolley stop is this little museum, set up by the National Park Service. It documents the Klondike gold rush of the late 1800s through a number of different media. (See the "Museums" section of Chapter 7.)

Seattle Fire Department Headquarters

Corner of S. Main and Second Ave.
(206) 386-1400

The station is not set up for drop-in guests, but half-hour tours can be arranged in advance. If you're just passing by, check out the sculptures of firefighters that decorate the exterior corners of the building.

> ### ESSENTIALS
> The station has a very convenient public rest room on the Main Street side.

Waterfall Park

Corner of S. Main and Second Ave., across from the fire station

Heading east from Occidental Park, you wouldn't guess this small place is a park because of the large surrounding fence. Though it is privately maintained, it is open to the public and provides a nice, peaceful setting for a snack. It marks the site of the original offices of United Parcel Service. With several fountains, the park's main feature is (yep!) a waterfall. Use it as a bargaining tool, if you want some time for your own shopping: "Just let me go into this one last shop, and then we'll go see the . . ."

Pioneer Place and First Avenue

You'll probably walk past **Pioneer Place** without noticing it. But the triangular area, where Yesler Way, First Avenue, and James

Waterfall Park is a small oasis.

Street intersect, is where the word "pioneer" really comes into play. Adorned with a 1905 pergola, it marks the site of Seattle's first settlement.

Underground Tour

610 First Ave. S.
(206) 682-4646 or (888) 608-6337
www.undergroundtour.com
Season: Tours daily year-round
Tickets: $6.50/adults,
$5.50/seniors, $5/students ages 13-17, $2.75/children ages 6-12. Children age 5 and under might find the tour too challenging

This 90-minute tour takes you beneath Pioneer Square to see what's left of 1889 Seattle. As stated previously, Pioneer Square was literally rebuilt over the old city, after the Great Seattle Fire of 1889. The tours are offered daily, year-round, and include many interesting histori-

cal facts (as well as several corny jokes). Reservations are suggested, as tours fill quickly; advance reservations are required for groups. Arrive at least 20 minutes early. The tour is not wheelchair or stroller accessible; wear comfortable walking shoes. Be warned that some kids don't find this tour at all interesting; it requires a penchant for history, a vivid imagination, and an appreciation of subterranean scents and scenes.

Across the street from Pioneer Place is **Magic Mouse Toys** (603 First Ave.; 206-682-8097), a two-story toy store with a wide assortment of art supplies, games, collectibles, and toys. One small room is devoted entirely to puzzles. Nearby, a very good, but often missed, book selection is tucked downstairs in the back of the store. The staff is knowledgeable and amicable; kids are welcome and encouraged to do what comes naturally: play!

North, the only store of interest is **Metsker Maps** (702 First Ave.; 206-623-8747), and that's mainly for geography fans. It's full of maps, globes, atlases, and travel books.

Heading south toward the Kingdome, First Avenue is lined with shops, restaurants, and seedy hotels. Some highlights:

Animation U.S.A. (104 First Ave. S.; 206-625-0347) is a small gallery that sells comic-strip stats and cartoon "cels" from all the major animation studios, including Hanna Barbera, Disney, and Warner Bros. The bright colors and familiar characters will surely enchant your child, but don't expect cheap art. The pieces are very spendy.

The Elliott Bay Book Company (101 S. Main St.; 206-624-6600; www.elliottbaybook.com/ebbco) is a favorite bookstore of local literary buffs. It boasts a large kids' book section, complete with a two-story castle where kids can relax and read their selections. Elliott Bay also has a good storytelling program for children; call for the latest schedule. Downstairs, a gourmet cafe/deli sells delectable scones, muffins, salads, and sandwiches.

Other stores of note include **Sports Den** (319 First Ave. S.; 206-624-2550), **Wood Shop Toys** (320 First Ave.; 206-624-1763), and the **Seattle Seahawks EndZone Store** (88 S. King St.; 206-682-2900).

Snacks/Restaurants

You won't go hungry on First Avenue, which offers an assortment of pizza places, snack shops, sweets, and sit-down restaurants. If you didn't carbo load at Grand Central Bakery at Pioneer Square, stop in at **A La Francaise Bakery** (417 First Ave.; 206-624-0322) for heavenly breads. **The Candy Barrel** (First Ave. and Yesler Way; 206-624-5542) will sate any sweet tooth; so will a giant cookie from **Cow Chip Cookies** (102-A First Ave.; 206-292-9808). **Walter's Waffles and Snack Cafe** (106 James St.; 206-382-2692) features "Serious Snack Waffles, Hot to Go." Walter should add the words "delicious" and "inexpensive" to his description.

Other Area Attractions
Kingdome
201 S. King St.
(206) 296-3128; www.kingdome.org
Hours: Mon.-Sat., 11 a.m., and 1 and 3 p.m., mid-April through late September; holiday tours in mid- to late December 1998; call to confirm in 1999
Admission: $5/adults, $2.50/children ages 6-12 and seniors, free/children age 5 and under

This is your last chance to tour the Seattle landmark. Scheduled to be torn down in 2000 to make way for the new Seahawks football stadium, the Kingdome offers one-hour behind-the-scenes public tours of the playing field, a locker room, the press box, and the luxury lounge. The Kingdome Sports Museum features a collection of sports memorabilia dating back to the 19th century.

Smith Tower
Second Ave. S. and Yesler Way
(206) 622-4004

Though the elevator at the 42-story Smith Tower was closed to

Visit the Kingdome before it's too late.

the public for most of 1997, tours are slated to begin again in spring 1998. Hours and cost had not been determined as of publication. Call for more information and to confirm operations.

The Smith Tower was built between 1911 and 1914, and was, at that time, the tallest building west of the Mississippi. The entire building was constructed with various stones and metals, in a pyrophobic attempt to make the building fire resistant.

When the lift is open, it offers one of the best elevator rides in Seattle. The attendant will give you a brief rundown of the Smith Tower's history on the way up, but your kids will likely be more captivated by his actions than his words. This is a true, old-fashioned elevator—metal gate and all—run not by pushing buttons, but by maneuvering a brass lever. The shaft and pulley are visible from inside, a thrilling sight for aspiring engineers. When you get out on the 35th floor, look to the right of the elevator and you will see the Otis elevator motor that just pulled you up.

Rialto Movie Art
81 1/2 S. Washington St., lower level; (206) 622-5099)

Warp back to the 1970s with movie posters, TV show collectibles, Pez dispensers, and original period dolls.

Ruby Montana's Pinto Pony
(800) 788-7829; rubymontana.com

The wacky store, which sells some of the best knickknacks in

TIPS

North of Smith Tower on Yesler Way is the Pioneer Square Station downtown transit tunnel, with underground bus service south to the International District Station and north to the Westlake Center. You can ride buses between Jackson and Battery streets and the waterfront and Sixth Avenue free all day.

town for kids and adults, had to leave its Pioneer Square location in spring 1998. It hadn't found a new home as of this printing, so call for the new address. Store items include small toys, funky gadgets, 1950s kitsch, and antique salt and pepper shakers.

A friendly dragon decorates a wall at Hing Hay Park.

INTERNATIONAL DISTRICT / CHINATOWN

Between Fifth Ave. S.
and 12th Ave. S.
S. Dearborn St. to W. Washington St.

Shops, businesses, and restaurants representing all Asian cultures—Chinese, Japanese, Korean, Vietnamese, Filipino, Thai, and others—anchor this dilapidated but spirited section of town.

Though the International District's boundaries are somewhat defined, there is no dragon gate to say you've arrived, no tourist strip that contains all the must-see shops and sights, and no 24-hour bustling crowd. Instead, it is a scattered, undeveloped treasure of Seattle, with some highlights and an overwhelm-

ing amount of potential. Make sure to point out the details on the street lamps and phone booths to your children, and plan on holding up the younger ones so that they can see some of the more lively store windows, especially along the north side of S. King Street, where they'll come face to glass with large fish,

TIPS

We don't recommend going on a leisurely tour in the early evening or after dark, because the area is fairly desolate and can be intimidating. However, this shouldn't stop you from taking the kids to one of its many great restaurants for dinner.

roasted delicacies, and other colorful spectacles. Note also some of the colorful portals and balconies along Seventh Avenue S.

Chinatown Discovery Tours

419 Seventh Ave. S.
(206) 236-0657
Tickets: $9.95-$34.95/adults,
$6.95-$19.95/children, based on
tour of four adults or more

The Chinatown Discovery Tours were started by Vi Mar, a prominent Chinese woman, to educate people and to promote understanding, acceptance, and support of the city's Asian community. She offers several different tour packages, including the one-and-a-half-hour Touch of Chinatown; the one-and-a-half-hour Chinatown by Day, featuring a six-course dim sum lunch; the two-hour Nibble Your Way through Chinatown; and the three-and-a-half-hour Chinatown by Night, with an eight-course banquet. Tours are also offered for schools and youth groups.

With 128 nieces and nephews,

and three children of her own, Vi is no stranger to children, and she spends the first part of the tour (which is spent in the office) getting the kids' minds in motion—asking pointed questions and engaging them with stories of her own experiences as a Chinese woman born and raised in the area.

Though the walking part of the tour is short, Vi says she will tailor the tour to cover whatever interests the group, so be sure to state your expectations up front, especially if you wish to spend more time exploring the area.

Danny Woo International District Community Garden

Kobe Terrace Park
S. Main and Maynard Ave. S.

In 1976, Seattle's Japanese sister city, Kobe, gave the International District a stone lantern, with the stated hope that it would "shed light on the friendship between the peoples of Kobe and Seattle forever." The cement lantern, which sits upon a bed of rocks, is not going to make your kids jump up and down with excitement, but the walk through the park and the Danny Woo Community Garden below is entertaining enough. The garden does exhibit a certain charm, with its winding cobblestone and gravel paths, and small produce gardens.

Hing Hay Park

S. King and Maynard Ave. S.

Marked by an ornate red and orange pavilion, which was donated by the Taiwanese government, Hing

Hay Park is a central gathering place for people—and pigeons. Hing Hay means "good fortune" in Chinese, and maybe if your family has a seat on one of the many benches in this red-bricked park, some luck will rub off on you.

Check out the colorful wall mural on the north side of the park, which tells the history of Asians in Seattle, from their early efforts in building the railroads to their modern-day involvement in the community. Kids will notice the primary figure in the mural is a dragon—a powerful but good symbol in this piece.

International Children's Park
S. Lane St. and Seventh Ave. S.

If you are exploring the area with young children, take them to this little park for a break. The park, which is primarily a big sandbox, features a winding slide, a bridge, some big climbing rocks, and a dragon sculpture kids can sit on (with a little help). There is a small patch of grass and several benches. Don't bother heading farther south of this park if you're on foot.

Wing Luke Museum
407 Seventh Ave. S.
(206) 623-5124
Hours: Tues.-Fri., 11 a.m.-4:30 p.m.; Sat.-Sun., 12-4 p.m.
Admission: $2.50/adults, $1.50/seniors and students, 75 cents/children ages 5-12 years, free/all ages on Thursdays
Annual membership: $50/family

The Wing Luke Asian Museum showcases the many contributions of Seattle's Asian cultures and their diversity. Part of the museum is devoted to teaching people about the hardships and discrimination Asians have suffered here, an important and sometimes forgotten chapter of history that kids should learn. (See the "Museums" section of Chapter 7.)

Uwajimaya
519 Sixth Ave. S.
(206) 624-6248
Free one-hour parking in lot

Even if you're not out of canned bananas, dried fish, or Thai chiles, Uwajimaya is an irresistible stop in the International District. Whether you take your kids down the food aisles to show them the culinary delights of Japan, China, Korea, or the Philippines, or take them upstairs to see the colorful assortment of dolls, stationery, and textiles, this place is sure to arouse their curiosity.

A trip to Uwajimaya is never complete without examining some of the less familiar fruits and vegetables; visiting the live geoduck, crab, and clam tanks; sampling the fresh sushi (or at least watching the sushi chefs in action); and browsing through the book area. The books and magazines, sold on the upper level of the store, have an amazing visual appeal, with most titles in elegant characters instead of English letters, and covers that open on the left instead of the right. If you're hungry, check out the small restaurant and deli.

As you walk around, notice the packaging and labels on soda, candies, and toys (three things bound to appeal to the kids) and treat everyone to a box of rice candy as you leave—they won't believe they can eat the transparent wrapping!

Tsue Chong Noodle Co.
801 S. King St.
(206) 623-0801

The company, which has been operated by four generations of the Louie family since 1917, makes 19 kinds of Chinese noodles and fortune cookies. There's not much to see in the retail store (you can buy cheap bags of broken fortune cookies); tours of the factory are offered for groups of 15 or more people age 9 and up.

Snacks/Restaurants

With half a dozen bakeries and more than 60 restaurants, the International District is not short on snack spots. Although many Seattleites have their favorites, each place has a different charm and appeal (some even have photos of their dishes in the window). Be adventurous and try something new. Have a dim sum brunch or head to a sushi bar so you'll learn more by testing what each culture has to offer.

Sun Ya Seafood Restaurant
605 Seventh S.
(206) 623-1670

This restaurant near the park doesn't have a children's menu, so you either have to split an order or pay for a full-priced meal ($6-$8, plus rice). It does have high chairs and a changing table in the women's rest room. Kids will be delighted by a large fish tank and another tank with live crabs and lobsters.

Green Village
721 S. King
(206) 624-3634

Green Village II
514 Sixth Ave. S.
(206) 621-1719

See "Restaurants" in Chapter 11.

DOWNTOWN

Don't venture near the corner of Sixth Avenue and Pike Street unless you've got a big wad of cash or a credit card with a high spending limit. With Planet Hollywood and Nike Town on one side, GameWorks down the way, and FAO Schwarz across the street, this is sort of a Bermuda Triangle for money: You'll wonder where it disappeared.

FAO Schwarz
Sixth Ave. and Pike St.
(206) 442-9500

A giant teddy bear greets you outside the two-story store; once inside, you'll spy a fanciful tower decorated with a talking clock, dancing ruby slippers, and an ani-

The FAO Schwarz bear greets downtown visitors.

mated Humpty Dumpty. (If you stay very long, listening to the same short song over and over will make it seem a lot less cute.) Upstairs, an animated dinosaur and a talking tree populate the stuffed animal section; a giant keyboard à la the movie "Big" (filmed in FAO Schwarz's New York store) runs along the floor nearby. The store is part of the upscale City Centre shopping mall, which encompasses the block between Fifth and Sixth avenues and Pike and Union streets.

GameWorks
1511 Seventh Ave.
(206) 521-0952
www.gameworks.com/seattle/index
.html
Hours: Mon.-Thurs., 10 a.m.-11 p.m.; Fri.-Sat., 10 a.m.-1 a.m.; Sun., 11 a.m.-10 p.m.
Admission: Free; games cost $1-$4

To call this a video arcade is like calling Disneyland an amusement park. Parents who never mastered Pac-Man (or Pong, for that matter) will find themselves feeling even more out of it; those who got into video games will be challenged by interactive and multiplayer games. One game allow players to "race" a car that moves while a live announcer keeps track of the status of each vehicle. Another game allows one player to pitch virtual balls to another player, who hits them on a virtual screen. Still other games let players fish, snowboard, ski, and bike. There are also traditional video games, an Internet lounge, low-tech pool and air hock-

195

ey tables, and plenty of food. The Southwest Chili Fries are famous (or infamous, for calorie counters): a pound of potatoes slathered in chili and cheese sauce.

Nike Town
1500 Sixth St.
(206) 447-6453

Besides clear tubes that send shoes between floors and a variety of TVs playing sports videos, there is nothing gimmicky to attract kids to this store except buying lots of expensive Nike merchandise.

Planet Hollywood
1500 Sixth St.
(206) 287-0001

Planet Hollywood is less a restaurant than an attraction. Owned by movie stars, including Demi Moore, Bruce Willis, and Sylvester Stallone, it is dramatically decorated with movie posters, cutouts of movie characters, life-size props (including

TIPS

Make sure to visit the rest room, which is decorated all in black and has a giant pair of sunglasses functioning as a mirror. There is a changing table.

The commercial machine chugs on: T-shirts are $18 to $22; a variety of other logo merchandise is also available.

an airplane), and displays with costumes from movies and TV shows (for example, the medical scrubs worn by George Clooney's Dr. Ross on "ER," and an ape costume from "Planet of the Apes"). Don't expect to carry on any sort of conversation, because a half-dozen TVs continually play movie montages and clips. The food is overpriced and on one visit, ranged from mediocre to bad. The pomodoro (a pasta dish) tasted like Spaghetti-Os and the bun on a grilled chicken sandwich was cold. Adult meals run $7.50 to $10 for basics such as pizza, hamburgers, and sandwiches. A glass of pop is another $2. Kids' meals are $5.95 for pizza, burgers, or pasta. If you have teens who insist on going in, splurge on some specialty drinks or desserts (which are quite good) and eat real food someplace else.

The Bon Marche
Third Ave. and Pine St.
(206) 506-6000

Your kids will not want to go beyond the lowest level (the Metro level, with direct access to the Westlake Center bus tunnel), since that's where the extensive toy department, **Toytropolis,** is located.

Westlake Center
1601 Fifth Ave.
(206) 467-1600

Westlake has the usual selection of shopping mall stores. The center's food court, Pacific Place, offers an array of reasonably priced food choices. Across Pine Street is Westlake Park, a busy downtown gathering place where concerts are offered during the summer and kids can't resist a walk through the park's cascading fountains. You can catch the Monorail to the Seattle Center on the top level.

INSIDE SCOOP Downtown Holiday Fun

The holiday season from Thanksgiving to New Year's is a wonderful time to visit downtown. Most stores have holiday displays, carolers are often out, and kids enjoy riding on the carousel at Westlake Park. Some activities to check out:

The Bon Marche's Holiday Train invites hands-on participation outside The Bon's window at Fourth and Stewart. Heat-sensitive handprints and a remote-control device allow spectators to run the trains during designated hours.

The Enchanted Forest transforms Rainier Square (1301 Fifth Ave.) into a holiday fairyland, with playful and elegant theme-decorated trees and daily entertainment.

The Holiday Carousel at Westlake Park (Fourth Ave. and Pine St.) takes riders for a spin on lovely antique animals in exchange for a $1 donation.

A **Gingerbread Village** created by local architects and the culinary staff of the Seattle Sheraton Hotel and Towers (1400 Sixth Ave.) is displayed in the hotel's lobby.

The **Teddy Bear Suite** is the most popular room in the Four Seasons Olympic Hotel (411 University St.) during the holiday season. Anyone can visit this merry suite filled with hundreds of teddy bears, teddy bear toys, and teddy bear books. Stop by the front desk or the concierge desk to get the VIP Teddy Bear Suite key.

Visit Santa at **Nordstrom's Santa Lane** (Fifth Ave. and Pine St.), Westlake Center's **Winter Wonderland** (Fourth and Pine, on the second level), and the **Bon Marché's Santaland** (Third and Pine, on the sixth floor).

THE SEATTLE CENTER

No child would pass up a visit to the Seattle Center: Any place that maintains a carnival atmosphere is bound to be a hit. But this 74-acre area on lower Queen Anne is not just an amusement park with dizzying rides and garish frills it is a place where families can see first-rate children's theater productions, get into some hands-on science experiments and art projects, sample foods from all over the world, and roll and tumble on soft green lawns.

Constructed for the 1962 World's Fair, the Seattle Center has continued to host events, celebrations, and festivals to bring the community together. Its vast expanse offers a multitude of indoor and outdoor activities and encompasses various fine-arts and sports facilities. Some of its better-known residents are the Pacific Science Center, the Children's Museum, Seattle Children's Theatre, Seattle Opera, the SuperSonics, and the Seattle Repertory Theatre.

Many of the Center's residents are expanding or remodeling, with

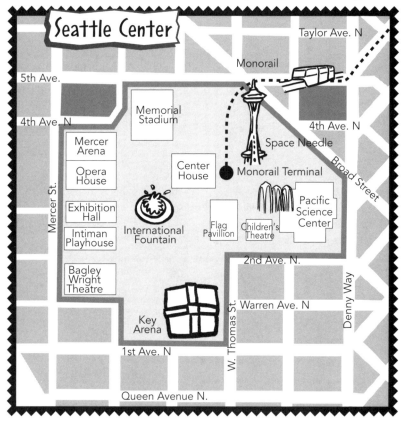

TIPS

Going to the Seattle Center for the entire day to "do it all" would not only transform your sweet angels into snarling brats, but it would likely deplete their college funds. With so much to do at the Center, you are better off deciding as a family which appeals to you most (e.g., the Fun Forest or the Pacific Science Center) and then seeing where you stand—or if you can still stand—at the end of that activity.

ongoing projects at the Pacific Science Center and the Fun Forest. Major renovations are also planned for the Space Needle, Mercer Arena, and Opera House, though all were in the preliminary stages as of press time. A long-term proposal is for the construction of a hotel at the Center.

The Charlotte Martin Theatre

Seattle Children's Theatre
(206) 443-0807, (206) 633-4567
(tickets)

See "Theaters" in Chapter 7 for details.

Construction on an expansion project (a rehearsal studio and technical area) is expected to begin in July 1998 and finish about a year later. It should not affect performances.

Children's Museum

Seattle Center House, lower level
(206) 441-1768

The Children's Museum offers the best in creative, interactive play for young children in the city. See "Museums" in Chapter 7.

Experience Music Project

Fifth Ave., between Thomas and Harrison
(425) 450-1997;
www.experience.org

Scheduled to open in 1999, the Experience Music Project won't be hard to find. The funky, controversial metallic structure designed by Frank O. Gehry will sit directly

ESSENTIALS

You can expect to pay for parking around the Seattle Center, and there may be tedious traffic if an event is happening. Fortunately, parking lots are plentiful, except on the south side. A new 11-acre surface parking lot recently opened east of Seattle Center at Fifth Avenue and Harrison.

If you are heading to the Center from the downtown area, opt for taking the Monorail (206-684-7200) from Westlake Center (Fourth Ave. and Pine St.). The ride is just under two minutes, and it will land you smack in the middle of the Center's action. Kids age 4 and under ride free; one-way fares are $1/adults and 75 cents /children ages 5-12. The Monorail runs about every 15 minutes and can be accessed from the third floor of the Westlake Center or from just outside the Seattle Center House, near the Fun Forest (these are its only stops). It runs 7:30 a.m.-11 p.m. on weekdays and 9 a.m.-11 p.m. on weekends.

The Pacific Science Center is an ideal destination for all ages.

COURTESY OF THE PACIFIC SCIENCE CENTER

north of the Space Needle and encompass 130,000 square feet. In addition to traditional museum displays of collections such as musicians' costumes and sheet music, the Project will offer live performances and educational programs. According to a fact sheet about the museum, it will "encourage visitors to listen, learn, participate in making music, and experience the power and joy of music in all its forms." For example, a "Sound Lab" will allow visitors to make and listen to music; a "Crossroads" exhibit will examine rock music's sources and influences, with an emphasis on the Northwest.

International Fountain
Located across from KeyArena, north of the Seattle Center House

Kids can't resist water, so they probably won't notice how ugly this giant, spiky metallic fountain is. Set in a huge cement bowl, the fountain plays music and shoots up water in different patterns. Kids can venture as far down as they like and get as soaked as they would like (or you'll permit). And hey, it's one of the few free things at Seattle Center, so enjoy it.

Pacific Science Center
(206) 443-2001

An ideal destination for any age child, the Science Center is a veritable science playground. A $18 million expansion, including a new IMAX theater and additional gallery space, should be completed by late 1998. See "Museums" in Chapter 7.

Fun Forest
(206) 728-1585
Hours: June 1-Labor Day, daily, noon-11 p.m.; weekend operation the remainder of the year. Indoor pavilion, daily, 11 a.m. year-round
Tickets: 95 cents/ticket, $6/book of 8, $12/book of 18; book tickets can be used throughout the Fun Forest season

The Seattle Center's aforementioned carnival atmosphere—complete with the requisite sights, sounds, and smells—is captured in an area at the foot of the Space Needle called the Fun Forest. Before you enter its confines, however, be sure to prepare your child for the mighty temptations of giant stuffed bears, clouds of cotton candy, and rides that are over much too quickly. Negotiate the terms of the outing—type of snacks, number of rides—so you won't have to be the cruel fun squasher when you get asked for more of everything.

The Fun Forest is in the middle of a four-year redevelopment project. The first phase in 1996-97 included the construction of an indoor pavilion with miniature golf, laser tag, amusement games, and a kiddie ride (sort of a small-scale Dumbo ride). The outdoor kiddie rides were moved from their old location to a site east of the new pavilion. In June 1998, a new self-service cafe with burgers and fries should open in a spot north of the monorail. The final project, in 1999-2000, will be the relocation of the big rides (such as the Orbiter, Wild River, and the Windstorm Roller Coaster) and the addition of some new ones (these had not been selected as of press time). The carnival games area is also slated for a facelift.

Seattle Center House

If you're hungry, this is the place to go. The second floor is lined with restaurants of all types, including Subway, Pizza Haven, Roaster's Chicken, Rico Burrito, Quincy's Burgers, Kabab Corner, Frankfurter, and, of course, Starbucks. Bean Pod Deli offers baked potatoes, salads, sandwiches, and soup in a bread bowl. Seattle Fudge and Bubble's Ice Cream can satisfy any cravings for sweets.

If you have younger kids, take your food upstairs and eat while they enjoy a free play area on the top floor with a Lego table, tricycles, cars, and a gazebo. If the stage on the lower level isn't in use for some sort of dancing or special event, the riding toys are often brought down so kids can have a wide, open space to tool around in.

The Center House gears up for a variety of celebrations year-round, many highlighting Seattle's different cultures. Admission is free and most feature entertainment, crafts, and other activities. (See Chapter 10 for more detailed information.)

INSIDE SCOOP

Best Bets for Tourists

Alki, Discovery, or Lincoln Parks (Chapter 3)

Children's Museum (Chapter 7)

Hiram M. Chittenden Government Locks (Chapter 3)

Museum of Flight (Chapter 7)

Northwest Trek Wildlife Park (Chapter 1)

Pacific Science Center (Chapter 7)

Pike Place Market and Seattle Waterfront

Seattle Aquarium

Seattle Center

Space Needle

Woodland Park Zoo (Chapter 1)

STEPHANIE DUNNEWIND

Seattle wouldn't be Seattle without the Space Needle.

Space Needle

(206) 443-2111

www.spaceneedle.com

Tickets: (for elevator ride to Observation Deck): $8.50/adults, $7/seniors, $4/children ages 5-12, free/children age 4 and under; $1/person discount from 8-10 a.m. and 9 p.m.-midnight

Built for the World's Fair 40 years ago, the Space Needle still makes Seattle's skyline distinctive. The 605-foot landmark, though now dwarfed by downtown buildings, remains one of the best vantage points. Visitors can take one of the elevators (nicknamed "beetles" because of their color and design) up 518 feet to the recently remodeled Observation Deck for a panoramic view of the city, the Olympic and Cascade mountains, Puget Sound, and Mount Rainier. Don't bother going if rain will spoil the view; there's not much else to do besides look out. The Needle also features two revolving restaurants at the 500-foot level (one full rotation every hour), but some don't think the thrill is worth the price for family dining (the elevator ride is free if you're eating).

Though the project had not been officially approved as of press time, the Space Needle's ground level is expected to go through a major renovation. The new entry will feature a two-story glass building with an expanded gift shop, lounge, and more space for ticket lines. The new look will also include landscaping and a series of plazas.

Snacks/Restaurants

The Center grounds are littered with concession stands, selling all the usual treats for exorbitant prices. If the kids are up for a more filling (though not necessarily healthier) snack, brace yourself and head to the Center House.

Or venture north just off the Center grounds to Mercer Street. between First Avenue N. and Queen Anne Avenue N., where tasty take-out can be found at **Larry's Market** (206-213-0778), **Kidd Valley Hamburgers** (206-284-0184), **World Wrapps** (206-286-9727), and the kid-pleasing **McDonald's Express**.

Chapter 9

OUT-OF-TOWN EXCURSIONS

Seattle neighborhoods have become so self-sufficient and self-contained that you rarely need to travel beyond your own community to find a decent park, a good book store or video shop, and life's other little necessities. But when you realize that quality time with the kids has become routine or predictable, then it's time to blow out of town—at least for a few hours. Hop on a train for a day trip to Tacoma, go to Olympia and see our legislators in action, visit a nearby city's children's museum, or tour an airplane factory. You won't need suitcases or motel reservations, and everyone will benefit from the change of scenery.

Boeing Tour Center

Boeing Everett Plant, exit 189
from I-5
(800) 468-1476 or (206) 544-1264[
Public tours: Mon.-Fri., hourly 9-11
a.m. and 1-3 p.m.
Admission: Free

Free tours of Boeing's Everett
Plant are offered for families with
children who are at least 4 feet, 2
inches tall. The tours run weekdays
on a first-come, first-served basis.

TIPS

Summer tours at the Boeing Tour
Center are very popular, so if possible,
come as early as 8:30 a.m. and get
tickets for a later tour. Afternoon
tours often fill up by noon.

Before or after your tour, check
out the Museum of Flight's restoration center nearby. Visitors can walk
around and watch volunteers repair
old planes and helicopters. From the
tour center, return to eastbound
Highway 526 and take the first exit,
Airport Road. Go south on Airport
Road about a mile to 100th St. S.W.
Turn right onto 100th; Building C-72
is immediately on your right. The
center is open Tues.-Sat., 10 a.m.-5
p.m. Admission is free. For more information, call (425) 745-5150.

They begin with a half-hour video
presentation in the plant's theater,
and continue at a moderate pace
through the factory, covering about
one-third of a mile in all, including
some steep stairs. The tour ends
with a drive along the flight line.
Photographic equipment, purses,
and cellular phones are not permitted. Group tours for 10 or more are
by reservation only.

Capitol Tours

State Capitol, Olympia
(360) 586-8687
Tours: Daily year-round, on the
hour 10 a.m.-3 p.m.
Legislative sessions: Odd years,
Jan.-April; even years, Jan.-March
Admission: Free

The more a parent knows about
the workings and wonders of government, the more difficult it is to
explain it to kids. It's hard to
describe the nuts and bolts of the
system (how it is supposed to
work) without getting into the com-

TIPS

Bring a lunch and enjoy a picnic
on the beautiful Capitol grounds. The
Governor's Mansion is open for tours
on Wednesday afternoons by reservation only; children's groups must be
sixth-grade level or older to be
admitted.

› ESSENTIALS

› Between sessions, parking is
available just outside the Capitol
Building for 50 cents an hour
(bring quarters). During the session, parking is available in designated Visitor Center parking areas
only. A free shuttle bus provides
rides to the Capitol from some
parking areas.

plexities of donkeys and elephants
and all the muddling issues and
scandals (why it doesn't always
work). One-hour docent tours are
led year-round, but the most interesting time to visit is during the legislative session, when tours include
a visit to Senate and House galleries
whenever possible, for a close-up
view of Washington's elected offi-
cials in action. Tours during this
time tend to be very crowded;
reservations are suggested.

Specialty tours of the legislative,
judicial, and executive branches, as
well as of the Governor's Mansion,
the State Capitol Museum, and historical landmarks, can be arranged.
These tours most often run two to
four hours and can be tailored to
any visitors, from preschoolers to
adults, physically and mentally challenged persons, school groups, or
individuals. Reservations for specialty tours are required.

Chateau Ste. Michelle Winery

14111 N.E. 145th, Woodinville
(425) 488-3300
www.ste-michelle.com
Hours: Daily, 10 a.m.-4:30 p.m.;
closed Christmas, New Year's, and
Easter.

Admission and tours: Free
Directions: From Interstate 405,
take exit 23 (Highway 522 toward
Monroe) to the Woodinville exit.
Turn right at the end of the exit
ramp and go three blocks to N.E.
175th Street. Turn right, cross the
railroad tracks, and then turn left at
the stop sign at Highway 202. Continue two miles to the Chateau's
gates on the right.

Don't worry: the award-winning
Ste. Michelle Winery offers kids
grape juice during its daily cellar
tours and wine tastings, so you
won't have a tipsy first-grader. The
free tours leave from the lobby and
last about 45 minutes. They are
stroller- and wheelchair-accessible,
and groups are welcome.

Take a walk on the lovely estate,
making sure to visit the terraced
trout ponds above the chateau and
the duck pond out by the vineyards.
Watch for the resident peacocks.

TIPS

Ste. Michelle Winery is a good
turn-around point for families riding
the Sammamish River bike trail from
Marymoor Park in Redmond. (See
"Biking" in Chapter 4 for more
information.) Young riders should
walk their bikes on the short strip
of busy road between the trail and
the winery, but otherwise the ride is
fairly safe.

Picnic tables are available if you want to bring a lunch or purchase food from the gift shop.

During the spring and summer months, the grounds of Ste. Michelle are host to a variety of big-name entertainment; jazz, classical, and contemporary music concerts; theatrical presentations; and dance performances. Admission fees vary; some shows are free. The public is invited to bring a picnic and spread out on the lawn.

Children's Museum of Tacoma
936 Broadway, Tacoma
(253) 627-6031
Hours: Tues.-Sat., 10 a.m..-5 pm.; Sun., 12-5 p.m.
Admission: $4.25/person, free/children under age 2

The Children's Museum of Tacoma devotes much of its space to a major thematic exhibit, which changes every 18 months. Specific programs, workshops, and hands-on activities are designed in conjunction with the exhibit's theme to

NEIGHBORHOOD NOTES

WOODINVILLE

Just across the street from Ste. Michelle is **Columbia Winery** (14111 N.E. 145th St.; 425-488-3300; www.columbiawinery.com), which offers weekend tours by request. A cozy wine-tasting room with a fireplace is open daily, 10 a.m.-4:30 p.m.

Next door to the Columbia Winery is the giant **Redhook Brewery** (14300 N.E. 145th St.; 425-483-3232). Besides a restaurant and beer garden, the brewery offers one-hour tours at 1, 3, and 5 p.m. daily.

If you can still drive after all that, visit **Molbak's** (13625 N.E. 175th; 425-

483-5000). The supersized nursery offers special events throughout the year, including **Molbak's Fairyland** in October, when local theater groups perform a favorite children's story and the store creates displays fitting the theme. For Christmas, the store features live music, Santa visits, and hundreds of poinsettias.

The **Woodinville Farmers Market** is held Saturdays, May-Oct., 9 a.m.-4 p.m., in downtown Woodinville, next to City Hall. Call (425) 788-3697 for more information. The city also puts on a Fourth of July bash with live entertainment in a field near Ste. Michelle.

enhance children's creativity, comprehension, and learning.

The current exhibit, "Omokunle," is a replica of a rural Nigerian village. Inside the exhibit children can explore what the people of Yorubaland eat, where they live, what clothes they wear, and how they shop. "Omokunle" will be on display through September 1998.

"Insecta Perspecta—A Bug's-Eye View," featuring ladybugs, dragonflies, and carpenter ants, opens in March 1998. This introduction to bugs allows children to learn about where insects live, what they eat, and their role in the environment. Inside the exhibit children can dress up in bug costumes, create a big bug sculpture, play computer bug games, and use a field guide. "Insecta Perspecta" will be on display through December 1998.

Quarterly revolving exhibits include "Personal Collections," which offers multicultural and multigenerational opportunities for children and their families to learn about the concepts of collecting, and the "Kids Gallery," which features art for, by, and about children.

Children's Museum of Snohomish County

3013 Colby Ave., Everett
(425) 258-1006
Hours: Mon.-Sat., 10 a.m.-3 p.m.
Admission: $3/person, free/children age 2 and under

Hands-on activities at the museum in downtown Everett include a grocery store, café, and stage with costumes. The Shadow Wall freezes your shadow in whatever position you choose. In an 1890s pioneer section, children can groom a horse, build a Play Mobile fort, or wash clothes on a washboard. Toddlers get their own corner with beanbag chairs, storybooks, and playful displays. School-age children will enjoy computers and a giant Lego table. Kids will be captivated as balls are sucked up a tube and wind their way through the maze suspended from the ceiling.

Enchanted Village and Wild Waves Water Park

36201 Enchanted Pkwy. S.,
Federal Way
(253) 661-8001
Hours: Open mid-April through Labor Day and December; seasonal hours vary
Admission: Enchanted Village only, $9/children under 48 inches, $11/all persons over 4 feet tall; Wild Waves and Enchanted Village combination, $17.95-$19.95; free/children age 2 and under
Season passes: $59.95-$79.95

Pack a picnic and spend the day enjoying 70 acres of family fun and excitement at Wild Waves Water Park and Enchanted Village in Federal Way. The price of admission is steep, so plan on getting there early and spending time at both Wild Waves and Enchanted Village to get your money's worth.

Enchanted Village is a magical

TIPS

Though this may be an expensive outing for parents, we haven't met a child yet (including teenagers) who doesn't consider Enchanted Village and Wild Waves a favorite destination. It works well to arrive around 10 or 11 a.m., have a picnic at lunchtime, and then leave about a half hour before the park closes to avoid the traffic jam right at closing time. Several fast-food places (Dairy Queen, McDonald's, etc.) are located nearby on 320th in Federal Way, so you can get dinner before you get back on the freeway. Food is not allowed in the Wild Waves area (very strictly enforced), but Enchanted Village, which is a short, easy walk from Wild Waves, sells food and has many pleasant picnic areas where you can bring your own food and beverages.

As you would expect, the crowds are enormous at Wild Waves on hot summer days, especially on weekends (Saturday is busiest). Expect long lines for everything except the water park for very young children, where toddlers and preschoolers can come and go without waiting.

Enchanted Village and Wild Waves are well supervised. The staff is helpful and courteous; the rides and facilities are exceptionally clean and well maintained.

place for young children. It has a quiet, forested setting, a pleasant switch from the carnival atmosphere at most amusement parks. It offers several activities and attractions likely to drive any kid to delirium, including 20 amusement rides, wading pools, bumper boats, the Antique Doll and Toy Museum, and the Wax Museum. The "Wild Thing" ride, with a triple corkscrew loop, is billed as the Northwest's largest roller coaster. Admission to Enchanted Village includes an unlimited number of rides and other attractions, including live entertainment, puppet shows, and magic shows; there are additional fees for arcade games, video games, remote-controlled boats, and face painting.

Wild Waves is the Northwest's largest water park, with 30 acres of water mania including giant water slides, a river ride, and a 24,000-square-foot wave pool. There are a few smaller slides and water rides for the younger set, but this park is most popular with age 8 and up. The giant water slides are best reserved for older children and adults.

Admission to Wild Waves always includes admission to Enchanted Village. Birthday parties, company picnics, and other kinds of group events are welcome and receive discounted admission.

ESSENTIALS

There is no admission to Wild Waves only. Food concessions, raft rentals, video games, and lockers are available for additional fees. Parking costs $2.

Jetty Island

10th St. and Marine Park, Everett
(425) 257-8300
Open: July-Labor Day, Wed.-Sun.

Take a free ferry ride to Jetty Island, a 2-mile-long, half-mile-wide artificially made island a quarter-mile off the Everett waterfront in Port Gardner Bay. Visitors can explore the island's environment on their own or participate in special activities. There is also a shallow, warm-water beach. Naturalists often lead special programs.

Pioneer Farm Museum

7716 Ohop Valley Road, Eatonville
(south of Puyallup)
(360) 832-6300
Hours: Seasonal hours vary; closed Thanksgiving-Feb.
Admission: $4.50-$5.50/person, free/children age 2 and under

After the long (about one and a half hours) ride from Seattle, you and your kids might be disappointed when you first see the sparse, drab setting of Pioneer Farm. The owners of this farm have aimed to give an authentic (i.e., not Disneyfied) depiction of life in pioneer times. Once the 90-minute tour begins, however, most school-age children will be enthralled to learn how people lived 100 years ago. The tour includes a visit to a log cabin, schoolhouse, barn, blacksmith, and wood shop and allows children to participate in more than 100 activities, such as scrubbing clothes, sawing wood, carding

TIPS

The Pioneer Farm is not a pristine museum tour but a hands-on experience where participants jump in the hay, work a forge, and pet the pig, so dress accordingly.

Pioneer Farm also offers a variety of programs for school and private groups that explore the Native American culture and pioneer heritage. These programs include storytelling, participatory activities, history, Indian lore, and the environmental history of the region. Groups may also register for an overnight adventure to extend their pioneering activities into cooking over an open fire and sleeping in the hayloft.

wool, grinding wheat, and milking the cow.

Point Defiance Park

5400 N. Pearl St., Tacoma
(253) 305-1000
Hours: Open daily year-round
Admission: Free; there is a fee for some attractions
Directions: From I-5 take exit 132, and follow signs to Hwy. 16. Turn left at the Sixth Ave. exit from Hwy. 16, turn right onto Pearl St., and follow the signs to Point Defiance Park.

STEPHANIE DUNNEWIND

Never Never Land features life-size characters from children's literature.

Don't go to Point Defiance Park expecting to see and do everything in one visit; you can't possibly experience all it has to offer in one day. Owned and operated by the Metropolitan Park District of Tacoma, Point Defiance is among the 20 largest city parks in the United States.

About an hour's drive from Seattle, the park covers 698 acres and includes the Point Defiance Zoo and Aquarium (see Chapter 1), Never Never Land, Fort Nisqually (a restored Hudson Bay Company fort), the Camp 6 Logging Museum, and Boat House Marina. The park terrain consists of scenic floral gardens, old-growth forests, playgrounds, tennis courts, and superb picnic areas featuring grills, electricity, water, and covered shelters. There are two beaches as well, where you can rent boats, fish,

swim, or sunbathe.

On Saturday mornings, the park's wooded Five-Mile Drive is closed to automobile traffic until 1 p.m., making it a good time to take the kids for a stroll or bike ride.

If your kids are suffering from a reality overdose, take them into **Never Never Land**, a children's storyland featuring a 10-acre forest full of two dozen tableaus with life-size characters from favorite children's literature, including Peter Rabbit, Humpty Dumpty, Hansel and Gretel, and Goldilocks and the Three Bears. Though most are just for viewing, a couple of displays have small houses children can enter—a thrill after a constant refrain of "Don't touch." It ends with a small playground where kids can slide down the tongue of the Old Lady Who Lived in a Shoe's giant shoe and steer Captain Hook's ship. It's all geared to kids from preschool to early elementary age; older children will likely think it's hokey. Never Never Land is open daily during the summer (June-August), 11 a.m.-6 p.m. A small concession booth sells snacks. Admission is $3/adults, $2.50/seniors, $2/children ages 3-12, free/children age 2 and under. Group tours and birthday parties are welcome by reservation; call (253) 591-5845.

Fort Nisqually is a restored Hudson's Bay Company fort complete with a working blacksmith shop and several restored buildings, as well as a gift shop. The best time to visit is Wednesday through Sunday between Memorial Day and Labor Day, when all the historic buildings are open for viewing and are staffed by costumed workers.

Summer admission is $1.50/adults and 75 cents/children (admission is free during the remainder of the year, but the historical buildings are not always open); call ahead to confirm hours of operation, (253) 591-5339. Special events include the Brigade Encampment in August, a reenactment of the 1855 arrival of a brigade to the fort; the Candlelight Tour, the first weekend in October; and 19th Century Christmas, the first weekend in December. Fees vary for these events.

The big attraction of **Camp 6,** a replica of a logging camp, is the train ride. The short loop, with a mid-ride talk about logging equipment, is just right for young children, though older ones might be underwhelmed. (As of publication, the camp's steam locomotive was out of commission, waiting for a

Kids can ride a short loop on the Camp 6 train at Point Defiance.

TIPS

In September, the Camp 6 train makes a good end-of-the-day activity after the zoo closes. A special Santa Train runs the first three weekends in December; call (253) 752-0047 for more information.

$50,000 repair and renovation.) The train runs Saturdays, Sundays, and holidays, noon-4 p.m., in April and May, and noon-6:30 p.m. from Memorial Day through the end of September. Fares are $2/adults, $1/children age 11 and under and seniors, free/children age 2 and under. The outdoor exhibits are open year-round, but the indoor ones are closed every Monday and Tuesday, as well as from November to January. They are free. For more information, call (253) 752-0047.

The **Boat House Marina** rents small motorboats year-round; call (253) 591-5325 for detailed information. Next door is a full-service restaurant operated by Anthony's. A half-mile paved promenade trail connects the marina beach with Owen Beach. Be sure to read the poetry carved into the sidewalk.

Sea-Tac International Airport
Metered parking: $1/every 20 minutes; 40-minute minimum, 2-hour maximum

Instead of pulling your child through the airport on a quick dash to the plane, make Sea-Tac the final destination for a novel and relatively inexpensive outing.

The terminals for Horizon Air, one of the smaller, locally based airlines, offer a first-rate opportunity to observe the entire travel process from landing to takeoff. Look out the windows lining the C concourse for close-up views of planes being fueled and loaded with luggage and passengers boarding and disembarking.

You can ride the subway to the S and N gates from the main terminal, a thrill for any little ones who enjoy trains. A bizarre interactive light display and a few small toys are located at the entrance to the B concourse.

Wander through the gift shops, check out the abundant art, witness a few tearful greetings and good-byes, and then head back home for lunch and a nap—just the right amount of travel and adventure for a preschooler.

Snoqualmie Falls Park
Located 25 miles east of Seattle; take exit 27 from I-90
Open year-round
Admission: Free

Just outside the town of Snoqualmie, the Snoqualmie River plunges 270 feet over a rock gorge. Go in late spring or early summer, when the snow is melting, for the most dramatic cascade. This scenic two-acre park, located in the foothills of the Cascade Mountains, is owned and operated by Puget Power. The Snoqualmie Falls Hydroelectric Project has been gen-

Snoqualmie Falls offers an easy and close view of a spectacular waterfall.

erating electricity since 1898.

The park's grounds feature observation platforms to view the falls, plus picnic areas, rest rooms, a gift shop, and cafe. For the ambitious, the half-mile River Trail leads down to the river's edge for a spectacular view of the cascading falls. The trail is steep, however, so be prepared to help the little ones on the trip back up.

Tacoma Art Museum
1123 Pacific Ave., Tacoma
(253) 272-4258
Hours: Tues.-Sat., 10 a.m.-5 p.m.; Thurs., 10 a.m.-7 p.m.; Sun., 12-5 p.m.
Admission: $4/adults, $3/seniors and students, free/children 12 and under.

A special feature of the Tacoma Art Museum is ArtWORKS, a work-

space devoted to hands-on activities for the entire family. The activities explore the themes presented in the current exhibits being showcased in the museum's main galleries. Admission to ArtWORKS is included in museum admission.

Washington State History Museum
1911 Pacific Ave., Tacoma
1-888-BE-THERE
Hours: Labor Day-Memorial Day: Tues.-Sat., 10 a.m.-5 p.m.; Thurs., 10 a.m.-8 p.m.; Sun., 11 a.m.-5 p.m. Memorial Day-Labor Day: Mon.-Sat., 9 a.m.-5 p.m.; Thurs., 9 a.m.-8 p.m.; Sun., 11 a.m.-5 p.m.
Admission: $7/adults, $6/seniors, $5/students and military, $4/children ages 6-12, free/children ages 3-5, $20/family group, free every Thurs., 5-8 p.m.
Parking: $1/0-3 hours, $2/3-5 hours, $5/all day, free/Sat., Sun., and holidays.
Directions: Take exit 133 (City Center) from Interstate 5. From there, take the E. 26th St. exit and turn left on 26th. Head three blocks to Pacific Ave. and turn right. The museum is on the right five blocks down on Pacific.

The museum's Great Hall of Washington History allows visitors to not only walk through the history of our state, but to listen in on personal experiences. In the traditional Southern Coast Salish plank house, you can hear a conversation between a basket maker and her

Interactive exhibits put you into historical situations.

granddaughter; in a Seattle Hooverville shack, two residents, Mac and Leon, discuss the Depression. History becomes something you can experience as you sit on the seat of a covered wagon and explore a coal mine or dress up in pioneer clothing. The 49 interactive exhibits in the enormous museum put you right in historical situations.

The 1,800-square-foot model railroad exhibit depicts the rail lines that ran from Tacoma's Point Defi-ance Park to the Stampede Pass tunnel in the Cascades during the golden age of railroads.

Both indoor and outdoor theaters offer live presentations, re-enactments and films.

Whale Watch

Mosquito Fleet
1724 W. Marine View Dr., Everett
(800) 325-ORCA (6722)
(425) 787-6400 or (425) 252-6800
Season: April-Oct.
Spring and fall, $59/adults,
$29.50/children age 17 and under;
mid-June to Sept., $79/adults,
$39.50/children.

Mosquito Fleet offers one-day cruises to the San Juan Islands from Marina Village in Everett. The vessels have inside seating with large windows or outdoor decks. Kids will enjoy listening to whales on hydrophones. Boarding starts at 8 a.m. with departure at 8:30 a.m. The boat returns at 6 p.m.

Whatcom Children's Museum

227 Prospect, Bellingham
(360) 733-8769
Hours: Tues.-Wed., 12-5 p.m.;
Thurs.-Sat., 10 a.m.-5 p.m.; Sun,
12-5 p.m.
Admission: $2/person

Located in downtown Bellingham, the children's museum offers hands-on fun for children from toddlers to about age 12. Exhibits, which in the past have included a puppet theater, model trains, natural history displays, and an "Our Town" role-playing area, change at least yearly. A 1998 exhibit will center on dinosaurs.

TIPS

The first Saturday of the month is Family Activity Day, when the museum provides hands-on activities, storytelling, and entertainment. There is a museum cafe.

TRAIN RIDES

A train ride is one of the best outings you can take with your child. The immensity of the engine, the commotion and flurry of departure, and the soothing motion once you are under way never fail to fascinate children (and most adults). On your short journey you can sit back and have a real visit, leaving behind the stress and strain of everyday life. Bring snacks and books if you think your fellow traveler might get restless.

Amtrak Stations

Third Ave. at S. Jackson, Seattle
1001 Puyallup Ave., Tacoma
(800) 872-7245
Schedule: Trains leave Seattle at 8 a.m. and 10 a.m., arriving in Tacoma at 8:50 and 10:57 a.m. respectively. You can catch the 6:53 p.m. train back, arriving in Seattle at 7:50 p.m.
Ticket prices: Round trip Seattle-Tacoma, $11-$20/adults, $5.50-$10/children

A day trip on Amtrak will give your child the thrill of a ride on a real train without the hassle of overnight travel. Tacoma is a perfect destination since the ride lasts just about as long as a child's attention span, thus ensuring that the trip home will be eagerly anticipated, not dreaded. Spend the bulk of the day exploring Tacoma's many attractions, including Point Defiance Zoo and Aquarium (see Chapter 1). Plan it so that you jump back on board just as your stomachs are beginning to rumble

and have dinner in the dining car. You'll get the kids home just in time for bed.

When you call Amtrak, an automated system lets you find the departure and arrival times that best suit your needs. Reservations are strongly recommended.

Lake Whatcom Railway

Located 10 miles north of Sedro Woolley on Hwy. 9, about two hours from Seattle, in Wickersham
P.O. Box 91, Acme, WA 98220
(360) 595-2218
Schedule: Special excursions year-round; call for complete schedule
Ticket prices: $10/adults; $5/children; rates vary for special events

Throughout the year, the Lake Whatcom Railway offers scenic tours of Whatcom County Passengers travel seven miles roundtrip on the Northern Pacific railway, built in 1903. The 90-minute journey passes through forest land, with views of Mount Baker. The train runs through a tunnel (always a highlight) and stops for a 20-minute break near a lake so passengers can check out the engine up close or stretch their legs. Special excursions, complete with entertainment, refreshments, and appearances by special characters, occur on Valentine's Day, Easter, and December (the Santa Train). In addition, the train runs twice daily every Saturday, mid-July through August. Reservations are required as space is limited; send a self-addressed stamped envelope to the above address for tickets.

Mount Rainier Scenic Railroad

Located about 40 miles southeast of Tacoma on Hwy. 7, in Elbe (360) 569-2588 or (888) STEAM-11 *Schedule:* Departs daily from mid-June to Labor Day, 11 a.m., 1:15 p.m., and 3:30 p.m.; departs weekends only from Memorial Day to mid-June, Labor Day through the end of September, and in December *Ticket prices:* $9.50/adults, $8.50/seniors, $7.50/juniors ages12-17, $6.50/children under age 12

Mount Rainier Scenic Railroad's vintage steam locomotives depart Elbe for hour-and-a-half steam train excursions through the foothills of Mount Rainier. The extraordinary scenery on the 14-mile trip to Mineral Lake includes spectacular bridges. No reservations are required. The Snowball Express with Santa runs December weekends. Bring a coat if you want to sit in the open car.

If you want to give an older child a real treat, the Cascadian Dinner Train offers a complete five-course prime rib, ostrich, or salmon dinner during a four-hour train ride through the foothills of Mount Rainier. The Dinner Train departs Elbe from April through Memorial Day and October through November at 1 p.m. on Sundays, and from Memorial Day through September at 5:30 p.m. on

---

INSIDE SCOOP Museums for Kids

Some museums kids might enjoy if you're visiting any of these cities:

The African American Museum, 925 Court C, Tacoma; (253) 274-1278. Open Tues.-Sat., 10 a.m.-5 p.m. $3.75/person, free/age 3 and under. Exhibits vary in appropriateness for children. Plan to visit during one of the museum's special events, which usually take place twice a month on Saturdays. Call for a calendar of events.

Log Cabin Museum, 202 Sidney Ave., Port Orchard; (360) 876-3693. Free, but donations accepted. The 1914 log cabin features changing exhibits that portray family life at various times in south Kitsap County's history.

Naval Undersea Museum, 610 Dowell St., Keyport; (360) 396-4148. Free. Open Wed.-Sun., 10 a.m.-4 p.m. Exhibits on U.S. Navy history, operations, and technology, including deep-diving vehicles. Several hands-on stations.

Poulsbo Marine Science Center, 18743 Front St. N.W., Poulsbo; (360) 779-5549. $4/adults, $3/children ages 13-17, $2/children ages 2-12. Open daily, 11 a.m.-5 p.m. An aquarium, touch tanks, and exhibits on biology and geology of Puget Sound.

Saturdays. Prepaid reservations are required; the cost is $65/person. Call (888) RRDINER.

Puget Sound and Snoqualmie Valley Railway

38625 S.E. King St., Snoqualmie
(425) 888-2206 or (425) 746-4025
Schedule: April-Sept., Sat.-Sun.; Oct., Sundays only. Trains depart hourly 11 a.m.-4 p.m. from Snoqualmie, and hourly 11:30 am.-3:30 p.m. from North Bend
Ticket prices: $6/adults, $4/children, free/children under age 3

Travel aboard the historic Puget Sound and Snoqualmie Valley steam train for a one-hour round trip through the scenic Snoqualmie Valley, from the town of Snoqualmie to North Bend. The tracks run along the South Fork of the Snoqualmie River, over trestles, and through rural areas in the shadow of Mount Si. The train runs each weekend from Memorial Day through Labor Day, as well as on select days during the spring and fall. No reservations are necessary.

Make a one-hour stopover to eat a picnic lunch in the parks around the depots at both ends, or visit a local restaurant. Make sure you walk through the park in Snoqualmie, which has a giant log on display.

The railway offers two special events during the year: the Spook Train, offering young ghosts and goblins a special Halloween treat, and the popular Santa Train, complete with Old Saint Nick and lots of goodies. The Santa Train sells out long before December; call for reservations in early fall.

The Snoqualmie Railway Museum, located at the depot, is open Thurs.-Mon., 10 am.-5 p.m., and features railroad artifacts and photographs. Admission is free.

Chapter 10

SEASON BY SEASON

Seattleites don't need to experience blizzards, hurricanes, and monsoons to know when a new season has arrived. We can take the family for a drive just an hour north or east to show them the wonder of snow in winter. We can pack them up and drive five hours to eastern Washington to feel real heat in the summer. And we can take part in the many local festivals and events that mark the holidays and capture the spirit of spring, summer, winter, and fall.

Here, you'll find a calendar of events and activities that can take your family out of the doldrums in any month. Ride on a Santa train at Christmas time, catch a glimpse of the whales as they migrate in April, visit a berry farm in the hot summer sun, or harvest a pumpkin for Halloween.

For up-to-date information on these and many more special events and seasonal activities held throughout the Puget Sound area, check the monthly Calendar and Going Places listing inside *Seattle's Child, Eastside Parent, Snohomish County Parent, South Sound Parent,* or *Puget Sound Parent,* Northwest Parent Publishing's newsmagazines for families. Call (206) 441-0191 for information on obtaining a complimentary copy or a subscription.

WINTER

JANUARY

Bavarian Ice Fest
Downtown Leavenworth (20 miles west of Wenatchee)
Leavenworth Chamber of Commerce, (509) 548-5807
The Bavarian Ice Fest is held over the Martin Luther King Jr. holiday weekend and features snowshoe races, tug-of-war contests, and special children's activities.

Chinese New Year
Children's Museum, Seattle; (206) 441-1768
Wing Luke Asian Museum, Seattle; (206) 623-5124

Children can learn about Chinese art and culture and celebrate the New Year in hands-on workshops at the Children's Museum. Wing Luke Asian Museum offers an exhibit each winter on Asian New Year traditions.

Kids and Critters Naturefest
Northwest Trek Wildlife Park, Eatonville; (800) 433-TREK
For three days in mid-January, Northwest Trek features special fun and interesting lessons about the wildlife in this immense park.

Martin Luther King Jr. Day
Seattle Center House, Seattle (206) 684-8582
The "Keeping the Dream Alive Celebration" at the Seattle Center provides entertainment, children's activities, speakers, and exhibits that commemorate the life of Martin Luther King Jr.

Celebrate Tet
Seattle Center House, Seattle (206) 684-8582
The Vietnamese New Year is welcomed with a weekend-long festival featuring two stages with continuous live entertainment, plus food, and arts and crafts.

FEBRUARY

Celebrating African-American History Month
Public libraries, community groups, private organizations, and others sponsor special events and

The Burke Museum hosts Dinosaur Days in February.

festivals celebrating African-American History Month each February.

Dinosaur Day
Burke Museum, Seattle
(206) 543-5590

Watch the museum's fossil preparator at work, look at dinosaur eggs under a microscope, and check out tables full of dinosaur bones and ancient minerals, plants, and invertebrates.

Festival Sundiata
Seattle Center, Seattle
(206) 684-7200

This festival celebrating African and African-American cultures features arts and crafts, history, musical performances, and children's activities.

Legislature in Session
State Capitol, Olympia

Visit Olympia and see our lawmakers in action, (see Chapter 9).

Northwest Flower and Garden Show
Convention and Trade Center, Seattle; (206) 224-1700

This annual event features demonstrations, exhibits, products, and especially hard-to-find plant varieties for sale. Special children's programs include a Children's Garden competition, as well as hands-on activities.

Valentine Train
Lake Whatcom Railway, Wickersham; (360) 595-2218

The Lake Whatcom Railway train departs Wickersham, 10 miles

north of Sedro Woolley on SR 9 (about two hours north of Seattle), for a one-hour tour of scenic Whatcom County. The ride features live entertainment, Valentine goodies, and fun.

SPRING

MARCH

Children's Hospital Health Fair
Children's Hospital and Medical Center, Seattle; (206) 526-2201

This annual fair is designed to help children form positive views about health-care experiences. Includes a tour of an operating room, a hospital play kit, lots of hands-on fun, and a hearing screening for children age 4 and up.

Irish Week Festival
Seattle Center, Seattle
(206) 684-7200

This annual event features traditional Irish music, singing, dancing, displays, workshops on Irish history, and contests to find the child with the reddest hair or the most freckles!

St. Patrick's Day Parade
City Hall to Westlake Center, Seattle; (206) 623-0340

Annual downtown parade begins at noon, featuring bagpipes, singing, dancing, and the laying of a green stripe down the center of Fourth Ave.

Kent Kids Arts Day
Kent Parks and Recreation and Kent Arts Commission
(253) 859-3991

Hands-on crafts and entertainment are presented for the younger set.

Purim Carnival
Stroum Jewish Community Center, Mercer Island; (206) 232-7115

Purim, the happiest of all Jewish holidays, is celebrated one month before Passover. The carnival includes entertainment, Israeli dancing, traditional Purim foods, a Passover book and gift sale, and a kosher hot dog lunch. A special carnival for preschoolers features over 40 game booths.

Redmond Toddler Indoor Carnival
Redmond
Redmond Parent/Toddler Groups,
(425) 869-5605

This popular spring carnival is designed for children ages 1-5, and features face painting, cake walks, door prizes, fishing, balloons, hands-on crafts, entertainment, and more. Proceeds benefit the Redmond parent/toddler programs.

Whirligig

Seattle Center, Seattle
(206) 684-7200

Every spring, the Seattle Center presents a special monthlong indoor carnival, which includes indoor rides, special events, workshops, entertainment, and more designed for children age 10 and under.

Whale Migration

Westport Chamber of Commerce, Westport; (360) 268-9422

Once the cold weather is on its way out, gray whales return to Alaska from Baja California, where they winter and calve. Take a whale-watching excursion sometime between March and August to get an unforgettable look at these magnificent creatures.

Orca-watching cruises around the San Juan Islands leave from Bellingham and Anacortes.

APRIL

Daffodil Festival/Grand Floral Street Parade

Downtown Tacoma
Daffodil Festival Association, (253) 627-6176

The annual Junior Daffodil Parade, designed specifically for children, features kids, pets, music, and nonmotorized floats. Held in early April, the parade goes through Tacoma's downtown area. The Grand Floral Street Parade is also held in Tacoma each April, and features floats decorated with fresh daffodils, as well as bands, drill teams, and clowns.

Puyallup Spring Fair

Puyallup Fairgrounds, Puyallup
(206) 841-5045

Puyallup's celebration is replete with carnival rides, a petting farm, livestock shows, and the Daffodil Parade.

Seattle Cherry Blossom and Japanese Cultural Festival

Seattle Center, Seattle
(206) 684-7200

This annual festival celebrates traditional Japanese culture with arts and crafts, tea ceremonies, origami demonstrations, and performing arts.

Skagit Valley Tulip Festival

Throughout the Skagit Valley
(800-) 4TULIPS (488-5477)

This annual event features 1,500 acres of tulips, irises, and daffodils in full bloom, as well as many family activities, including arts and crafts, sporting events, pancake breakfasts, bicycling, pony rides, and tours aboard the Tulip Transit Vans.

Wild-n-Wooly Sheep Shearing

Kelsey Creek Community Farm Park, Bellevue; (425) 455-6885

The annual sheep-shearing event features wagon and pony rides, crafts, heritage demonstrations, sheepdog herding trials, and snacks.

Worldfest

Northgate Shopping Center,
Seattle; (206) 362-477

This special two-day spring
event celebrates the diverse ethnic
communities of the Seattle area
with song, dance, arts, crafts, and
ethnic cuisine. One highlight is the
Children of the World Parade, in
which children representing over 50
nationalities parade in their native
costumes.

Seattle Mariners Baseball

Kingdome, Seattle; (206) 628-3555

The Seattle Mariners play their
season opener in early April and
continue through September (and
fans hope into October post-season
play). Special discounts and promotional events offer fun for the entire
family (See Chapter 6.)

Tacoma Rainiers Baseball

Cheney Stadium, Tacoma;
(253) 752-7707

Tacoma's Class AAA affiliate of
the Mariners plays baseball outdoors at Cheney Stadium from April
to September. Promotional activities
for families are held throughout the
season. (See "The Little Guys" in
Chapter 6.)

Artspring: A Very Special Arts Festival

Very Special Arts Washington
(206) 443-1843

Artspring celebrates the visual
and performing arts achievements
and talents of children and adults
with disabilities, and features interactive hands-on activities and workshops for persons with and without
disabilities.

MAY

Boating Day

Seattle

Considering that Seattle has
more small boats per capita than
almost any other city in the world,
it seems fitting that the first Saturday of every May is set aside for
celebrating the opening of boating
season. Locals climb into anything
that will float and make merry.

The noon parade of decorated
boats proceeds eastbound through
the Montlake Cut, near the University of Washington. The parade is
preceded by crew races beginning
at about 10 a.m. Popular viewing
spots include East Montlake Park (at
the southwest end of the cut) and
the Lake Washington Ship Canal
Trail on the south side. Another
choice location is the large deck
area at the east end of the cut, easily accessible via a sidewalk at the
east end of Shelby St. near the
Museum of History and Industry.
Get there early for a good view.

Children's Day at the Japanese Garden

Washington Park Arboretum,
Seattle; (206) 325-4510

Storytelling, drum performances,
martial arts demonstrations, and
origami are some of the activities
offered at this annual event.

Intergenerational Fair

Seattle Center, Seattle
(206) 684-7200

Young and old can enjoy "A Time for All Ages" celebration.

Mom and Me at the Zoo

Woodland Park Zoo, Seattle
(206) 684-4800
Point Defiance Zoo, Tacoma
(206) 591-5337

This annual Mother's Day event held on the Saturday before Mom's Day features special activities, entertainment, animal talks, and hands-on crafts.

Northwest Folklife Festival

Seattle Center, Seattle
(206) 684-7300

This annual Memorial Day Weekend festival celebrates the Northwest's diverse cultural heritage with music, dance, and more. The International Children's Village features hands-on activities, workshops, and special stage performances just for kids.

Pike Place Market Festival

Pike Place Market, Seattle
(206) 587-0351

Enjoy a variety of entertainment and activities for the entire family on Memorial Day weekend. Don't miss the Kids' Alley, featuring a variety of hands-on activities and entertainment.

Seattle International Children's Festival

Seattle Center, Seattle
(206) 684-7346

Don't miss this truly exceptional opportunity to see world-class children's entertainment. Every May, the festival showcases premier children's performers from around the world, including puppeteers, musicians, storytellers, dance troupes, and more. School and community groups attend the weekday performances, but Saturday offers a full day of entertainment for families.

Seattle Maritime Festival

Waterfront, Seattle
Downtown Seattle Association,
(206) 443-3830

A full week of activities and special events showcases the maritime industry in the Seattle area. Activities include vessel tours, tugboat races, free admission to many waterfront attractions for kids, and more.

University District Street Fair

On University Way (west of the UW campus), Seattle; (206) 527-2567

This granddaddy of Northwest street fairs features 500 booths, music, a children's festival area, an ethnic dance stage, plenty of good people-watching, and food.

Bicycle Saturdays and Sundays

Lake Washington Blvd. (from Mount Baker Beach to Seward Park), Seattle
Seattle Parks and Recreation,
(206) 684-8021

From May to September, the

second Saturday and third Sunday of each month are designated as Bicycle Day along Lake Washington Boulevard. Free bicycle safety checks and first-aid stations are provided along the route, which is closed to motorized vehicles.

Velodrome Bike Racing
Velodrome, Marymoor Park, Redmond; (206) 527-9345

A full season of bike racing and events runs from mid-May to early September. (See "The Little Guys" in Chapter 6.)

SUMMER

JUNE

Dad and Me Fun Run
Marymoor Park, Redmond
(206) 296-2964

A full day of family fun surrounds the annual Dad and Me Classic Fun Run. Held at Marymoor Park in Redmond, this special event features a 5K competitive run, as well as a 5K family walk, a special half-mile course for children age 6 and under, and loads of activities and entertainment. The Fun Run is usually held over Father's Day weekend.

Edmonds Waterfront Festival
Edmonds Community College, Edmonds; (425) 771-1744

Entertainment, food and craft vendors, and special kids' activities highlight this celebration.

Everett Salty Sea Days
Waterfront, Everett
Salty Sea Days Association
(425) 339-1113

Everett's annual maritime festival features carnival rides, log-rolling contests, athletic events, demonstrations, ongoing entertainment, celebrity appearances, and children's activities.

Fire Festival
Pioneer Square, Seattle
Pioneer Square Association,
(206) 622-6235

Visit Pioneer Square and help your kids learn about the Great Seattle Fire of 1889. Antique fire trucks are on display, and the fire department demonstrates some of its know-how. It's a good mix of history, entertainment, and children's activities.

Fremont Fair
Fremont neighborhood, Seattle
(206) 633-4409

Seattle's funkiest neighborhood celebrates summer with a Solstice Parade, a huge crafts marketplace, ethnic food, live entertainment, and children's activities.

KidsDay
Every year in June, Seattle celebrates kids with one day of enter-

tainment, arts activities, and free admission to many popular attractions throughout Seattle, including the Woodland Park Zoo, the Seattle Aquarium, the Monorail, the Center for Wooden Boats, the Children's Museum, and more.

Everett AquaSox Baseball
Everett Memorial Stadium, Everett
(425) 258-3673

A Class A affiliate of the Mariners, the AquaSox play outdoor baseball on real grass from June to September. Look for a future star and experience great family entertainment. (See "The Little Guys" in Chapter 6.)

Kinderfest
Downtown Leavenworth (20 miles west of Wenatchee)
Leavenworth Chamber of Commerce, (509) 548-5807

The faux-Bavarian town of Leavenworth dedicates a weekend in June to children with a festival featuring entertainment, activities, and hands-on exhibits.

Marysville Strawberry Festival
Downtown Marysville
(360) 659-7664

The Northwest's favorite red berry gets its due, in a celebration complete with carnival rides, a food and crafts market, and a parade.

YMCA Run for Kids
Downtown Tacoma
Downtown Tacoma YMCA,
(253) 597-6444

This annual event, which benefits YMCA programs, features a family walk/run, prizes, drawings, and fun!

JULY

Bite of Seattle
Seattle Center, Seattle
(206) 684-7200

Food booths from more than 50 local restaurants, nonstop live entertainment, and kids' activities attract the multitudes.

Camlann Medieval Faire
Carnation
Camlann Medieval Association,
(425) 788-1353

Visit the annual Medieval Faire on weekends during July and August. Special attractions include armored knights in combat, minstrels, dancing, juggling, storytelling, and demonstrations in blacksmithing, tile making, spinning, weaving, and candle making.

Chinatown/International District Summer Festival
International District, Seattle
(206) 382-1197

Highlights include three entertainment stages, martial arts demonstrations, an Asian food bazaar, and Asian arts and crafts.

Fourth of July Celebrations
Lots of fun activities for children and families are held throughout the area to celebrate America's birthday. Activities and sites include Downtown Park, Bellevue (425-452-4106); a Carnation festival (425-333-4055);

Edmonds (425-776-6711); Everett (425-257-8300); Gas Works Park fireworks over Lake Union (206-682-4FUN); Issaquah's Down Home Fourth of July (425-392-0661); Fourth of Jul-Ivar's Fireworks Celebration at Myrtle Edwards Park, Seattle (206-587-6500); the Naturalization Ceremony at the Seattle Center, Seattle (206-684-7200); and Woodinville's fireworks (425-4898-2700).

FlyerWorks
Museum of Flight, Seattle
(206) 764-5700

The museum presents an aerial show during the Fourth of Jul-Ivar's celebration each July 4 at Myrtle Edwards Park in downtown Seattle. The flying parade features antique flying machines, World War II-era aircraft, and modern military planes. Down on the ground, the museum hosts the Fun Zone, with entertainment and hands-on workshops.

Kent International Balloon Classic
Kent; (253) 859-3991

This annual festival features hot-air balloon launches and races. An evening event includes lighted balloons, entertainment, and booths.

Kid's Fair
Bellevue Square, Bellevue
Pacific Northwest Arts and Crafts
Fair, (425) 454-4900

Part of the popular Pacific Northwest Arts and Crafts Fair held each summer in Bellevue, the Kids Fair features arts and crafts for kids, by kids, and with kids, plus lots of hands-on creative and imaginative play.

King County Fair
King County Fairgrounds, Enumclaw, (206) 296-8888 or (360) 825-7777

King County's fair, the state's oldest, offers country performers, children's entertainment, a rodeo, carnival rides, and fair food. Admission is $6.50/adults, $3/children ages 6-15, free/children age 5 and under.

Kirkland SummerFest
Downtown Kirkland; (425) 822-7161

This annual arts festival features fun for all.

Marymoor Heritage Festival
Marymoor Park, Redmond
(206) 296-2964

Held over the Fourth of July, the festival includes musicians, dancers, arts and crafts demonstrations, foods from around the world, entertainment, and a Children's Corner with hands-on activities.

Mercer Island Summer Celebration
Downtown and Mercerdale Park, Mercer Island; (206) 236-7285

This low-key festival includes a parade, live entertainment, an arts-and-crafts fair, food, boat tours, games, and hands-on activities for kids.

Pacific Northwest Scottish Highland Games and Clan Gathering
King County Fairgrounds, Enumclaw; (206) 522-2541

Everyone is welcome at this two-day event; a bagpipe competition, drummers, dancers, and athletes are only part of the fun. One evening features a traditional Scottish party with music, stories, sing-alongs, and country dancing.

Tivoli—Viking Days
Nordic Heritage Museum, Seattle
(206) 789-5707

The annual family event transforms the museum's grounds into a Viking marketplace with colorful craft and food booths, musicians, dancers, and lots of children's events, games, and amusements.

Wooden Boat Festival
Center for Wooden Boats (south end of Lake Union), Seattle
(206) 382-BOAT

The center displays a variety of wooden boats, from skiffs to square riggers, both in the water and out. Activities include a wooden yacht race, small-boat races, working exhibits, music, food, contests, and more. Children will enjoy activities designed to teach maritime skills. Usually held over the Fourth of July weekend.

Outdoor Concerts
Many communities throughout the Puget Sound region present outdoor family concerts during July and August, spotlighting the area's best local talent at little or no cost. Bring a picnic and enjoy the sounds. (See"Music" in Chapter 7.)

Redmond Derby Days
City Hall, Redmond; (425) 885-4014

Parades, carnival rides, canoe rides, a medieval fair, petting zoo, and bike races are part of this four-day festival.

Seafair Summer Festival
Throughout the Seattle area
Seafair, (206) 728-0123, ext. 6001

For four weeks during July and August, Seattle and neighboring communities celebrate the Seafair Summer Festival, featuring ethnic and community celebrations and parades, children's parades, sporting events, the U.S. Navy Fleet, the Torchlight Parade, the Unlimited Hydroplane Races, and awe-inspiring aerial performances by the Navy's Blue Angels. Highlights include the International District Summer Festival, Redmond Derby Days, the Milk Carton Derby on Green Lake, and West Seattle's Hi-Yu Festival. Call the Seafair office or your local community group or parks department for a complete schedule of events in your area. The kiddie parades are especially popular with young audiences.

AUGUST

Bubble Festival
Pacific Science Center, Seattle
(206) 443-2001

Learn everything there is to know about bubbles at the Pacific Science Center's popular festival. Attractions include lots of hands-on activities and loads of information on how bubbles are used in everyday life.

Island County Fair
Island County Fairgrounds, Langley, Whidbey Island; (360) 221-4677

The Island County Fair is held each August, with everything a genuine county fair has to offer: hot scones, Ferris wheels, displays of the finest produce in the county, logging demonstrations, and a first-class parade. On Sunday there is a Barnyard Scramble—small animals and children under 7 are turned loose together in a corral. But beware! You may bring a live chicken home with you. What the kids catch, they get to keep!

Kent Canterbury Faire
Mill Creek Canyon Earthworks Park, Kent; (253) 859-3991.

South King County's premier arts festival offers Renaissance and medieval villages, children's activities, food booths, and continuous performances of music, dance, and theater.

Kids' Carnival
Robinswood Park, Bellevue
(425) 452-4106

Bellevue Parks Department's annual day of fun for kids features clowns, carnival games, crafts, face painting, and free live entertainment.

KOMO Kidsfair
Seattle Center, Seattle
(206) 684-7200

An afternoon of free activities and entertainment for the entire family is presented by KOMO Radio and Television and held at the Seattle Center. Attractions include a ride on the KOMO Air 4 whirlibird, hands-on activities, informational and educational exhibits, and visits by television and radio personalities.

Renton River Days
Several sites throughout Renton
(425) 235-2587

Nearly a week of family events and entertainment includes arts and crafts, art shows, sporting events, and the popular Yellow Rubber Duck Derby.

Evergreen State Fair
Evergreen Fairgrounds, Monroe
(360) 794-4344 or (425) 339-3309

With all the attractions of a large state fair but on a smaller scale, the Evergreen State Fair features top name entertainment, agricultural exhibits, pig races, clowns, a carnival, and lots more.

FALL

SEPTEMBER

Autumn Leaf Festival
Leavenworth (20 miles west of Wenatchee)
Leavenworth Chamber of Commerce, (509) 548-5807

Held on the last weekend of September, this festival celebrates the splendor of fall foliage in the Tumwater Canyon with a parade, food, Bavarian music, and hands-on activities for kids.

Bumbershoot

Seattle Center, Seattle
(206) 682-4386
www.bumbershoot.org

Held each year over the Labor Day weekend, Bumbershoot is a huge arts festival, with a full lineup of family entertainment, including first-rate live music, art exhibits, food, theater, arts and crafts, and more.

Fiestas Patrias

Seattle Center, Seattle
(206) 684-7200

Held every September in celebration of Mexican and Latin American independence, this event features dancing, music, crafts, ethnic foods, and exhibits.

Western Washington Fair

Puyallup Fairgrounds, Puyallup
(253) 841-5045

The sixth-largest fair in the United States features a wide variety of family events and activities, top name entertainment, a petting farm, farm animals, home crafts, carnival rides, agricultural displays, and food, food, food (a bag of hot raspberry scones is a must)! Metro buses (206-553-3000) provide excellent direct service right to the fairgrounds, a good way to avoid the parking and traffic hassles.

St. Demetrios Greek Festival

St. Demetrios Greek Orthodox Church, Seattle; (206) 325-4347

Authentic Greek food, arts and crafts, games for children, folk dancing, and entertainment are offered for one weekend in September. Very popular.

Wallingford Wurst Festival

St. Benedict School (Wallingford neighborhood), Seattle
(206) 633-3375

This annual free festival includes children's games, carnival rides, live entertainment, international food, dancers, music, and more.

OCTOBER

Halloween Fun and Pumpkin Picking

Communities throughout the Puget Sound area offer a variety of Halloween activities for children of all ages. Check with local parks departments, Camp Long in West Seattle, the Seattle Aquarium, the Pacific Science Center, local shopping malls, and Northwest Trek for details about special programs.

Also, many farms just outside the city have pumpkin patches where your children can pick their own jack-o'-lanterns straight off the vine. (See Chapter 2.)

Festa Italiana

Seattle Center, Seattle
(206) 684-7200

Music, dancing, and food are presented in celebration of Italian culture.

Kelsey Creek Farm Fair

Kelsey Creek Farm, Bellevue
(425) 452-7254

Families can enjoy a variety of old-time activities and entertainment, including music, dancing, heritage craft demonstrations, antique tractor displays and rides, an animal petting area, kids' crafts, and a gathering of mountain men.

King County Library Used Book Sale
(206) 684-6605

This annual sale offers great deals on furniture, children's books, records, and cassettes.

Issaquah Salmon Days
Downtown Issaquah
(425) 392-0661

This annual weekend festival, celebrating the return of the salmon up Issaquah Creek, features a parade, arts and crafts, children's activities, sporting events, continuous entertainment, food, and more.

Molbak's Fairyland
Molbak's Greenhouse and Nursery, Woodinville; (425) 483-5000

Each October, Molbak's is transformed into a floral fairyland with scenes that re-create a favorite children's story. Local theater groups perform dramatizations of the story; families are invited to drop in, browse, and enjoy the displays.

"World Music in Motion"
Seattle Philharmonic Orchestra, (206) 528-6878

The orchestra presents its annual family concert each fall.

NOVEMBER

"A Christmas Carol"
ACT Theatre, Seattle; (206) 292-7676

Introduce your child to the holiday morality tale of Scrooge and Tiny Tim with this outstanding production. Recommended for age 5 and up.

The Bon Marche Holiday Parade
The Bon Marche, Seattle
(206) 506-4FUN

The annual parade is held the morning of the day after Thanksgiving in downtown Seattle. Holiday festivities continue throughout the day.

Celebration Especially for Children
Bellevue Art Museum, Bellevue
(425) 454-3322

Each year, the Bellevue Art Museum presents a special exhibit as part of its Especially for Children Series. Designed specifically for kids, the program may also include workshops and special activities based on the subject of the exhibit. The program continues through December.

Chipupugwendere African Harvest Festival
Langston Hughes Cultural Arts Center, Seattle; (206) 684-4757

This three-day celebration includes traditional African cuisine, live entertainment, arts and crafts, and dance and drum workshops.

Discover Music!

Seattle Symphony, (206) 443-4747

Each year from November to June, the Seattle Symphony presents a special series of musical performances designed to introduce children ages 6 to 10 to the world of classical music.

Festival of Light

Children's Museum, Seattle
(206) 441-1768

The Children's Museum's annual event celebrates winter holidays from around the world with music, hands-on activities, and storytelling.

Model Railroad Show

Pacific Science Center, Seattle
(206) 443-2001

This annual event over Thanksgiving Day weekend features model train layouts, music from the heyday of railroads, workshops, and hands-on activities.

Tellebration

Seattle Storytellers Guild
(206) 621-8646

The two-hour storytelling concert features Northwest storytellers.

Yulefest

Nordic Heritage Museum, Seattle
(206) 789-5707

Celebrate the beginning of the holiday season at the annual Nordic Yulefest, which highlights the crafts, music, dance, and food of Scandinavia.

KING 5 Winterfest

Seattle Center, Seattle
(206) 684-7200

The winter festival features daily entertainment, a model train display, ice skating on a tiny outdoor rink, arts and crafts, workshops, and loads of activities. Held each year from Thanksgiving until the first part of the new year on the Seattle Center grounds.

DECEMBER

Brunch with Santa

The Bon Marche, Seattle
(206) 506-4FUN
Four Seasons Olympic Hotel, Seattle; (206) 528-2777
Seattle Sheraton Hotel and Towers, Seattle; (206) 667-6264
Woodland Park Zoo, Seattle
(206) 632-9664

Chanukah Celebration

Stroum Jewish Community Center, Mercer Island; (206) 232-7115

A large community gathering with games, menorahs, and lots of golden latkes.

Children's Christmas in Scandinavia

Nordic Heritage Museum, Seattle
(206) 789-5708

This celebration is for children, by children. Children from the Swedish Cultural Society present the traditional St. Lucia ceremony, a children's dance group performs with participation from the audience, and children sing carols and dance around the Christmas tree.

Maurice Sendak designed the sets and costumes for the Pacific Northwest Ballet's "The Nut-cracker."

COURTESY OF THE PACIFIC NORTHWEST BALLET

Christmas Ship
Argosy Cruises, Seattle
(206) 623-1445

During December, nightly cruises depart from various locations on Lake Washington and Puget Sound for the annual Christmas Ship Festival. Carol with the on-board choirs, cruise among the parading boats, and wave at thousands of onlookers at beach bonfires. The cruises last two to three hours.

Christmas Tree Lighting
Downtown Leavenworth (20 miles west of Wenatchee)
Leavenworth Chamber of Commerce, (509) 548-5807

The Christmas Tree Lighting Ceremony is held on the first two weekends in December.

Enchanted Village Lights
Federal Way; (253) 661-8001

The amusement park is open and adorned with holiday lights and decorations most nights from December to early January.

Family Fest
Museum of History and Industry, Seattle; (206) 324-1125

Each year during the holidays, the Museum of History and Industry hosts special activities and events celebrating holiday traditions from around the world.

Great Figgy Pudding Street Corner Caroling Competition
Westlake Center, Seattle
(206) 467-1600

Costumed caroling groups sing

both traditional and original carols on downtown Seattle streets. Shoppers can then vote for their favorite act.

"The Nutcracker"
Pacific Northwest Ballet, Seattle
(206) 441-2424; www.pnb.org
Olympic Ballet Theatre, Edmonds
(425) 774-7570
Emily's Dance Arts, Bellevue
(425) 746-3659
Evergreen City Ballet, Auburn
(253) 833-9039
Cameo Dance Theatre, Seattle
(206) 528-8183

Each year, Pacific Northwest Ballet performs "The Nutcracker" at the Seattle Opera House with a spectacular Maurice Sendak set. There are also backstage tours after some performances. Many local dance studios and dance companies also perform this holiday favorite, often featuring young performers. These smaller-scale productions are low priced and often a great hit with young audiences.

Santa's Reindeer Farm
Cougar Mountain Zoo, Issaquah
(425) 391-5508

Visit the elves' workshop, pet Santa's reindeer, sit in the sleigh, and meet Santa at Santa's Reindeer Farm. After dark, the farm sparkles with thousands of lights.

Santa Trains
Camp 6, Point Defiance Park,
Tacoma; (253) 752-0047
Lake Whatcom Railway,
Wickersham; (360) 595-2218

Snoqualmie Valley Railroad,
Snoqualmie; (425) 888-2206

These organizations offer special Santa Trains during December. Children get a ride, receive goodies, and visit with Santa. Call early in the fall for reservations, as tickets sell quickly.

Science Wonderland
Pacific Science Center, Seattle
(206) 443-2001

The Science Center's annual holiday extravaganza features loads of hands-on, educational fun. Held during the winter holiday break, late December through early January.

Teddy Bear Suite
Four Seasons Olympic Hotel,
Seattle; (206) 621-1700

Every December, the Four Seasons Olympic Hotel in downtown Seattle converts one of its rooms into a teddy bear wonderland, complete with an antique bed, lots of teddy bears dressed for bedtime, a decorated Christmas tree, music, treats, and a special place for parents to read from a collection of teddy bear books. A fun place to take a break on a busy shopping day. There is no charge.

Tickle Tune Typhoon
(206) 632-9466

The group presents an annual family holiday concert, featuring original and traditional music and dance. The cast includes waltzing snowflakes, a dancing Christmas tree, and Santa (doing his famous "Belly Boogie").

Voices of Christmas
Seattle Group Theatre, Seattle
(206) 441-1299

Designed for the entire family, this popular show features winter holiday traditions from around the world in a unique theatrical revue including music, comedy, poetry, and storytelling. Tickets go on sale in early September.

Zoobilee
Woodland Park Zoo, Seattle
(206) 684-4800

Zoobilee, held on December weekends, features Santa visits and photos, storytelling, and carolers.

Zoolights
Point Defiance Zoo and Aquarium, Tacoma; (253) 591-5337

Each December, the Point Defiance Zoo and Aquarium are transformed into a fantasy land of lights. Thousands of lights cover pathways, trees, and buildings and illuminate figures in the shapes of animals, nursery-rhyme characters, and local landmarks. Crowds are smallest early in the month.

Chapter 11

BASICS

Restaurants
Shopping
Transportation
Resources
Web Sites

RESTAURANTS

I t's hard to have a good dining-out experience with a young eater, and when grown-ups are brave or foolish enough to venture into a restaurant with a child, we believe they deserve all the good food and helpful service they can possibly get. We are talking real family eateries here—where your toddler can fling a fistful of rice without shaming you out of the place, the high chairs aren't quaint antiques that can be flipped over with one good arch of the back, and the food and service are worth the effort and money.

This list was compiled from our own experiences as parents and from the recommendations of fellow parents. The selections were made with the following criteria in mind.

Good Food. For the adults and the kids.

Kid Friendly. You and your kids should feel genuinely welcome, even if your kids don't always act like short British diplomats. Your server will hopefully distract a fussy baby and cheerfully clean up spilled milk, instead of glowering unsympathetically as the behavior at your table begins to deteriorate.

Fair Prices. A typical kid goes through numerous eating stages, ranging from nibbling two bites per meal to inhaling everything in sight and still feeling "starved." Both phases are costly if you are eating out. The period between these two extremes seems to occupy a very small window of time, so the prices for kids' meals should give parents a break.

Fast Service. Most young kids sitting in a restaurant are time bombs waiting to blow. In everyone's interest, your server should go for top efficiency, recognizing you are here to refuel and leave, not to linger over meaningful conversation. We don't think any meal is worth a long wait when you are dining with kids.

Entertainment. This is not essential for placement on our list, but it does give the adults that extra two minutes to gulp down their meals. A floor show is not necessary, but it sure helps to offer a cup of crayons or a balloon.

Seattle

Alki Homestead
2717 61st Ave. S.W. (West Seattle), Seattle
(206) 935-5678
Dinner, Wed.-Sat.; reservations required

There is a very narrow slice of the population that is perfectly suited for this old-fashioned restaurant: little girls, ages 5 to 10, who are charmed by old-fashioned elegance. They will be enchanted, while everybody else has an OK dining experience. Located in a genuine log cabin (built in 1904) and decked out with lace tablecloths and fine crystal, it is not a place to take preschoolers. The specialty of the house is a pan-fried chicken dinner with all the fixings ($11.95). This is an ideal restaurant for a night on the town with one child, not a feeding stop for a hungry brood.

Blue Star Cafe and Pub
4512 Stone Way N., Seattle
(206) 548-0345
Lunch, Sat.-Sun.; dinner daily

Granted, it is called a pub and there are no crayons or other kid attractions provided, but this spacious spot at the west end of Wallingford has such fast service you probably won't need anything to entertain your kids. There's a good standard children's menu, featuring generously dished helpings for $3.95, including a small soda or milk. Older kids with big appetites will find a good selection on the regular menu since the theme of the place is home-style cooking. There is plenty of elbow room and the cheerful hum of folks having a good time, so you won't feel conspicuous if your kids get wiggly while you savor the last morsels of your delicious meal.

Chinook's at Salmon Bay
1900 W. Nickerson St., Seattle
(206) 283-4665
Lunch daily; dinner, daily; breakfast, Sat.-Sun.

Little Chinook's
1735 W. Thurman
(206) 283-4665

There is plenty for kids to look

at while gazing through the large windows that enclose this big, bustling restaurant at Fisherman's Terminal near Ballard. While the view of the working marina will provide diversion for small fry, the wide selection of good food (over 125 items on the dinner menu, plus daily specials) will delight the adults. This is also a good place to bring out-of-town relatives—they'll get a taste of the city's maritime life and the chance to eat well-prepared seafood, and you won't get wiped out by the check (dinner entrees are $7.95 to $14.95). There is often a short wait for breakfast on weekends, but kids can easily be distracted by a walk among the hundreds of fishing boats. Once you are seated, a basket of scrumptious freshly baked scones arrives at your table, accompanied by orange butter.

Little Chinooks, located adjacent to the main restaurant, offers fish (ling cod, halibut, prawns or oysters) and chips in a more casual fast-food environment. Tables don't fit more than four people, so this isn't the spot for groups.

If you want to work off your meal, drive a few blocks west to Discovery Park and take a walk in the city's largest park (see entry in Chapter 3).

Green Village
721 S. King St., Seattle
(206) 624-3634
Dinner, Wed.-Mon.

Green Village 2

514 Sixth Ave. S., Seattle
(206) 621-1719
Dinner, Mon.-Sat.

At Green Village on S. King, your toughest moment will be choosing from the menu of over 100 items. Don't agonize too much, though; we haven't found a bad choice yet. The dishes are mostly Szechwan specialties and curries, so you be careful not to order foods that will be too hot for young palates. All the noodle dishes are wonderful; the seafood dishes are also exceptional (however, stay away from the seafood if you are dining on a tight budget). There are several big, round tables that can comfortably seat eight, so this is a fine place to come with a big group.

If you hanker for Chinese food but you want a quicker and less expensive alternative, head to Green Village 2. This little hole-in-the-wall has a very limited menu (House Special Rice Noodles, $4.50 with soup; Three Types of Seafood Noodles, $4.95; Vegetables Over Rice, $4.25). There are no high chairs at Green Village 2. After your meal, walk across the street to browse in Uwajimaya (see "International District" in Chapter 8).

Iron Horse

311 Third Ave. S. (Pioneer Square), Seattle
(206) 233-9506
Lunch, dinner daily

We broke a few of our standards by including this place, especially rule number one: The food must be good. The food is not bad here, just mediocre. But go anyway, because children will be thrilled to have a toy train deliver their hamburger. A toot of the whistle announces your order is on its way, and when you see your preschooler's face as the train pulls up at her table, you'll be glad you came. Fare is standard: salads, burgers, and sandwiches at moderate prices; train paraphernalia covers the walls. This is also a good place to have a birthday party (the train delivers a complimentary sundae to the birthday boy or girl).

Ivar's Acres of Clams

Pier 54, Seattle
(206) 624-6852
Lunch, dinner daily

Ivar's Indian Salmon House

401 Northlake Way, Seattle
(206) 632-0767
Lunch, Mon.-Fri; dinner, daily; brunch, Sun.

Ivar's Mukilteo Landing

710 Front St., Mukilteo
(425) 742-6180
Lunch, dinner daily

With a children's menu that doubles as a colorful mask, friendly servers who go out of their way to make kids feel welcome, and good food at very reasonable prices (salmon, cornbread, and slaw for $8.75), Ivar's is a quintessential family restaurant. All three restaurants have the added attraction of being located on the water, so there's always a good view of the boat activity. All three restaurants also have a take-out counter outside, a great option on a summer night.

Our favorite of the three is the Indian Salmon House. The setting is a replica of an Indian longhouse, with magnificent canoes, masks, and photographs decorating the dining area. Cod and salmon are cooked over a smoky alder fire, and kids enjoy watching the cooks working over the big flames. This is an ideal place to take an out-of-town family to give them a glimpse of Northwest Indian culture along with a good salmon meal and a water view.

Julia's
1714 N. 44th (Wallingford), Seattle
(206) 633-1175
Breakfast, lunch, and dinner, daily

Voted the best breakfast spot by readers of *Seattle's Child* and *Eastside Parent*, Julia's will downsize its famous breakfasts for children. A kids' menu is available for lunch and dinner. Expect a wait at breakfast/brunch time on weekends.

Luna Park Cafe
2918 S.W. Avalon Way
(West Seattle), Seattle
(206) 935-7250
Breakfast, lunch, and dinner, daily
Directions: From I-5, take the Spokane St. exit, then the Harbor Ave. exit. Turn left onto S. Avalon; the restaurant is on the right.

Jukeboxes all over the place, a batmobile right in the joint, a genuine soda fountain that serves up thick, creamy milkshakes, and a child's menu that includes Mickey Mouse pancakes—when you think

about it, West Seattle is not that far away. Take lots of quarters and show your kids what a record (as opposed to a CD) looks like. And if the '50s decor isn't enough to lure you there, the tasty, down-home food should be. Kids' meals range from $1.75 to $2.95; adult meals are $6 to $7. The servers will happily split a $2.95 milkshake into two still-generous portions for you and your child to share.

The Old Spaghetti Factory
2801 Elliott Ave., Seattle
(206) 441-7724
Lunch and dinner, daily; reservations not accepted

The first clue that this place is good for families is its name: "Factory" is not a word usually associated with elegant dining. Even so, the Spaghetti Factory has managed to create a festive atmosphere, with Victorian-style decor, a beautiful old scale (only kids love to weigh themselves before and after dinner), and a real caboose that sits in the middle of the main dining area (good luck waiting for one of its few tables). What is factory-like is the speed and efficiency of the wait staff and the sheer size of the place.

The food is delicious and very reasonably priced (spaghetti with clam sauce, $5.60; meatballs and spaghetti, $6.75; combo plate of meat sauce, mushroom sauce, and specialty cheese, $6.55). All dinners include salad, a loaf of sourdough bread (served with plain and garlic butters), and spumoni for dessert. Kids get a choice of special meals that come on plastic dinosaur plates (so popular they will sell you the dinner sets). A popular young kiddie meal includes spaghetti with tomato sauce, plus applesauce, beverage, dinosaur cookie, and frozen treat, for $2.95 ($3.35 with a meatball; $3.95 for lasagna instead of spaghetti). A junior meal, for bigger or hungrier children, costs $4.45 and includes spaghetti, salad, bread, beverage, and spumoni. Since you aren't the only parent in town looking for good food and service at a great price in a fun setting, plan to go early (before 5:30 p.m.) if you want to avoid a wait.

Palisade Waterfront Restaurant

2601 W. Marina Pl., Seattle
(206) 285-1000
Lunch and dinner, daily; brunch, Sun.

Although it's not your typical "family restaurant," Palisade nevertheless offers one meal with great appeal for kids and adults alike: Sunday brunch. The "Palisade Cityview Brunch" ($14/adults, $6/kids age 12 and under) begins with freshly squeezed orange juice (mimosas available for the grownups) and a basket of blueberry and raspberry muffins. Proceed next to the fruit bar, which includes fresh seasonal fruits, granola, and several salads. The buffet also features the brunch's signature item—banana-macadamia nut-sourdough griddlecakes, served with pineapple butter and maple-rum syrup.

If these all-you-can-eat offerings aren't enough to fill the kids, spend just a dollar more to order a "wacky waffle" (bearing a striking resemblance to Mickey Mouse, complete with a strawberry nose) or scrambled eggs with cheese and apple sausages. Adults can add on to their brunch too for $1 to $6 more, choosing from stuffed French toast, spit-roasted salmon hash, a very good vegetable omelet, and seven other brunch entrées, as well as several meat, seafood, and pasta choices.

Besides tasty food, the Polynesian-themed Palisade has some unique features that make it especially fun for kids, such as a grand piano above the bar that plays all by itself, ponds filled with live tropical fish, an ice sculpture that tempts touching by little hands (despite parental admonitions not to do so), and views of boats with fun-to-read names in Elliott Bay Marina below and the city skyline beyond.

Roy's Restaurant

1900 Fifth Ave. (in the Westin Hotel), Seattle
(206) 256-7697
Breakfast, lunch, and dinner, daily

It is surprisingly difficult to find a good meal in downtown Seattle that will satisfy both adults and children without breaking the budget. At this cheery cafe located off the main lobby of the Westin Hotel (close to the Monorail station), you and your child will find a wide variety of healthy and delicious choices and a kitchen that is exceptionally accommodating to the finicky eater. Crayons are provided, and service is excellent. The owner himself has children, and thus the entire menu is very kid friendly. There is a children's menu, which features delicious homemade pizzas for $3, and if you're lucky, the chef might take you in the back and let your kids ball their own dough! This is a good place to take a child before a night out at the theater.

Seattle Crab Company
1000 N.E. Northgate Way, Seattle
(206) 366-9225
Lunch and dinner, daily

When this north-end restaurant opened several years ago in a former Skipper's location, customers stood in a Skipper's-style line to order their food, but now it's a sit-down restaurant with fast and friendly service. The varied menu of reasonably priced seafood includes three kinds of crab—available chilled, steamed, or as crab cakes— plus prawns, halibut, cod, scallops, salmon, mussels, and clams. For non-fish- eaters, there's hamburgers, steak, chicken sandwiches, and several pasta dishes. Chowders, salads, and four yummy desserts round out the offerings. Kids have a choice of hamburgers, chicken, or fish (all with fries), or noodles and cheese, served with animal crackers and applesauce, for $2.95.

Upright rolls of paper towels serve as napkins, handy for shellfish eaters and even handier for kid clean-ups.

The 5 Spot
1502 Queen Anne Ave. N., Seattle
(206) 285-7768
Breakfast, lunch, and dinner, daily

This cheery eatery, perched at the summit of Queen Anne Hill, aims to be child-friendly and adult-welcoming in equal proportions. The 5 Spot features a permanent menu of eclectic dishes and a rotating menu, changed quarterly, based on a culinary theme, which the decor also reflects. For example, when the theme was "Baja Border Grill," an array of dishes from that region of Mexico was offered and decorations included piñatas hung suspended from the high ceilings and walls festooned with strings of chili pepper lights. The main dining room and bar are large and noisy; a smaller room in back offers quieter dining.

The children's menu offers the usual picky-eater standbys: a foot-long hot dog , peanut butter sandwich, fish and chips, charcoal-broiled chicken breast, and quesadillas ($3.50-$4.75). The fresh lemonade arrives in frosty mason jars. For dessert, a parade of ice cream treats is offered, along with other goodies. For adults, the permanent menu features entrees from five U.S. regions. Small and entree-size salads are available, as well as a respectable variety of vegetarian entrees. Prices for most entrees range from $8 to $13. Servings are enormous. The attention to detail is exceptional: the cilantro vinaigrette on a side salad of gourmet greens was a treat.

The 5 Spot's child-friendliness extends to the rest rooms. Both men's and women's feature baby-changing tables. After your meal, walk off some calories in the inviting urban neighborhood. Stroll along Queen Anne Avenue, past the bistros, bakeries, and bookstores, or stop at the playground at First Avenue West and Blaine.

Eastside

Alexa's Cafe
10115 Main St., Bothell
(425) 483-6275
Breakfast and lunch, daily
(8 a.m.-3 p.m.)

If you want to take a little more time to enjoy lunch than it takes for your child to scarf down a sandwich, try this friendly cafe in downtown Bothell. A giant Barney doll sits near the entrance, and a doll house, books, crayons, and a basket full of toys occupy a section of this otherwise grown-up place. A cozy couch invites little ones to curl up and read, and just beyond are tables where parents can enjoy lunch while perusing local artwork and sculptures. All sandwiches are made on inch-thick homemade bread, and the delicious soups are also homemade. The only drawback is that the kids' sandwiches come on the same bread and are too cumbersome for little mouths without a lot of extra cutting. The result can be a big mess. The desserts, such as fresh pies and brownies, are also wonderful.

The Eating Factory
10630 N.E. Eighth St., Bellevue
(425) 688-8202
Lunch and dinner, daily

Trust Bellevue to be the place where even smorgasbords get yuppi-

fied. The Eating Factory offers a Japanese buffet with all-you-can-eat sushi. And you'd better eat all you take, because the restaurant charges $1 for any leftover pieces of sushi that your eyes thought your stomach could accommodate. Even those who aren't big on raw fish and rice wrapped in seaweed can enjoy noodle, chicken, and seafood dishes; miso soup; tempura; fresh fruit; and a Japanese salad bar. The sushi isn't of the highest quality, but it's a great place to sample different kinds without having to tally the cost up in your head each time you (or your kids) take one. The decor is bright, clean, and colorful; high chairs are plentiful. A television playing Japanese music videos makes for a sort of multi-pop-cultural experience. A tip: Go for lunch rather than the more expensive dinner (which includes crab legs and jumbo shrimp). Adults pay $9.95 for lunch and $16.95 for dinner. Children under 4 feet 2 inches tall eat for half price, while little ones under 3 feet 2 inches eat free.

Jay Berry's Restaurant
385 N.W. Gilman Blvd., Issaquah
(425) 392-0808
Lunch daily except Sunday;
dinner daily

Voted as serving the best pizza in Issaquah by the local newspaper, Jay Berry's also makes wonderful pasta dishes. Prices range from $7 for all-you-can-eat spaghetti to $11 for chicken Parmesan. A large specialty pizza is $18.50. If you come during a slow time, you might get a seat by the long window that overlooks a small creek.

Various Locations

Azteca

Seattle: Ballard, Lake Union, Northgate area, Shilshole, and University Village
Eastside: Bellevue, Kirkland (Totem Lake), and Redmond
South: Burien, Federal Way, Southcenter, and Tacoma
Lunch and dinner, daily

Azteca does an outstanding job of serving good Mexican food quickly and at reasonable prices. Children are made to feel welcome by the gracious attitude of the staff, an excellent children's menu, and crayons and balloons. The prices are good every day (regular entrées are $5 to $10; a meal from the children's menu is $2.95), but Sundays are an even better deal for families, when a child's meal is only 95 cents!

Billy McHale's

4065 128th S.E. (Factoria), Bellevue; (425) 746-1138;
1800 S. 320th, Federal Way
(253) 927-4450
10115 S. Tacoma Way, Lakewood
(253) 582-6330
15210 Redmond Way, Redmond
(425) 881-0316
241 S.W. Seventh, Renton
(425) 271-7427
Lunch and dinner, daily

The big hit at this restaurant is the miniature train running on a track hung just below the ceiling. Watching for it to come chugging by as it circles the dining area has kept many a preschooler entertained until the food came. Some restaurants also have play areas set off from the waiting area so parents don't have to strain to amuse kids before and after they're seated. Kids' meals are a little pricier than some, ranging from $3 for a hot dog to $4.50 for barbecued ribs, but they are served with French fries, carrot sticks, applesauce, and a packet of cookies. Drinks are $1 extra. On Sundays, children age 12 and under receive any kids' entrée for half off. Most adult meals fall into the $7-$10 range, with soup, burgers, and seafood options. There are free refills on pop and "bottomless" fries, which is likely to please teenagers (and husbands).

Chang's Mongolian Grill

7601 Evergreen Way, Everett
(425) 347-1925
24060 104th S.E., Kent
(253) 850-6264
1827 Broadway, Seattle
(206) 325-6160
Lunch and dinner, daily

This is a good place to get children to eat their vegetables, as they'll likely think even carrots taste good after they watch chefs stir-fry their chosen mix of meat and veggies on a flaming grill.

Diners fill a bowl with options from a long buffet, which includes pieces of beef, chicken, fish, and shrimp; noodles; and vegetables. They can then top their selection with a number of flavorings, such as garlic and soy sauce. Two cooks dump the bowls on a large, round grill, and kids can watch their dinner being fried. Meat juices often spark a blaze, which is always an attention-getter. Servers bring rice to accompany the meal, or better yet for kids, rice pancakes that can be filled and rolled. Meals also include soup and a dish of ice cream. Adults pay $6.25 for lunch and $9.95 for dinner. Children ages 4-10 are half price; children 3 and under are $2.

Circo Circo!

23223 Pacific Hwy. S., Kent
(206) 878-4424
12709 N.E. 124th (Totem Lake),
Kirkland; (425) 821-9405
Lunch and dinner, daily

It's hard to go wrong with Mexican food, but Circo Circo tries a little harder than most restaurants to improve standard Mexican offerings by using ingredients that are obviously fresh and by allowing a variety of options (such as what kinds of beans you'd like, e.g., refried, regular, or black). A separate vegetarian menu is available, though many items on the regular menu are meatless. The menu also notes which items are low-fat. The decor is bright, and kids are offered crayons. Prices range from about $6 to $8.

Cucina!Cucina!

800 Bellevue Way N.E. (Bellevue
Place), Bellevue; (425) 637-1178
2220 Carillon Point, Kirkland
(425) 822-4000
2902 228th S.E. (Pickering Place),

Issaquah; (425) 391-3800
901 Fairview N. (Chandler's Cove),
Seattle; (206) 447-2782
4201 S. Steele (north side of Tacoma Mall), Tacoma; (253) 475-6000
17770 Southcenter Pkwy. (Parkway Plaza), Tukwila; (206) 575-0520
Lunch and dinner, daily

Upon entering Seattle's Cucina!Cucina! your child is offered a balloon—an instant hit. Though crayons and a menu to color are de rigueur in family restaurants now, Cucina! expands the concept further by having the entire table serve as a canvas (it's covered with white butcher paper). Servers also offer pieces of raw pizza dough that kids can treat like Play-Doh.

The child's menu offers individual pizzas ($2.95-$3.75 includes milk or soda) and a good selection of pasta dishes, such as plain buttered pasta and spaghetti with meatballs. Be forewarned: A basket of bread costs $3. (Complimentary bread is sorely missed when you are a parent with a kid on the verge of a hunger breakdown, and a surprising oversight for a restaurant that caters to kids.) Adult meals run from $7 for an authentically wood-fired cheese pizza to $10 for calzone.

The decor is festive and playful, with all sorts of bicycles hanging from the ceiling. In Seattle, kids can watch activity on Lake Union out the windows. You won't dine on the finest Italian cuisine in town, but you will eat decent and sometimes inspired food at moderate prices. And your kids will probably come away feeling they have had a fun treat.

Pasta Ya Gotcha

11025 N.E. Eighth, Bellevue
(425) 637-7019
123 Lake St. S., Kirkland
(425) 889-1511
Lunch and dinner, daily
823 Third, Seattle; (206) 223-4788
Lunch only

Pasta Ya Gotcha's quick service (under three minutes), casual dining atmosphere (food is served on paper plates even if you're eating in), and goofy name might lead to you expect uninspired dishes, but you'll actually find a pleasant balance between standards (spaghetti with red sauce) and more unusual offerings such as BBQ pasta, Thai peanut noodles, and Caesar salad linguini. The à la carte dishes start at $3.95 and end at $5.50. A side salad or soup is an extra $1.50. Kid's meals are $2.95 for spaghetti with red sauce or circle noodles with alfredo sauce or butter and cheese.

Vince's Italian Restaurant and Pizzeria

15223 Fourth SW, Burien
(206) 246-1497
32411 Pacific Hwy. S., Federal Way
(253) 839-1496
2815 N.E. Sunset Blvd., Renton
(425) 226-8180
8824 Renton S., Seattle
(206) 722-2116
Lunch and dinner, daily

From the Italian trivia placards on the tables to the hand-tossed pizza dough, Vince's is not about Pizza Hut-style Italian food, but something a lot more authentic. The offerings include pizza loaded with fresh top-

pings, calzone, and four-course pasta dinners with soup, salad, and dessert. Kids' meals include mini-pizzas and spaghetti. Depending on how many courses you add, dinners are about $7 to $10. Kids will enjoy the profiteroles, tiny cream puffs covered with chocolate sauce. Kids meals are $2.75-$3.25.

Zoopa

1070 Bellevue Square (inside the mall), Bellevue; (425) 453-7887
463 Northgate Mall (outside the mall by J.C. Penney), Seattle;
(206) 440-8136
1901 S. 72nd, Tacoma;
(253) 472-0900
393 Strander Blvd. (near Southcenter Mall), Tukwila; (206) 575-0500
Lunch and dinner, daily

The problem with most buffet-style restaurants is that they sacrifice quality for quantity. Sure, you can eat your fill, but who would want to? Zoopa rises above this pitfall. It offers a full meal, from salad to dessert, focusing on pasta and soups. Besides the huge salad bar, diners can choose between three kinds of pasta sauce, four kinds of soup, a baked potato bar, and a variety of fresh breads, including mini-muffins. Kids have all the adult options plus a special bar just for them with favorites such as fruit, crackers, and Jell-O. After- dinner treats include low-fat, soft-serve ice cream, toppings, and several tempting desserts. Meals are $7.39/adults, $3.99/children ages 5-10, free/kids under age 5. Drinks are extra, but there are free refills on pop.

Tacoma

Freighthouse Square

2501 E. D St. (green building just
north of the Tacoma Dome)
(253) 305-0678
Hours: Mon.-Sat., 10 a.m.-7 p.m.;
Sun., noon-5 p.m.

If your family's tastes are impos-
sibly varied or if you crave ethnic
food, check out Freighthouse
Square's food court, with almost a
dozen locally owned eateries. The
cuisine circles the globe: Mexican,
Korean, Vietnamese, Italian, Indian,
Greek, and German. Espresso, a
bakery, and an ice cream shop
round out the meal.

Harmon Pub and Brewery

1938 Pacific Ave. (across the street
from the Washington State History
Museum), Tacoma
(253) 383-2739
Lunch and dinner, daily

From the outside, the Harmon
doesn't look like a family place, but
inside you'll find crayons, a coloring
sheet, cozy booths, and possibly the
most interesting kids' menu in Tacoma. While parents can sample the
"Brew Ski" and classic pub grub
($6.95-$8.95), kids can choose from
a quarter-pound burger and fries
($3.95), rainbow pasta with cheese
sauce ($3.25), bratwurst with garlic
mashed potatoes ($3.95), chicken
strips ($3.95), pizza ($3.95), or
peanut butter and jelly sandwich
with fries ($2.95). Unlike the bland
fare found on most kids' menus,

many of these items are scaled-
down versions of the adult offerings.
The mild garlic-herb flavoring on the
fries, the herbs in the pizza crust,
and the multicolored pasta could be
surprising (and possibly distressing)
for less adventurous eaters.

The Antique Sandwich Co.

5102 N. Pearl (two blocks south of
Point Defiance Park), Tacoma
(253) 752-4069
Breakfast, lunch, and dinner, daily

If you are looking for a place to
relax with good, simple food, this
old-fashioned coffee house makes a
perfect stop after an outing to Point
Defiance Park. In the summer, outdoor dining is possible in the "'Garden of Eatin'.'" The Antique Sandwich offers a long list of deli sandwiches served with salad or chips
(average price: $5.50), with the flex-
ibility to serve even plain cream
cheese and bread (bread choices
are whole wheat and rye). Quiches
and a few other entrées are also
available, along with home-style
desserts. A large collection of toys
will keep kids busy as parents
linger and enjoy a free coffee refill.

The Old Spaghetti Factory

1735 Jefferson S. (two blocks west
of Union Station), Tacoma
(253) 383-2214
(See review under "Seattle.")

Rock Pasta Brick Oven Pizza
and Brewery

1920 Jefferson St., Tacoma
(253) 272-1221
Lunch, and dinner, daily

If the wait at the Spaghetti Factory is more than you can stand or if you want some something you wouldn't cook at home, step across the street for an eating adventure. Don't worry: The kids can still have a plain cheese or peanut butter and jelly pizza or plain buttered noodles ($2.50-$3), but you can have the Elvis Sighting, sun-dried tomato and ricotta- filled ravioli in a rich pesto cream sauce served with tomatoes and roasted pecans ($9.25 includes salad and bread) or a Philadelphia Freedom pizza, which is shaved sirloin, caramelized onions, roasted peppers, and Romano and Swiss cheeses topped with a horseradish-Dijon- sour cream sauce ($8.25 or $12.95).

Pastas and pizzas are named for legendary rock songs and performers, but the background music sticks pretty much to mellower '70's- style rock. Kids receive a blob of pizza dough to entertain them. Be sure to check out the bear skeleton to the right of the entry. It is Jessie, a relic from the TV series "*Northern Exposure.*"

Fast-Food Alternatives

If you're looking for an alternative to the assembly-line burger places most kids adore, check out the following. All offer affordable take-out meals, with the option of a casual eat-in environment too.

Boston Market
Various locations throughout the region
Lunch and dinner, daily

Boston Market sells the kind of meat-and-potatoes comfort food that many of us grew up with: roasted chicken and turkey breast, ham, meat loaf, pot pie, mashed potatoes, baked beans, and casseroles. Individual meals ($4.50-$6.49) and family "feasts" ($14-$26) are available with a variety of side dishes and cornbread. If kids age 10 and under insist on ordering a meal of their own, both the macaroni and cheese ($1.99) and kid- size serving of meat ($2.49) include a side dish, corn bread, and a drink. Parents love the convenience and quality of Boston Market and voted it the best take-out in *Eastside Parent's* 1997 Golden Bootie Awards.

The restaurants also sell fixings for big holiday or special-occasion meals, including whole and half glazed hams, rotisserie turkey breasts, and banquet-size containers of side dishes. You can transfer the food to your own serving dishes before your guests arrive and no one will know you didn't make it yourself (maybe).

Cucina Presto
Various locations in Seattle, Bellevue, Mercer Island, Kirkland, Renton, Lynnwood, and Everett
Lunch and dinner, daily

An offshoot of the highly successful Cucina!Cucina! chain, Cucina Presto has proven to be especially popular with families. Many of the same or similar wood-fired pizzas, specialty pastas, and salads are on the menu, but the prices are lower, the service is (usually) faster, the atmosphere is more casual, and (dare we say it?) you won't need to leave a tip.

Kids' meals are a real bargain—a mini-pizza (cheese or pepperoni) goes for $1.99 or pasta lovers can "mix and match" from the available pastas and sauces for $2.49. Both meals include all-you-can-drink milk or pop.

Five nine-inch hand-tossed piz-

INSIDE SCOOP

Supermarkets with Restaurants

One of the tastier convenience trends of the decade has been the emergence of supermarkets that offer take-out and eat-in meals. Delis with fried chicken, salads, soups, and a variety of other cold and hot prepared foods, including Chinese entrées, have been available for a while now. Few new supermarkets open without these "basics."

Two local chains—**Larry's Market** and **QFC**—have taken the concept even further, with restaurants within some of their stores.

At QFC's University Village flagship store, for instance, shoppers will find Noah's Bagels, Juba's juice bar, Starbucks, Cinnabon, Viva Gelato, Banzai Sushi (besides sushi, you can order freshly made hot entrées like fried rice and yakisoba), a Cucina!Cucina! pasta bar, and QFC's own panini bar, with a variety of Northwest-inspired grilled sandwiches.

This QFC also has eating tables inside and outside, a fireplace sur-

rounded by chairs, a piano that visiting pianists sometimes play, and a free child-care center if you'd like to enjoy a kid-free meal. No other QFC is quite as extensive as this, but many have at least the panini bar and one or two other restaurant options.

Larry's Markets boast impressive deli counters, including many unique items. Known as "the" place to go for gourmet foods, including exotic produce and hard-to-find delicacies, the grocery section is surprisingly affordable if you shop the advertised specials. The store's cafeteria is open from early morning till evening, with a cook-to-order menu featuring traditional cafe fare. Most stores also feature a "panizza," where you can order grilled panini sandwiches, a "taqueria" for Mexican-inspired specialties, a sushi bar, and a juice bar. You're welcome to munch on any store-bought edibles in the cafe eating area.

zas ($3.99-$4.99) are on the menu, including one with goat cheese, artichokes, pesto, and pine nuts for decidedly adult tastes. If you're watching your fat intake, pizzas can be ordered with low-fat mozzarella or no cheese at all, and a few of the pastas (4.49-$5.99) are also designated as heart-healthy.

While some of the locations have drive-throughs and all offer take-out, we recommend this option for pastas and salads only, as the pizzas definitely lose some appeal when transported and reheated. Besides, Cucina Presto is a fun place to eat: The outlets are as brightly decorated and colorful as their parent restaurants, and kids can enjoy playing with pizza dough at the table here too (you'll have to ask the cashier for the dough, though).

Kidd Valley
Various locations in Seattle and the Eastside
Open for lunch and dinner

Though this local burger chain has expanded into malls and lost some of its uniqueness in the process, it still manages to retain a neighborhood feel at its stand-alone restaurants, including those in the University District, Kenmore, Capitol Hill, Queen Anne, and Bellevue. Several locations are quite handy for picnickers, such as the branches on Lake Washington Blvd. in Kirkland (across from a waterfront city park), near Green Lake, and at Coulon Park in Renton.

The menu doesn't differ greatly from national fast-food chains, but the quality often does. Thick and creamy milkshakes, hefty sauce-dripping burgers, and original items like deep-fried mushrooms make Kidd Valley a local favorite. Naturally, they offer kids' ("Kidds"?) meals too—burgers, cheeseburgers, hot dogs, and grilled cheese sandwiches, with fries, a drink, and a toy—for $2.59 to $2.79.

Taco Del Mar
World Wrapps
Various locations in Seattle and the Eastside

Take your basic tortilla and start adding funky fillings such as fish, in the case of Taco Del Mar, or various ethnic types of ingredients, in the case of World Wrapps, and you've got a reasonably healthy and affordable fast food. World Wrapps also offers fruit smoothies, which kids should enjoy. Both places also offer traditional Mexican-style burritos for children with less adventuresome palates. The meals range from $4 to $7 and are quite filling.

SHOPPING LIST
Malls

Alderwood Mall, 3000 184th St. S.W., Lynnwood; (425) 771-1121

Bellevue Square, N.E. Eighth and Bellevue Way N.E., Bellevue; (425) 454-2431

Country Village, 23730 Bothell-Everett Hwy., Bothell; (425) 483-2250

Crossroads Shopping Center, 15600 N.E. Eighth St., Bellevue; (425) 644-1111

Everett Mall, 1402 S.E. Everett Mall Way, Everett; (425) 355-1771

Factoria Mall, S.E. 39th and 128th Ave. S.E., Bellevue; (425) 747-7344

Factory Stores at North Bend, 461 South Fork Ave. S.W., North Bend; (425) 888-4505

Gilman Village, 317 N.W. Gilman Blvd., Issaquah; (425) 392-6802

Lake Forest Park Towne Centre, 17171 Bothell Way N.E., Lake Forest Park; (206) 367-6617

Northgate Mall, Northgate Way, Seattle; (206) 362-4777

Pacific Place (opening Sept. 1998), Sixth Ave. and Olive Way, Seattle

Redmond Town Center, 16495 N.E. 74th St., Redmond; (425) 867-0808

Southcenter, junction of Interstate 405 and Interstate 5, Tukwila; (206) 246-7400

Supermall of the Great Northwest, Supermall Way, Auburn; (253) 833-9500

Totem Lake, 12620 120th Ave. N.E., Kirkland; (425) 820-2399

University Village, 4500 25th Ave. NE, Seattle; (206) 523-0622

Westlake Center, 400 Pine St., Seattle; (206) 467-1600

The greater Seattle area offers an exceptionally diverse assortment of toy, clothing, book, and furniture stores that specialize in products for children. Here are some of the best.

ON THE EASTSIDE

CLOTHING

Baby Guess-Guess Kids
Bellevue Square, Bellevue
(425) 454-1992

The Bon Marché
Bellevue Square, Bellevue
(425) 688-6490 (boys' clothing department)
(425) 688-6451 (girls' clothing department)

Brat Pack
7335 N.E. 164th, Redmond
(425) 883-1006

Fine Threads
Redmond Town Center, Redmond
(425) 558-5888

Fleece Farm Kotton Kids
3020 Issaquah-Pine Lake Road, No. 91, Issaquah
(425) 392-5369

GapKids
Bellevue Square, Bellevue
(425) 454-1539

Gymboree
Bellevue Square, Bellevue
(425) 450-9460

Kids Club
Crossroads Shopping Center, Bellevue
(425) 643-KIDS

Kids Cottage
13300 N.E. 175th, Woodinville
(425) 481-2106

Lil' People
Bellevue Square, Bellevue
(425) 455-4967

Merry Go Round Baby News
11111 N.E. Eighth, Bellevue
(425) 454-1610

Nordstrom
Bellevue Square, Bellevue
(425) 455-5800

Oilily
Bellevue Square, Bellevue
(425) 688-0663

**Stars—The Children's Wear
Super Store**
55 N.E. Gilman Blvd., Issaquah
(425) 392-2900

Talbot's Kids
Bellevue Square, Bellevue
(425) 450-3375

SHOES

The Shoe Zoo
240 N.W. Gilman Blvd., Issaquah
(425) 392-8211
Redmond Town Center, Redmond
(425) 558-7534

Stride Rite
Bellevue Square, Bellevue
(425) 453-0101

CONSIGNMENT CLOTHING AND TOYS

Kids Again Consignment
519 156th Ave. S.E., Bellevue
(425) 957-9746

The Tree House
15742 Redmond Way, Redmond
(425) 885-1145

Re-Dress Consignment
513 156th Ave. S.E., Bellevue
(425) 746-7984

**Saturday's Child Consignment
Shoppe**
18012 Bothell-Everett Hwy., Bothell
(425) 486-6716

TOYS

Disney Store
Bellevue Square
(425) 451-0540

Eastside Trains
217 Central Way, Kirkland
(425) 828-4098

Ernie's Toys
16122 N.E. 87th, Redmond
(425) 861-5823

FAO Schwarz
Bellevue Square, Bellevue
(425) 646-9500

Great Train Store
Bellevue Square, Bellevue
(425) 452-9244

Imaginarium
Bellevue Square, Bellevue
(425) 453-5288

Imagination Express
1175 NW Gilman Blvd., Issaquah
(425) 392-3847

Lakeshore Learning Materials
11027 N.E. Fourth, Bellevue
(425) 462-8076

Learning Express
15600 N.E. Eighth, Bellevue
(425) 746-2750

Thinker Toys
10680 N.E. Eighth St., Bellevue
(425) 453-0051

Tree Top Toys
15752 Redmond Way, Redmond
(425) 869-9713

Turn Off the TV
Bellevue Square, Bellevue
(425) 646-1070

Whitehorse Toys
Gilman Village, Issaquah
(425) 391-1498

BOOKSTORES

All for Kids
170 Front St. N., Issaquah
(425) 391-4089

Barnes & Noble
626 106th Ave. N.E., Bellevue
(425) 451-8463
15600 N.E. Eighth, Bellevue
(425) 644-1650
Pickering Place, Issaquah
(425) 557-8808

Half-Price Books
Crossroads Mall, Bellevue
(425) 747-6616
7805 Leary Way, Redmond
(425) 702-2499

Island Books
3014 78th Ave. S.E., Mercer Island
(206) 232-6920

Little Professor Book Store
612 228th Ave. N.E. (on the Redmond Plateau), Redmond
(425) 868-7894

Parkplace Book Co.
Park Place Center, Kirkland
(425) 828-6546

University Bookstore
990 102nd Ave. N.E., Bellevue
(425) 632-9500

CHILDREN'S FURNITURE

A Child's Room
15123 N.E. 24th St., Redmond
(425) 643-7050

Bellini's
201 Bellevue Way N.E., Bellevue
(425) 451-0126

Go To Your Room
13000 Bellevue-Redmond Road,
Bellevue
(425) 453-2990

Merry Go Round Baby News
11111 N.E. Eighth, Bellevue
(425) 454-1610

MATERNITY WEAR

A Designer Maternity Factory
11010 N.E. Eighth, Bellevue
(425) 451-1945

Mimi Maternity
Bellevue Square, Bellevue
(425) 637-8785

Moms 'N Tots
137 106th Ave. N.E, Bellevue
(425) 454-1355

Motherhood Maternity
Bellevue Square, Bellevue
(425) 454-1355

PARTY SUPPLIES

Birthday Express
11220 120th Ave. N.E., Kirkland
(425) 641-0075

Confetti Junction
17181 Redmond Way, Redmond
(425) 861-0567

Partytime
Loehmann's Plaza, Bellevue
(425) 643-7355
1100 N.E. Bellevue Way, Bellevue
(425) 747-5555

Play for Less
10015 N.E. 137th St., Kirkland
(425) 820-4751
975 N.W. Gilman Blvd., Issaquah
(425) 392-3777

SEATTLE— DOWNTOWN

CLOTHING

The Bon Marché
1601 Third Ave., Seattle
(206) 344-2121

KidGear
1420 Fifth Ave. (City Centre),
Seattle
(206) 624-0756

Li'l People
Westlake Center, Seattle
(206) 623-4463
Nordstrom
1501 Fifth Ave., Seattle
(206) 628-2111

TOYS

The Disney Store
Westlake Center, Seattle
(206) 622-3323

Great Wind Kite Shop
402 Occidental Ave. S. (Pioneer Square), Seattle
(206) 624-6886

Magic Mouse Toys
603 First Ave. (Pioneer Square), Seattle
(206) 682-8097

The Nature Company
2001 Western Ave., Seattle
(206) 443-1608

Toytropolis
The Bon Marché (downtown and Northgate only)
1601 Third Ave., Seattle
(206) 344-2121

Turn Off the TV
Westlake Center, Seattle
(206) 521-0564
Wood Shop Toys
320 First S. (Pioneer Square), Seattle
(206) 624-1763

BOOKSTORES

Borders Books and Music
1501 Fourth Ave., Seattle
(206) 622-4599

Brentano's Bookstore
Westlake Center, Seattle
(206) 467-9626

Elliott Bay Book Company
101 S. Main St., (Pioneer Square), Seattle
(206) 624-6600

MATERNITY WEAR

Pea in the Pod
Westlake Center, Seattle
(206) 292-9200

SEATTLE—QUEEN ANNE, MAGNOLIA, CAPITOL HILL, UNIVERSITY AND NORTH SEATTLE

CLOTHING

Boston Street. Baby Store
1815 N. 45th St. (Wallingford), Seattle
(206) 366-9802
Northgate Mall, Seattle
(206) 366-9802

Cotton Caboodle
203 W. Thomas, Seattle
(206) 285-0075

Me 'n Mom's
5514 24th Ave. N.W., (Ballard), Seattle
(206) 781-4827

Kids Club
University Village, Seattle
(206) 524-2553

Rising Stars
7404 Greenwood Ave. N. (Greenwood), Seattle
(206) 781-0138

Small Fry
3209 W. McGraw, Seattle
(206) 283-4556

SHOES

The Shoe Zoo
University Village, Seattle
(206) 525-2770

CONSIGNMENT CLOTHES AND BOOKS

Abigail's
7509 35th Ave. N.E. (Wedgewood),
Seattle
(206) 729-3849

Afont Fashions
4560 33rd Ave. S., Seattle
(206) 721-5279

Bootyland
1321 E. Pine St. (Capitol Hill),
Seattle
(206) 328-0636

Kid's On 45th
1720 N. 45th St. (Wallingford),
Seattle
(206) 633-KIDS (633-5437)

Kym's Kiddy Corner
11721 15th Ave. N.E. (Northgate),
Seattle
(206) 361-5974

Rainbow Boutique Consignment
9518 Roosevelt Way N.E.
(Northgate), Seattle
(206) 522-1213

TOYS

Archie McPhee's
3510 Stoneway Ave. N.
(Wallingford), Seattle
(206) 545-8344

The Disney Store
Northgate Mall
(206) 386-2656

Don's Hobbies
2943 N.E. Blakely, Seattle
(206) 525-7700

Imagination Toys
1815 N. 45th St. (in the Wallingford
Center), Seattle
(206) 547-2356
2236 NW Market St. (Ballard),
Seattle
(206) 784-1310

Math & Stuff
8926 Roosevelt Way N.E. (Maple
Leaf), Seattle
(206) 522-8891

Pinocchio's Toys
4540 Union Bay Pl. N.E. (behind
University Village), Seattle
(206) 528-1100

Teri's Toybox
University Village, Seattle
(206) 526-7147

Top Ten Toys
104 N. 85th St. (Roosevelt), Seattle
(206) 782-0098

Toytropolis
The BonMarché
Northgate Mall, Seattle
(206) 440-6753

BOOKSTORES

All for Kids Books & Music
2900 N.E. Blakely, Seattle
(206) 526-2768

Barnes & Noble
University Village, Seattle
(206) 517-4107

Fremont Place Book Company
621 N. 35th St. (Fremont), Seattle
(206) 547-5970

Half Price Books
4709 Roosevelt Way N.E.
(206) 547-7859

Madison Park Books
4105 E. Madison (Madison Park),
Seattle
(206) 328-READ

Secret Garden Children's Bookshop
6115 15th Ave. N.W. (Ballard),
Seattle
(206) 789-5006

University Book Store
4326 University Way N.E.
(University District), Seattle
(206) 634-3400

FURNITURE

Go To Your Room
University Village
(206) 528-0711

MATERNITY WEAR

Village Maternity
University Village, Seattle
(206) 323-4705

COSTUMES AND PARTY SUPPLIES

Display & Costume Supply
11201 Roosevelt Way N.E. (Northgate), Seattle
(206) 362-4810

SOUTH END— KENT, RENTON, AND TUKWILA

CLOTHING

The Bon Marché
Southcenter Mall, Tukwila
(206) 575-2121

Nordstrom
Southcenter Mall, Tukwila
(206) 246-0400

TOYS

The Disney Store
Southcenter
(206) 241-8922

Imaginarium
Southcenter Mall, Tukwila
(206) 439-8980

HobbyTown USA
17774 Southcenter Pkwy., Tukwila
(206) 575-0949

BOOKSTORES

Barnes & Noble
300 Andover Park W., Tukwila
(206) 575-3965

Children's Bookshop
225 W. Meeker, Kent
(253) 852-0383

Half Price Books
16828 Southcenter Pkwy., Tukwila
(206) 575-3173

CHILDREN'S FURNITURE

IKEA
600 S.W. 43rd, Renton
(425) 656-2980 or (800) 570-4532

MATERNITY

Baby Love
915 Southcenter Shopping Center,
Tukwila
(206) 246-7111

NORTH END— BOTHELL, EDMONDS, LYNNWOOD, AND SHORELINE

CLOTHING

The Bon Marché
Alderwood Mall, Lynnwood
(425) 771-2121

Nordstrom
Alderwood Mall, Lynnwood
(425) 771-5755 or (206) 233-5351

KinderBritches
422 Main St., Edmonds
(425) 778-7600

CONSIGNMENT CLOTHING AND TOYS

Just Bearly Kids Consignment and Maternity
17818 Aurora Ave. N., Shoreline
206-546-8581

Just For You
19918 Aurora Ave. N., Shoreline
(206) 542-3993

Kym's Kiddie Corner
17516 Aurora Ave. N., Shoreline
(206) 546-9230

Saturday's Child
18012 Bothell-Everett Hwy., Bothell
(425) 486-6716

TOYS

Imaginarium
Alderwood Mall, Lynnwood
(425) 771-7220

Teri's Toybox
526 Main St., Edmonds
(425) 774-3190

Tree Top Toys
17171 Bothell Way N.E. (Lake
Forest Park Towne Center),
Lake Forest Park
(206) 363-5460

Toys That Teach
23812 Bothell-Everett Hwy., Bothell
(425) 481-2577

FURNITURE

Forget Me Not
514 Fifth Ave. S., Edmonds
(425) 774-0889

MATERNITY WEAR

Baby Love Maternity
Alderwood Mall, Lynnwood
(425) 776-1262

COSTUMES AND PARTY STUFF

Display & Costume Supply
5209 Evergreen Way, Everett
(425) 353-3364

TRANSPORTATION

Metro Bus Transit
Throughout King County
(206) 553-3000 or (800) 542-7876
transit.metrokc.gov
Hours: Buses operate daily
Fares (as of June 1, 1998): One
zone, $1-$1.25/adults; two zones,
$1.25-$1.75/adults; 75 cents/chil-
dren ages 5-17 (anywhere in King
County); free/children age 4 and
under (up to four children with one
adult)

Getting there can be as much fun
as the destination itself if you let
Metro do the driving within King
County. Just call (206) 553-3000 and
tell the Metro representative where
you are and where you want to go,
and he or she will give you all the
information you need: where to
catch the bus at what time, where to
transfer if necessary, what time you'll
arrive at your destination, and how
much the ride will cost. Rates vary
depending on the time of day; fares
are higher during rush hour (Mon.-
Fri., 6-9 a.m. and 3-6 p.m.). Rides in

the downtown business district between Jackson and Battery streets and the waterfront and Sixth Ave. are free from 6 a.m. to 7 p.m., which makes travel between Pioneer Square, the International District, Pike Place Market, Westlake Center, the shopping district, and the waterfront a cheap thrill. You can also get on and off buses in the Downtown Transit Tunnel at Fifth and Jackson, University St., Westlake Center, and Convention Place and enjoy a free tour beneath the streets of Seattle. Subterranean attractions include a clock made out of tools, neon art, and ornate ironwork.

Metro offers monthly passes and ticket books for frequent riders, as well as special Saturday and Sunday day passes ($1.70). If you already know where you will board the bus, ask the Metro representative about Bus Time, an automated system with recorded information offering the next two or three departure times for your particular route. For Sunday or holiday travel, a Family Pass is available, which entitles up to four children age 17 and younger to ride free all day with the purchase of one adult ticket at $1 (one zone) or $1.25 (two zones). You can buy these passes from the driver as you board the bus.

Monorail
Runs between Seattle Center House and Westlake Center
(206) 684-7200
Hours: Mon.-Fri., 7:30 a.m.-11 p.m.; Sat.-Sun., 9 a.m.-11 p.m.

Fare (one way): $1/adults, 75 cents/children ages 5-12, free/children age 4 and under

Constructed for the 1962 World's Fair, the Monorail seats about 122 people and offers an elevated view of the downtown area, as well as convenient travel between two of the most popular areas in the city: the shopping district and the Seattle Center grounds. Board the Monorail from either the third floor of Westlake Center or in the Seattle Center's Fun Forest. The trip takes just under two minutes and runs about every 15 minutes throughout the day (more often during the lunch hour).

Washington State Ferries
(206) 464-6400 or (800) 843-3779
www.seattleonline.com/ferries
Schedules and rates vary for each route

Operating the largest ferry system in the United States, the Washington State Ferries system serves island and peninsula communities throughout the Puget Sound region. Passengers can ride aboard a variety of boats within the fleet, from the smallest passenger-only ferry, which carries 250 people, to the jumbo ferries, which carry 2,000 people and 206 cars. The passenger-only ferry is used for runs between downtown Seattle and Vashon Island, and downtown Seattle and Bremerton; the jumbo ferries are used for the Seattle to Bainbridge Island run. The shortest ride (15 to 20 minutes) is from Fauntleroy (West Seattle) to Vashon Island; some riders have reported eagle and whale sightings on this run. The longest ride is from Seattle to Bremerton, which lasts just about one hour. One of the more interesting runs is the Keystone run, which travels back and forth between Whidbey Island and Port Townsend, one of the most charming communities in the Puget Sound area.

Passengers are welcome to bring their own food on board, or enjoy something from the cafeteria. A children's meal is packaged in a "ferry box" to take home. Also, although the ferry system does not organize or schedule birthday parties, nothing prohibits people from having such a celebration on board.

Waterfront Streetcar
(206) 553-3000
Fares: $1/adults (non-rush hour), $1.25/adults (rush hour), 75 cents/children ages 5-17 (all hours), free/children age 4 and under
Seasons: Operates daily year-round every 20-30 minutes; seasonal hours vary. Closed Thanksgiving, Christmas, and New Year's Day

Metro's bright green waterfront streetcars travel between Pier 70 and the International District, with nine stops along the way. The route follows the scenic Seattle waterfront along Alaskan Way to Main St., through Pioneer Square, to Fifth and S. Jackson St. You can board a bus or another streetcar free within two hours. The conductors offer information on what sites are located at each stop, and can help you find your destination.

RESOURCES

Seattle's Child, Eastside Parent, Snohomish County Parent, Puget Sound Parent, and South Sound Parent monthly newsmagazines
2107 Elliott Ave., Suite 303, Seattle, WA 98121
(206) 441-0191
www.nwparent.com

Available free at family-oriented businesses or by subscription, *Seattle's Child, Eastside Parent, Snohomish County Parent, Puget Sound Parent,* and *South Sound Parent* are the best local sources for what to do and where to go with children. Regular features include a monthly calendar of events for children and detailed activity listings, as well as information on classes and support groups for parents. Articles address a wide range of issues that affect families, while monthly columns look at age-specific development, education, home, and work. Several supplements are published throughout the year, including "A New Arrival" in February and August (for new and expectant parents); "Preschool Directory" in February; "Summer Learning" in April (summer classes and activities for kids); the "Family Phone Book" in March (services, stores, and resources for families); "Birthday Guide" in May (entertainment and party information); "Summer in the City" in June (activities and special events); the "Activity Guide" in September; "Winter Times" in October (guide to cold-weather fun); the "Education Directory" in November (elementary, junior high, and high schools, including public, private, and special needs); and the "A to Z Holiday Buying Guide" in December. To pick up a complimentary copy or start a subscription, call (206) 441-0191 or send in the form at the back of this book.

Parent Resource Centers

Ballard Family Center, 2101 N.W. 77th, Seattle; (206) 706-9645

The Family Center on Beacon Avenue, 7301 Beacon Ave. S., Seattle; (206) 723-1301

The Family Net, Kirkland Boys and Girls Club, 10805 124th Ave. N.E., Kirkland; (425) 827-0132

Family Support Center of South Snohomish, 6309 196th S.W., Lynnwood; (425) 670-8984

Family Works, 4001 Aurora Ave. N., Seattle; (206) 633-6429

Garfield Family Center, 2323 E. Cherry, Seattle; (206) 461-4486

Maple Valley Community Center, 22010 S.E. 248th St., Maple Valley; (425) 432-1272

Meadowbrook Family Center, 10517 35th Ave. N.E., Seattle; (206) 366-9256

North Seattle Family Center, 13540 Lake City Way N.E., No. 5, Seattle; (206) 364-7930

Parent Education Resource Center of Seattle, Cobb Medical Building, 1305 Fourth Ave., Seattle; (206) 447-1738

Parent Place, 327 Third Ave. S., Kent; (253) 723-1301

Rainier Family Support Center, 4600 38th Ave. S., Seattle; (206) 723-8590

Shoreline Family Support Center, 17018 15th Ave N.E., Shoreline; (206) 362-7282

Southwest Family Center, 4555 Delridge Way S.W., Seattle; (206) 937-7680

West Hill Family Enrichment Center, 12704 76th Ave. S., Seattle; (206) 772-2050

Good Numbers to Know

Emergency (24 hours a day), 911

Washington Poison Center (24 hours a day), (206) 526-2121 or (800) 732-6985

Children's Hospital Resource Line (7 a.m.-11 p.m. daily), (206) 526-2500. For questions about your child's growth, development, and health.

Parent Info-Line, (206) 233-0139. Find parenting classes, support groups, and family activities in King County.

WEB SITES

Northwest Parent Connection
www.nwparent.com

The publishers of "Out and About Seattle with Kids" offers a web site where parents can chat with other parents, research after-school activities, get ideas on weekend getaways, read book reviews, and find out about fun family events.

Seattle Sidewalk,
seattle.sidewalk.com

The highlight of Microsoft's online guide book is the trail finder feature. Though many areas are still under construction (there's an icon for kid-friendly restaurant reviews, but there weren't any on the link at press time), the trail finder really works. You can search a database of trails and parks by clicking on what kind of hike you want: easy or hard, short or long, half-day or overnight adventure. Or just say you want a kid-friendly hike, specifying the region of western Washington, and it will pull up a list of short, easy hikes/walks. More detailed (but still brief) information can be found at individual links for each one.

SeattleOnline,
www.seattleonline.com

This site is basically like an online chamber of commerce, showcasing local attractions, shopping, and entertainment. You can link to dozens of home pages,

including the Rosalie Whyel Museum of Doll Art, Northwest Trek, and Point Defiance Zoo. A restaurant guide, when it works, lets you search a database for a variety of restaurant types ("family" is one category) in a given city or even neighborhood.

DiveIn Seattle,
www.diveinseattle.com

Another community Web site, this one offers information and links to entertainment, sports, education, and events. One helpful feature is a map service that lets you type in an address; it then creates a map that you can print out.

City of Seattle,
www.pan.ci.seattle.wa.us

The official Web site includes visitor information and a directory of city parks and other sites.

City of Bellevue,
www.ci.bellevue.wa.us

A searchable database allows you to search city parks and facilities for certain features, such as hiking trails or boat launches. You can also get online bicycling maps.

Other Web sites to check out:

All City, allcitynet.com/Seattle. Events, attractions, and local home pages.

Art in the Rain, www.wolfe.net/~fin/art. Info on museums, annual arts events, and kids' arts organizations.

Seattle-King County Convention and Visitors Bureau,

www.seeseattle.org. Pictures, hotels, calendar of events, and Seattle Frequently Asked Questions.

Great Places—Seattle, www.nia.com/greatplaces/Pacific_Northwest/Seattle. Places to eat, stay, and see.

Washington State Parks, www.parks.wa.gov. Winter recreation information, parks by region, and maps.

Issaquah Front Street Web, www.issaquah.org. Information on dining, entertainment, and things to do in Issaquah.

Northwest Restaurants, www.rossnet.com/seattlenet/restaurants. Search for restaurants by city and type.

Birthday Party Ideas

- Batting cages
- Bumper bowling
- Children's museum
- Ceramics painting
- Creation Station
- Enchanted Village and Wild Waves
- Family entertainment centers
- Farrel-McWhirter Park
- Forest Park Animal Farm
- Roller or Ice skating
- Kelsey Creek Community Park/Farm
- Miniature golf
- Northwest Puppet Center
- Pacific Science Center
- Remlinger Farms
- Seattle Mariners
- Swimming
- Woodland Park Zoo

Classes

- Bainbridge Performing Arts
- Bellevue Art Museum
- Camp Long
- Carkeek Park
- Children's Garden
- Children's Museum
- Discovery Park
- Farrel-McWhirter Park
- Forest Park Animal Farm
- Green Lake Small Craft Center
- Henry Art Gallery
- Ice skating
- Indoor rock climbing
- The Herbfarm
- Jewish Community Center's Youth Center

- Kelsey Creek Community Park and Farm
- Mount Baker Rowing and Sailing Center
- Museum of Flight
- Museum of History and Industry
- Nordic Heritage Museum
- Northwest Trek
- Olympic Game Farm
- Pacific Science Center
- Remlinger Farms
- Seattle Aquarium
- Seattle Art Museum
- Seattle Children's Theatre
- Seward Park
- Studio East
- Village Theatre
- Woodland Park Zoo
- Youth Theatre Northwest

Field Trips and Tours

- Bellevue Art Museum
- Boeing Tour Center
- Burke Museum
- Camp Long
- Carkeek Park
- Capitol Tours
- Center for Wooden Boats
- Children's Museum
- Chinatown Discovery Tours
- Cougar Mountain Zoological Park
- Discovery Park
- Local farms
- Farrel-McWhirter Park
- Fire stations
- Henry Art Gallery
- Hiram M. Chittendon Government Locks
- Kelsey Creek Community Park and Farm

INDEX

D

G

H

INDEX

L

INDEX

T

INDEX

FUNDRAISING

Raise money for your school or organization with books from Northwest Parent Publishing.

Schools, clubs, employee groups, and other organizations can raise funds by selling the books published by Northwest Parent Publishing.

Call (206) 441-0191 in Seattle for information about fundraising opportunities, or write to:

Northwest Parent Publishing
1530 Westlake Avenue North
Suite 600
Seattle, WA 98109

OUT AND ABOUT SEATTLE WITH KIDS FEEDBACK

We are interested in your comments on using this guide. Did we give you the information you needed? Did you have a terrific experience at one of the places we suggested? Or a disaster? Also, tell us about any places we left out. Give us the details!!!!

_____

_____

_____

_____

_____

_____

_____

_____

_____

_____

_____

_____

Your name _____

Address _____

City/State/Zip _____

Phone (   ) _____

Mail to: Northwest Parent Publishing, Inc.
1530 Westlake Ave. N., Suite 600, Seattle, WA 98109

Outstanding Resources for Parents
From Northwest Parent Publishing

BOOKS

Going Places: Family Getaways in the Pacific Northwest
The award-winning travel guide for families, covering Washington, Oregon, British Columbia, and Northern Idaho. Describes the hotels, dude ranches, resorts, and B&B's that are best for parents and children, as well as roadside attractions, family-friendly places to eat, and what to see and do once you arrive at your destination. 374 pages, $14.95 _____

Out and About Portland with Kids
The award-winning guide that tells where to go and what to see and do with kids around the Portland region. An invaluable resource for residents as well as out-of-town visitors. 242 pages, $12.95 _____

NEWSMAGAZINES

Northwest Parent publishes five award-winning regional news-magazines for parents. Each publication includes a comprehensive calendar of events, information about local resources and services, and articles about local issues of interest to parents and others concerned about children. Subscription includes special annual supplements: *The Education Directory, A Guide to Private and Public Schools, Birthdays! A Guide to Birthday Fun,* and *The Activity Guide: Information about After-school and Weekend Classes.* A one-year subscription costs $9 (special offer with this coupon–regular price $15). _____

Yes, send me one year (12 issues) of:
Eastside Parent _____
Portland Parent _____
Puget Sound Parent _____
Seattle's Child _____
Snohomish County Parent _____
South Sound Parent _____

Subtotal _____
Washington state residents add sales tax (sub-total x .086) _____
TOTAL _____

Your Name _____

Address _____

City/State/Zip _____

Phone _____

Mail coupon to: Northwest Parent Publishing, Inc.
1530 Westlake Ave. N., Suite 600
Seattle, WA 98109

Or call (206) 441-0191 in Seattle or (503) 638-1049 in Portland

Prices include shipping and handling. Allow 3 weeks for delivery. Satisfaction guaranteed or your money back.

Bellevue Art Museum

Located on the third floor
of Bellevue Square

Hours:
10 AM to 6 PM
Monday, Wednesday
thru Saturday

10 AM to 8 PM
Tuesday

11 AM to 5 PM
Sunday

(425)454-3322

Every Tuesday is FREE
www.bellevueart.org

Bellevue Art Museum

Located on the third floor
of Bellevue Square

Hours:
10 AM to 6 PM
Monday, Wednesday
thru Saturday

10 AM to 8 PM
Tuesday

11 AM to 5 PM
Sunday

(425)454-3322

Every Tuesday is FREE
www.bellevueart.org

The Burke Museum

Location:

Seattle
Located at 17th Ave. NE and
NE 45th St. on the UW campus

(206)543-7907
(206)543-5590

Hours:
Open daily 10-5
and until 8 on Thursday

OUT & ABOUT SEATTLE WITH KIDS

See Explore & Make Art

The Museum presents contemporary art of the region and programs to children and adults that connect art, community and everyday life with activities to See Explore and Make Art.

Bellevue Art Museum

Bellevue Art Museum

Located on the third floor of Bellevue Square

Hours:
10 AM to 6 PM
Monday, Wednesday thru Saturday

10 AM to 8 PM
Tuesday

11 AM to 5 PM
Sunday

(425)454-3322

Every Tuesday is FREE
www.bellevueart.org

OUT & ABOUT SEATTLE WITH KIDS

See Explore & Make Art

Saturday workshops inspired by *Bellevue Art Museum's* exhibitions. Students tour the exhibit and take part in an artist led, hands-on activity relating to the experience.

Bellevue Art Museum

Bellevue Art Museum

Located on the third floor of Bellevue Square

Hours:
10 AM to 6 PM
Monday, Wednesday thru Saturday

10 AM to 8 PM
Tuesday

11 AM to 5 PM
Sunday

(425)454-3322

Every Tuesday is FREE
www.bellevueart.org

OUT & ABOUT SEATTLE WITH KIDS

Get the inside story on Washington–Dinosaurs included! Visit the Burke for 545 million years of volcanoes, giant marine reptiles, whales, the Ice Age, and the fascinating cultural heritage of the Pacific Rim.

THE BURKE
MUSEUM OF
NATURAL HISTORY
AND CULTURE

The Burke Museum

Location:

Seattle
Located at 17th Ave. NE and NE 45th St. on the UW campus

(206)543-7907
(206)543-5590

Hours:
Open daily 10-5
and until 8 on Thursday

Cotton Caboodle

Store Location:

Lower Queen Anne
203 W. Thomas Street
Seattle, WA 98119
(206)282-2701

Go To Your Room

Store Locations:

Seattle
University Village
Seattle, Washington 98105

(206)528-0711

Bellevue
13000 Bel-Red Rd.
Bellevue, Washington 98005

(425)453-2990

Kingdome

Location:

Seattle
201 South King Street
Seattle, Washington 98104

(206)296-3128
TDD: (206)296-3191
www.metrokc.gov/stadium

The one-hour guided tour starts at Gate D at 11AM, 1PM & 3PM. Public tours operate mid-April through mid-Sept. and are accessible to strollers and wheelchairs. Tour prices: $5 adults and teens; $2.50 for children and seniors (65+). Parking is normally available in Kingdome North Lot. Call to verify tour times.

OUT & ABOUT SEATTLE WITH KIDS

Wholesale outlet for 100% cotton kids clothing in 45 colors. Ages 0-14. Some women's apparel. Hours: Tuesday – Saturday 10-4.

Cotton Caboodle
OUTLET STORE

Cotton Caboodle

Store Location:

Lower Queen Anne
203 W. Thomas Street
Seattle, WA 98119
(206)282-2701

OUT & ABOUT SEATTLE WITH KIDS

10% OFF Total Purchase
- Cribs • Changing Tables • Beds
- Frames/Prints • Chests
- Bedding/Rugs •Desks
- Clocks/Lamps • Rockers
- Toy Boxes • Posters and More!

Go To Your Room.
The Store for Children's Furnishings

Valid at time of purchase only. Only one coupon per customer.

Go To Your Room

Store Locations:

Seattle
University Village
Seattle, Washington 98105

(206)528-0711

Bellevue
13000 Bel-Red Rd.
Bellevue, Washington 98005

(425)453-2990

OUT & ABOUT SEATTLE WITH KIDS

We take you places you've never been before on a *Kingdome Tour* that includes a video of past events, a visit to the playing field, the press box, a locker room, VIP areas and a sports museum. Great fun and adventure for kids and their families.

Kingdome

Location:

Seattle
201 South King Street
Seattle, Washington 98104

(206)296-3128
TDD: (206)296-3191
www.metrokc.gov/stadium

The one-hour guided tour starts at Gate D at 11AM, 1PM & 3PM. Public tours operate mid-April through mid-Sept. and are accessible to strollers and wheelchairs. Tour prices: $5 adults and teens; $2.50 for children and seniors (65+). Parking is normally available in Kingddome North Lot. Call to verify tour times.

Northwest Trek
Wildlife Park

Location:

Eatonville
11610 Trek Drive East
Eatonville, Washington 98328

(800)433-TREK
(360)832-6117

www.nwtrek.org

Odyssey

Store Locations:

Pier 66
2205 Alaskan Way
Seattle, WA 98121

Olympic Game Farm

Office Locations:

Sequim
1423 Ward Road
Sequim, WA 98382
(800)778-4295

OUT & ABOUT SEATTLE WITH KIDS ▼

Climb aboard the tram and explore forests, meadows and high ridges to see native northwest wildlife. Stroll pathways to discover grizzly, wolves, cougar, birds-of-prey and small forest animals. Hands-on children's nature discovery center. **Call 800-433-TREK.**

▼

NORTHWESTREK
A Wildlife Park

Northwest Trek
Wildlife Park

Location:

Eatonville
11610 Trek Drive East
Eatonville, Washington 98328

(800)433-TREK
(360)832-6117

www.nwtrek.org

OUT & ABOUT SEATTLE WITH KIDS ▼

Ahoy mate!
Opening on the Seattle waterfront in July, *Odyssey* provides kids a place to explore their fascination with boats and ships, fishing, our marine environment, and more! Hands-on , interactive, state-of-the-art exhibits offer fun for the entire family.

▼

O D Y S S E Y
▪ ▪ ▪ ▪ > ▪
The Maritime Discovery Center

0001

Odyssey

Store Locations:

Pier 66
2205 Alaskan Way
Seattle, WA 98121

OUT & ABOUT SEATTLE WITH KIDS ▼

From the walk or driving tour you can feel the haunting power of a tiger's stare, hear the rich chorus of wolves howling or look a buffalo in the face. Come visit! Open daily 9:00 a.m.

▼

Spirit Wind Photo

Olympic Game Farm

Office Locations:

Sequim
1423 Ward Road
Sequim, WA 98382

(800)778-4295

Paint the Town

Studio Locations:

University Village
4527 University Village Ct. NE
Seattle, Washington 98105

(206)527-8554

Redmond Town Center
7329 164th Ave. NE
Redmond, Washington 98052

(425)861-8388

Painted Fire

Location:

Seattle
3601 Fremont Avenue North
Seattle, Washington 98103
(Just two blocks north of the
Fremont Bridge)

(206)545-2816

Saturday's Child

Store Locations:

Bothell
18012 Bothell-Everett Hwy
Bothell, WA 98012
(425)486-6716

Stone Gardens

Location:

Seattle
2839 NW Market Street
Seattle, Washington 98107
(next to Ballard Locks)

(206)781-9828

Washington State Historical Society

Museum Locations:

Tacoma
Washington State
History Museum
1911 Pacific Avenue
Tacoma, Washington 98402

Olympia
Washington State
Capital Museum
211 West 21st Avenue
Olympia, Washington 98501

1-888-BE THERE

Woodland Park Zoo

Location:

Seattle

5500 Phinney Avenue North
Seattle, WA 98103

(206)684-4800
TDD (206)684-4025

Northwest Parent Publishing

Mailing Address:

Northwest Parent Publishing
1530 Westlake Ave. N.
Suite 600
Seattle, WA 98109
(800)794-1018

Everything you need to know to plan a family vacation in the Pacific Northwest.

Northwest Parent Publishing

Mailing Address:

Northwest Parent Publishing
1530 Westlake Ave. N.
Suite 600
Seattle, WA 98109
(800)794-1018

Valuable resources for busy parents.

Northwest Parent Publishing

Mailing Address:

Northwest Parent Publishing
1530 Westlake Ave. N.
Suite 600
Seattle, WA 98109
(800)794-1018

Where to go and what to see with kids in Portland.

OUT & ABOUT SEATTLE WITH KIDS ▼

Going Places: Family Getaways in the Pacific Northwest.

Places to Stay.
Places to Eat.
What to See and Do.

▼

To receive your copy(ies) of Going Places please send coupon along with name, address, phone number, and $13.45 per copy to Northwest Parent Publishing.

Northwest Parent Publishing

Mailing Address:

Northwest Parent Publishing
1530 Westlake Ave. N.
Suite 600
Seattle, WA 98109
(800)794-1018

OUT & ABOUT SEATTLE WITH KIDS ▼

- Preschool Directory
- Family Phone Book
- Summer Learning
- Education Directory
- Winter Times
- A New Arrival

▼

Please send coupon and names of issues requested along with your name, address, phone number, and $3.00 per issue to Northwest Parent Publishing.

Northwest Parent Publishing

Mailing Address:

Northwest Parent Publishing
1530 Westlake Ave. N.
Suite 600
Seattle, WA 98109
(800)794-1018

OUT & ABOUT SEATTLE WITH KIDS ▼

Out and About Portland With Kids
The Ultimate Family Guide
for Fun and Learning

By Elizabeth Hartzell DeSimone,
editor of **Portland Parent**
monthly magazine.

▼

To receive your copy(ies) of Out and About Portland With Kids please send coupon along with name, address, phone number, and $11.65 per copy to Northwest Parent Publishing.

Northwest Parent Publishing

Mailing Address:

Northwest Parent Publishing
1530 Westlake Ave. N.
Suite 600
Seattle, WA 98109
(800)794-1018

Northwest Parent Publishing

Mailing Address:

Northwest Parent Publishing
1530 Westlake Ave. N.
Suite 600
Seattle, WA 98109
(800)794-1018

The monthly newsmagazine for parents.

OUT & ABOUT SEATTLE WITH KIDS

Seattle's Child · Eastside Parent

$12⁰⁰
Subscription - One Year
$20⁰⁰
Subscription - Two Years

Not valid with any other offer.

Northwest Parent Publishing

Mailing Address:

Northwest Parent Publishing
1530 Westlake Ave. N.
Suite 600
Seattle, WA 98109
(800)794-1018

The monthly newsmagazine for parents.

OUT & ABOUT SEATTLE WITH KIDS

PUGET SOUND Parent

$12⁰⁰
Subscription - One Year
$20⁰⁰
Subscription - Two Years

Not valid with any other offer.

Northwest Parent Publishing

Mailing Address:

Northwest Parent Publishing
1530 Westlake Ave. N.
Suite 600
Seattle, WA 98109
(800)794-1018

The monthly newsmagazine for parents.

OUT & ABOUT SEATTLE WITH KIDS

SNOHOMISH COUNTY Parent

$12⁰⁰
Subscription - One Year
$20⁰⁰
Subscription - Two Years

Not valid with any other offer.

OUT & ABOUT SEATTLE WITH KIDS

Decide to Subscribe!

▼

*To receive your subscription to
Seattle's Child or Eastside Parent
please send coupon along with name,
address, phone number, and
$12 (one year) or $20 (two years)
to Northwest Parent Publishing.*

▼
**Northwest Parent
Publishing**

Mailing Address:

Northwest Parent Publishing
1530 Westlake Ave. N.
Suite 600
Seattle, WA 98109
(800)794-1018

OUT & ABOUT SEATTLE WITH KIDS

Decide to Subscribe!

▼

*To receive your subscription to
Puget Sound Parent please send coupon
along with name, address,
phone number, and
$12 (one year) or $20 (two years)
to Northwest Parent Publishing.*

▼
**Northwest Parent
Publishing**

Mailing Address:

Northwest Parent Publishing
1530 Westlake Ave. N.
Suite 600
Seattle, WA 98109
(800)794-1018

OUT & ABOUT SEATTLE WITH KIDS

Decide to Subscribe!

▼

*To receive your subscription to
Snohomish Parent
please send coupon along with name,
address, phone number, and
$12 (one year) or $20 (two years)
to Northwest Parent Publishing.*

▼
**Northwest Parent
Publishing**

Mailing Address:

Northwest Parent Publishing
1530 Westlake Ave. N.
Suite 600
Seattle, WA 98109
(800)794-1018

Northwest Parent Publishing

Mailing Address:

Northwest Parent Publishing
1530 Westlake Ave. N.
Suite 600
Seattle, WA 98109
(800)794-1018

The monthly newsmagazine for parents.

Northwest Parent Publishing

Mailing Address:

Northwest Parent Publishing
1530 Westlake Ave. N.
Suite 600
Seattle, WA 98109
(800)794-1018

The newsletter for parents of children ages 10 to 18.

Northwest Parent Publishing

Mailing Address:

Northwest Parent Publishing
1530 Westlake Ave. N.
Suite 600
Seattle, WA 98109
(800)794-1018

The newsletter for parents of children ages 10 to 18.

OUT & ABOUT SEATTLE WITH KIDS ▼

Decide to Subscribe!

▼

To receive your subscription to South Sound Parent please send coupon along with name, address, phone number, and $12 (one year) or $20 (two years) to Northwest Parent Publishing.

Northwest Parent Publishing

Mailing Address:

Northwest Parent Publishing
1530 Westlake Ave. N.
Suite 600
Seattle, WA 98109
(800)794-1018

OUT & ABOUT SEATTLE WITH KIDS ▼

Get help answering questions like: What should I do if I don't like my child's choice of friends? What are reasonable rules for middle school boy-girl parties? How can I plan a productive summer for my teen?

▼

ten *to* eighteen

To receive a one year subscription send coupon along with name, address, phone number, and $22.50 to Northwest Parent Publishing.

Northwest Parent Publishing

Mailing Address:

Northwest Parent Publishing
1530 Westlake Ave. N.
Suite 600
Seattle, WA 98109
(800)794-1018

OUT & ABOUT SEATTLE WITH KIDS ▼

Gain greater understanding and appreciation of your child along with strategies to make you the most effective parent you can be.

▼

ten *to* eighteen

To receive a one year subscription send coupon along with name, address, phone number, and $22.50 to Northwest Parent Publishing.

Northwest Parent Publishing

Mailing Address:

Northwest Parent Publishing
1530 Westlake Ave. N.
Suite 600
Seattle, WA 98109
(800)794-1018